MODERN GERMAN POETRY

1910–1960

MODERN GERMAN POETRY

1910–1960

-+<-*+>-

AN ANTHOLOGY

WITH VERSE TRANSLATIONS

EDITED AND WITH AN INTRODUCTION BY

MICHAEL HAMBURGER
AND
CHRISTOPHER MIDDLETON

★

GROVE PRESS, INC.
NEW YORK

Library of Congress Catalog Card Number: 61-6602

First Evergreen Edition 1964

Second Printing

MANUFACTURED IN THE UNITED STATES OF AMERICA

In memory of William Rose

ACKNOWLEDGEMENTS

For permission to reprint copyright material, the following acknowledgements are made:

To Arche Verlag, Zürich, for the poems by Benn from *Statische Gedichte*, 1948, and by van Hoddis from *Weltende*, 1958; to Atlantis Verlag, Zürich, for the poem by Zollinger from *Gedichte*, 1956; to Atrium Verlag, Zürich, for the poem by Kästner from *Lyrische Hausapotheke*, 1935; to Frau Lilli Becher and Aufbau Verlag, Berlin, for the poems by Becher; to Bechtle Verlag, Esslingen, for the poems by Heissenbüttel from *Kombinationen*, 1954, and by Piontek from *Wassermarken*, 1957; to Benziger Verlag, Einsiedeln-Cologne, for the poem by Ball; to Siegbert Mohn Verlag, formerly C. Bertelsmann Verlag, Gütersloh, for the poem by Scholl from *Lyrik unserer Zeit* (1957); to Claassen Verlag, Hamburg, and to Mrs Margot Ruben, for the poems by Wolfskehl from *Gedichte*, 1960, and for the poem by Fried from *Gedichte*, 1958; to Deutsche Verlags-Anstalt, Stuttgart, for the poems by Krolow from *Die Zeichen der Welt*, 1952, and *Wind und Zeit*, 1954, for the poems by Celan from *Mohn und Gedächtnis*, 1952, and from *Von Schwelle zu Schwelle*, 1955, and for the poems by Meckel from *Nebelhörner*, 1959; to H. Ellermann Verlag, Munich, for the poems by Stadler from *Dichtungen* and for the poems by Heym from *Dichtungen und Schriften;* to S. Fischer Verlag, Frankfurt am Main, for the poem by Werfel from *Beschwörungen*, 1923; to Fretz und Wasmuth Verlag, Zürich, for the poems by Brambach from *Tagwerk*, 1959; to Günter Grass for his poem 'Wandlung' from *Akzente* (1959); to Hanser Verlag, Munich, for the poems by Höllerer from *Der andere Gast*, 1952; to Karl H. Henssel Verlag, Berlin, for the poems by Ringelnatz from *Und auf einmal steht es neben dir*, 1951; to Peter Huchel for his poems from *Gedichte*, 1948, and from 'Sinn und Form' (1959); to Insel Verlag, Wiesbaden, for the poems by Rilke from *Werke II*, 1956, for the poems by Morgenstern from *Alle Galgenlieder*, 1938, and for the poems by Hagelstange from *Zwischen Stern und Staub*, 1953; to the Jewish University Library, Jerusalem, for the poems by Ehrenstein, and to E. Rowohlt Verlag, Hamburg, for the poem

'Autofahrt' by Ehrenstein from *Mein Lied*, 1931; to Kösel Verlag, Munich, for the poems by Lasker-Schüler from *Gedichte*, 1959, and for the poem by Däubler from *Dichtungen und Schriften*, 1956; to Albert Langen-Georg Müller Verlag, Munich, for the poems by Herrmann-Neisse, and for the poems by Lichtenstein from *Gedichte und Geschichten, Bd. I*, 1919; to Limes Verlag, Wiesbaden, for the poems by Stramm from *Dein Lächeln weint*, 1956, for the poems by Arp from *wortträume und schwarze sterne*, 1953, and from *auf einem bein*, 1955, and for the poems by Benn from *Gesammelte Gedichte*, 1956; to H. Luchterhand Verlag, Darmstadt, for the poems by Goll from *Dichtungen*, 1960, and for the poems by Grass from *Die Vorzüge der Windhühner*, 1956; to O. Müller Verlag, Salzburg, for the poems by Trakl from *Gesammelte Werke : Die Dichtungen* [1938], 1948 (8th ed.), for the poems by Lavant from *Die Bettlerschale*, 1956, for the poems by Schmied from *Landkarte des Windes*, 1957, for the poem by Busta from *Die Scheune der Vögel*, 1958, and for the poem by Artmann from *med anna schwoazzn dintn*, 1958; to Andreas Okopenko for his poem (from *Expeditionen* [Munich] 1959); to Phaidon Press, London, for the poem by Klabund from *Gesammelte Gedichte*, 1930; to Piper Verlag, Munich, for the poems by Holthusen from *Labyrinthische Jahre*, 1952, and for the poems by Bachmann from *Die gestundete Zeit*, 1957, and from *Anrufung des grossen Bären*, 1956; to Rowohlt Verlag, Hamburg, for the poem by Schnack from *Tier rang gewaltig mit Tier*, 1920, and for the poems by Weyrauch from *Gesang um nicht zu sterben*, 1956; to Lambert Schneider Verlag, Heidelberg, for the poems by Steiner from *Unruhe ohne Uhr*, 1954, by Kolmar from *Das lyrische Werk*, 1955, and by Thoor from *Sonette und Lieder*, 1956; to P. Suhrkamp Verlag, Frankfurt am Main, for the poems by Brecht from *Gedichte und Lieder*, 1956 (also *Gedichte*, 6 vols, 1960–61), for the poems by Lehmann from *Meine Gedichtbücher*, 1956, for the poems by Loerke from *Gedichte und Prosa, Bd. I*, 1958, for the poems by Eich from *Botschaften des Regens*, 1955, and from *Träume*, 1954, for the poems by Schnurre from *Kassiber*, 1956, and for the poems by Enzensberger from *verteidigung der wölfe*, 1956, and from *landessprache*, 1960; to E. Tessloff Verlag, Hamburg, for the poems by Bauer from *Mein blaues Oktavheft*, 1954; and to Vereinigung Oltener Bücherfreunde, Olten, for the poem by Zemp from *Das Hochtal*, 1956.

The poems 'Altes Zimmer' and 'Die Blinden' by Erich Fried and the two poems by Hans Werner Cohn are printed by kind permission of the authors.

Acknowledgements are also made to the publishers of the following books and magazines in which some of the English translations have appeared: *New Zealand Poetry Yearbook* (Pegasus Press, Christchurch, N.Z.); *An Anthology of German Poetry from Hölderlin to Rilke*, ed. A. Flores (Doubleday, Anchor Books, New York); M. Hamburger, *Reason and Energy* (George Routledge and Sons, London, and Grove Press, New York); *Ohne Hass und Fahne*, ed. W. G. Deppe, C. Middleton, H. Schönherr (Rowohlt Verlag, Hamburg); *New World Writing June 1958* (New American Library, New York); Gottfried Benn, *Primal Vision*, ed. E. B. Ashton (New Directions, New York, and The Bodley Head Ltd., London); *Contemporary German Poetry*, ed. B. Deutsch and A. Yarmolinsky (The Bodley Head, London); *More Comic and Curious Verse*, ed. J. M. Cohen (Penguin Books, Harmondsworth, England); *Atlantic Monthly: Perspective of Germany* (March 1957: Intercultural Publications Inc., New York); *German Life and Letters; Harper's; New Departures; The New Statesman; The Painter and Sculptor; Poetry* (Chicago); *Texas University Quarterly; Tomorrow.*

The translations from Rilke, by Michael Hamburger, David Luke and Christopher Middleton, are printed by special permission of The Hogarth Press, Ltd., and of New Directions, New York, who published the authorized translation, by J. B. Leishman, of *Poems 1906-26.*

CONTENTS

xi

HANS ARP

GEORG HEYM

ALFRED LICHTENSTEIN

FRANZ WERFEL

KLABUND

JOHANNES R. BECHER

YVAN GOLL

ANTON SCHNACK

GERTRUD KOLMAR

ALBIN ZOLLINGER

BERTOLT BRECHT

CONTENTS

INTRODUCTION

This book is an anthology of modern German poems in English verse translation. The period involved is the half-century between 1910 and 1960; and the accent is on Expressionism. Since Expressionism initiated modern style in German poetry, most of this introduction is devoted to a discussion of it. And since the accent is on Expressionism, certain poets had to be omitted. Most of the poets omitted fall into four categories, which overlap at points: (1) those Naturalists, Impressionists and Symbolists whose work is either anchored in nineteenth century conventions, or not directly modern in style or outlook (e.g., Liliencron, Dehmel, George); (2) those poets whose work appeared well into this century but who were not affected by modernist techniques (e.g., Schröder, Borchardt, Carossa); (3) those poets who anticipated Expressionism in certain poems, but whose style or outlook is not central to it (e.g., Mombert, Dauthendey); and (4) poets of those bizarre, demi-prophetic, quasi-religious or otherwise quixotic groups which may be typical of the epoch but do not invariably claim attention as sources either of its best or even of its more charactered writing (e.g., Pannwitz, zur Linde, Derleth). There is, however, one other category of poets omitted: those, like Elisabeth Langgässer or Nelly Sachs, whose work resisted translation or could only be turned into versions which gave that impression. We hope that readers will have the charity to find this category not too large.

The word *Expressionist* is sometimes loosely applied to style in painting and poetry other and older than that which began to take shape in Germany around 1910. This is in part due to the fact that Expressionism was one of the slogans popularized by the revolution which affected all the arts soon after the beginning of this century, and which made it possible and desirable to revaluate certain antecedents. With this revaluation it was found that some of the work of older poets and artists (not to mention 'primitives') was not merely failed mimesis, art which failed to represent or to imitate observable realities, or art which was untrue to Classical principles. On the contrary, it was art which had distinct laws of its own, art which formed its image of reality by means never intended to be mimetic. Wilhelm Worringer, whose *Abstraktion und Einfühlung* (1909) was one of the pioneering works of revaluation, could thus in 1921 officially disparage mimesis to the extent of saying that imitation, though a basic impulse of the human mind, had nothing to do with art at all. The recognition of this other tradition in art, sometimes now called 'Asiatic', as opposed to 'Attic' or Classical art, was made largely possible after Expressionism in Germany and parallels in other European countries and in the United States had wrought radical changes in each of the arts in turn, not excluding music. The term *Expressionist*, first used in France to distinguish from the Impressionists certain new painters, was then applied to any art which was less mimetic than expressive, which did not present an image of an already realized or observable world, and which seemed to spring less out of eyesight than out of vision. The epoch of non-figurative art had begun. Benedetto Croce's esthetic, with its accent on intuition, helped to generalize the use of the term. But in German Expressionist poetry, it is less the intuition that matters than the modes in which such intuitive types as the early Expressionist poets reformed the idiom of German poetry, and made it into the proper creative speech of modern tensions and modern themes. Some of their formal innovations have parallels in other European literatures, including Russian literature. But though the modern movement was, from the start, an international one, German Expressionist poetry has certain unique features.

The modern movement as a whole began less with a formal program than with a polemical acclamation of the modern for its own sake. Marinetti's *Futurist Manifesto*, published in Paris in 1909, proclaimed that 'a roaring automobile is more beautiful than the Nike of Samothrace'. In Germany, too, the desire for a new outlook, an outlook that would be up-to-date and would also axe the bourgeois idols of the Wilhelmine period, preceded the appearance of any definite programs or of any new styles. The periodicals *Die Aktion* and *Der Sturm* were, however, founded in 1910; and a year later a German translation of Marinetti's manifesto appeared in *Der Sturm*. In 1911, also, the German Expressionist movement in poetry began with the publication of two poems, both in *Die Aktion*:

'Weltende' by Jakob van Hoddis, and 'Die Dämmerung' by Alfred Lichtenstein. At about the same time, the French poet Guillaume Apollinaire, impressed by the *Futurist Manifesto*, started the literary movement which he called *Orphisme*. The first Futurist exhibition was held in Paris in 1912; in 1913 there was a similar exhibition in London, where Marinetti himself lectured. The year 1913 also saw the publication of the Imagist group's *A few Don'ts*, which was to determine many future developments in poetry in the English language.

The best early German Expressionist poetry satisfies three of the Imagist requirements: the creation of new rhythms, freedom in the choice of subject, and concentration. But one must be cautious about attributing to the German poets the Imagist way of presenting an image. It is not that the German poets preferred generalities to the Imagist particulars, far from it: but what they wanted was less a clear rendering of a visual experience than a true rendering of visionary experience; and these two things are different. In Georg Heym or Georg Trakl, for instance, the image embodies tones of feeling to an extent which the Imagist, with his accent on the physical object of feeling, would not have admitted. Indeed, in early Expressionist poems the image can voice feelings precisely and be visually graphic, without using a realized or even realizable world as a source of objective correlatives. If it does not lean so heavily on the object as the image in Imagist poems, it does lean more heavily on tones of feeling as these crystallize in the configurations of images, of which the single image is an element. Accordingly, the early Expressionist image can seldom be isolated from context without losing some of its quality, whereas in Imagism it is precisely the isolated image of the particular realized object which exists to be appreciated. In Imagism the image's function is to isolate surface sharply; but the function of the early Expressionist image is to deepen the perspectives of the whole configuration of images within which it stands.

Yet Expressionism is more often distinguished from parallel movements in poetry less by contrasts like these, than by the tendencies which made it, after 1914, as much a sociological phenomenon as a literary movement. For, after 1914, its craft of imagery was vulgarized and, at the same time, its mental climate became predominantly political. We shall refer again to this development as 'Phase II Expressionism', in order to distinguish it from the early Expressionist poetry of the years 1911–14.

The Imagist program led to a diversity of individual achievements. Expressionist poetry, too, is really a body of work by poets who had little in common except certain apprehensions in the face of a disintegrating culture, and a need to create individual styles which would present their peculiar tensions. The early Expressionist poets did not subscribe to a common program. It has been suggested that the Imagist program was formulated in the face of crisis: in a world where all values were in doubt, sense-data were at least something to start from. But, as has been indicated, the German poets did not confine their attention to sense-data in this way. Neither were the best poets in a position to argue things out among themselves. Certainly, Berlin was the center. Here Jakob van Hoddis, Lichtenstein and Heym were working; here Herwarth Walden and Franz Pfemfert were editing their rival periodicals, *Der Sturm* and *Die Aktion*. Here, too, the literary club called the *Neuer Club* was active holding readings in its so-called 'Neopathetic Cabaret', which in some ways foreshadowed the Dadaist Cabaret Voltaire in Zürich—both expressed disapproval of 'literary' poetry and humbug. But Heym died early in 1912; and three other pioneers, Georg Trakl, Ernst Stadler and Franz Werfel, worked in places as remote from each other as from Berlin: Trakl in Salzburg and Innsbruck, Stadler in Strasbourg and Brussels, and Werfel in Prague and Vienna.

Jakob van Hoddis and Alfred Lichtenstein both lived in Berlin. The poem 'Weltende' by van Hoddis appeared before Lichtenstein's 'Die Dämmerung', and Lichtenstein admitted having used it as a model, though he rightly claimed to have improved on it. Both poems are rhymed and have regular stanzas. What was new about them was that they consisted of a deadpan concatenation of apparently dislocated images, derived from the contemporary scene, but not presenting a realistic picture. It was a new picture, because the viewpoint seemed to jump from line to line, and because the objects alluded to were not ones that can be ordinarily found in the same place at the same time. This was *collage*, a technique which was being tested at the same time in visual terms by Picasso (*Still Life with a Cane Chair*, 1911–12) and by Braque (*The Fruit Dish*, 1912), and which was to be developed drastically by the Zürich Dadaist poets five years later. Yet van Hoddis gave the game away in the title of his poem, 'End of the World', the strident sarcasm of which does not allow the images to speak for themselves. In Lichtenstein's poem, the images do speak for themselves, and the title, 'Twilight', is wryly ambiguous. The *collage* effect thus has much more force. 'Die Dämmerung' defied translation, so could not be included in the selection; but in the poem 'Prophezeiung' ('Prophecy')—an ironic title, considering the poem's present tense—there is a similar surreptitious scurrility, and a similar (if more obvious) vision of a dislocated world seen by an eye that has not been brutalized by habit.

In Lichtenstein, as in a number of early Expressionist poems, the quality of the vision is not some previously fixed, definite idea which can be detached from the images. The quality of the vision is absorbed into the images without residue, and it is the hidden nerve which governs their association. Such poems do not present the sensibility wasting in reflection of much nineteenth century verse (e.g., Lenau), but a sensibility absorbed and active in construction, presenting simultaneously the *what* and the *how* of the perception. Lichtenstein's images are accordingly full of piths and gists. Though not free from the self-deprecation made familiar by Heine and Laforgue, Lichtenstein's irony does not thus merely unsay what he seems to be saying and so negate his negative image of the world; rather his irony, without ever making discursive statements, simultaneously bewails and derides the world whose collapse his images embody. With his irony and his sense of the absurd, Lichtenstein developed one of the first and most appealing forms of Expressionist imagery: near-caricature, at once clownish and terrified. The new freedom of association asserted in his work also contributed to one of the main trends of modern poetry: the liberation of the image from the tyranny of the object.

Lichtenstein died in battle at the age of twenty-five, soon after war broke out in 1914. Of the other early Expressionist poets, Heym had died two years before, at the age of twenty-four; Trakl also died in 1914, while on active service; Ernst Stadler was killed on the Western front in the same year; and August Stramm, whose innovations are among the most extreme, was killed in 1915 on the Eastern front. The premature deaths of these poets is the chief reason why later developments in Expressionist poetry did not fulfill its early promise. Another reason is the increasingly political strain of Phase II Expressionism. And a third reason is that, besides lacking a definite program comparable to the Imagist manifesto, the poets could depend on no poet-critic with the stringent authority of Pound or Eliot. The lack of all conviction which had brought some greatness into the poems of the pioneers, was superseded all too soon by a passionate intensity which first lowered and then lost the aims of the early poets.

Between 1909 and 1912, however, Georg Heym was writing his roughly 130 poems, which explore the new apocalyptic mood, the theme of doom and the milieu of the city, which in varying proportions constitute the world of early Expressionist poetry. 'Umbra Vitae' is one of Heym's many poems in which the city is seen as a domain of demons. Heym's demons, as in his luridly macabre poem 'Die Dämonen der Städte', pervade modern existence as irrational destructive forces. Yet these are not death-wish poems, even though Heym is a poet of bile and brainstorm. The suicides in 'Umbra Vitae' are searching for their "lost selves". The German *verlorenes Wesen* also means "lost substance" or "lost being". And what Heym regards with horror is this loss of self and of substance (the medieval *inopia entis*) which hollows modern collective man. The only single individuals about whom he writes are outcasts and rebels (e.g., 'Judas'). Even in his pastoral poems, and in such massive visionary poems as 'Mond', the demons are near or present. Neither are the dead (as in the poem 'Die Morgue') exempted from their grasp; for death merely accelerates the disintegration which the dead knew in life, who "without name, poor, unknown, / Died in empty cellars, and alone."

In his massive poems, like 'Der Krieg', Heym frequently uses the device of personification to control perspective. But in 'Der Krieg' his graphic and tumbled imagery of the city offsets any literary quality that might weaken the device. The horror of war is compressed into the image: war "crumples the moon in his black hand." Personification is fortified by the typical dynamic verb-metaphor; and it is with such verb-metaphors as this that he transmutes and transvalues the observable world. The Expressionist poet is not, like the Impressionist poet, a passive reflector of sense-data, or, in Hofmannsthal's words, "a soundless brother of all things." Moreover, Heym's metaphors move in clusters and by association. Attention is fastened not on any objects of reference, but on the images themselves as they crystallize and cluster around a central visionary focus. The poem 'Und die Hörner des Sommers verstummten' exemplifies this procedure somewhat less forcefully than the massive poems like 'Mond' or 'Der Krieg'. But this is not to say that Heym's metaphors are graphic phantasms. In fact, one of the more subtle qualities of his poetry is his faculty for absorbing a plain observation into a visonary context. He does this often imperceptibly, by manipulating small parts of speech, like verb-prefixes. If it were done otherwise, or not at all, a number of his poems would be crass.

Another feature in Heym is the suppression of the analogical *as if* element in the poetic metaphor. This element had persisted in most previous modes of metaphor in German poetry, even in Romantic metaphor, despite certain Romantic theories about poetry as a kind of absolute word-music. The Romantic poet still worked from observation to construction, or vice versa, keeping his analogies usually explicit. Metaphor therefore never lost its fictive quality. The Expressionist, on the other hand, aims to eliminate this fictive element. Either he submerges the analogy, or he suppresses it. The older parallelism of image and idea is superseded by a fusion of image and idea, in which "the expressive element swallows the representational element." [1] This meant that the image could cease to refer to an observable world; it could become an end in itself, that is, *autotelic*. If it consists exclusively of images on this pattern, the poem exists as a discrete and self-contained world. It exists as an autonomous configuration of images which have affinity to each other, as consorted voices of the complex of feelings crystallized in

[1] W. Sokel, *The Writer in Extremis*. Stanford U.P., 1959, p. 51. This book is the most up-to-date and inclusive study of Expressionism.

the whole configuration, but need have no direct affinity to actual objects of reference. The poem becomes a *heterocosm*.[1] Many, if not most, of Trakl's later poems are heterocosms in this sense. To cite a familiar prose example: in Kafka's story *The Metamorphosis* (1914), Gregor Samsa, when he wakes up, is not in a state of mind which is insect-like; he wakes up to find that he has become an insect. In the image, object and idea are identical. Neither stands in an *as if* relation to the other; neither is a fiction based on the other; and the metaphor which results is free to conform to purely imaginative laws. Now the tendency of Expressionism after 1914 is to relax this principle, to write out in an often clumsy longhand what the pioneers had compressed into a vigorous and provocative stenography. In doing so, it ignored firstly the identification principle of early Expressionist metaphor; secondly, the Imagist (and not only Imagist) principle of concentration; and thirdly, T. E. Hulme's relevant precept about poetry being "a compromise for a language of intuition which would hand over sensations bodily",[2] a precept which also rejects the fictive element and to which Heym's and Trakl's metaphors do often conform.

The poems of Ernst Stadler, a slightly older contemporary of Heym and Trakl, are not so image-packed as theirs. Another difference is that Stadler's poems about the squalor of city life, poems about the Jewish quarter in the East End of London, do not express the obsessive foreboding of a general doom which is common to nearly all the early Expressionists. For Stadler, the age was an end, but the end was a fresh start. And he interpreted it less as an age of anxiety and disintegration than as one of transformation and hope. He is about the most literal of the foremost early Expressionists; and in his poems one can detect his starting-point more easily than in those of Heym or Trakl. This starting-point may fire the inner vision; but the inner vision seldom detaches itself from the frame of externals to become autonomous. Yet Stadler's poems are dithyrambic. His line is long and athletic, at times Whitmanesque. And many of his poems show the true dynamic mentality of the Expres-

[1] See M. H. Abrams, *The Mirror and the Lamp*. London, Oxford University Press, 1960, pp. 272–85.

[2] T. E. Hulme, *Speculations*. London, Routledge and Kegan Paul, 1949, p. 134.

sionist. Logical organization is, again, secondary; primary alone is the immediate presentation of a complex of feelings. The starting-point in experience may be a familiar one, a walk in early Spring, or waking as day breaks, or crossing a bridge in a train. In the poem 'On Crossing the Rhine Bridge at Cologne by Night', a recognizable world of sense-data persists almost to the end: the chimneys, roofs, lights, the train's rumbling. Yet this observed world is in the grip of an inner vision advancing toward a point of ecstasy. Only when it has reached this point, at which perception is extinguished in the intensity of pure self-consciousness, does the vision break free from the frame of sense. In this poem, it is the syntax which presents, gestically rather than logically, the simultaneous associations provoked by the sense-data. The gestic syntax is more highly developed in Stadler than in Heym; Stadler, too, unlike Heym, coins new words by linking old ones, like *nachtumschient* and *nachtentrissene* [*Luft*] in the Rhine Bridge poem. Heym, on the other hand, creates more surprising verb-metaphors than Stadler. Both poets, in different ways, were cultivating the "associative style" peculiar to Expressionism. It is a style which, by telescoping normally consecutive impressions and making them simultaneous in the poetic image, aims to rescue essence from time's chaotic flux. This is a far cry from the Impressionist style at the turn of the century, as in Liliencron's or Dehmel's poems, in which not verbs but nouns, not gestic syntax but logical syntax, had been predominant.

Stadler worked in his native Alsace, at Oxford and in Brussels. Even though he knew and praised work by Heym, and by Gottfried Benn, he had no contact with any of the Berlin poets. Of all the early Expressionists, it is the poet who was most remote from Berlin, the Austrian Georg Trakl, whose work probably comes closest to the early Expressionist idea of the visionary poet. Trakl does not seem to have been influenced by any of his contemporaries, with the possible exception of Else Lasker-Schüler, an older experimental poet, whom he did once meet on a brief visit to Berlin. Karl Kraus, the Austrian critic of literature and *moeurs*, may also have had some influence on Trakl's outlook; and Trakl dedicated one of his richest small poems to him. But the actual formative influences on Trakl's poetry are chiefly Baudelaire, Rimbaud, and Hölderlin. Not least, Dostoevsky had a certain influence on Trakl's thinking—his novels were in general congenial to writers of the period. Trakl's long poem 'Helian' (written during the winter 1912–13) also contains echoes from the Old and New Testaments; but here, as in other poems, Biblical motifs are wholly absorbed into Trakl's own image-world, even to the extent of being presented in the present tense.

One of the assumptions which Trakl shared with his contemporaries was that the materialistic bourgeois society of his time was doomed. But his attitude to this was as far from Stadler's vitalism as from Franz Werfel's utopian optimism. His apparent unconcern with political or other ideologies was shared by some of the best poets writing before 1914 (which is not to say that the age was not crazed by conflicting ideologies); but in Trakl, perhaps more than in any of his contemporaries, the vision of disintegration tells. He was certainly a poet of the generation which lay under Nietzsche's spell. Yet if we must look for beliefs in his work, we find that he believes in certain primitive Christian values: the reality of evil, and the expiation of guilt by suffering, values against which Nietzsche had levelled some of his harshest criticism. Trakl's beliefs, however, remain problematic—the decay of the faculty of belief does, after all, stigmatize the minds of many of the pioneers of modern poetry. Trakl's beliefs are implied in his poetry; but they are seldom stated, nor is it his intention to state beliefs. For he came closer than any of his contemporaries to creating a poetry of autotelic metaphor, in the sense outlined above. One approaches his meanings through the recurrent images and symbols which embody them; but even then it is hard to arrive at a generally acceptable interpretation, since much of his symbolism is ambiguous, and errors of interpretation arise equally if one assumes that his symbolism is systematic (a typology), or that it varies from poem to poem. Trakl was reticent about his work. He left little or no indication of how it is to be interpreted. In an age of manifestos and polemics, he was intent only on writing poems.

His poems must not be read as egocentric confessions in metaphoric disguises. One of his ablest critics has suggested just the converse, in fact: that his work evolves toward a transparency of vision, in which things enact and interpret themselves through autonomous metaphoric forms. This would account for the luminosity of Trakl's inscapes. And his mature work at least (1912–14) fulfills the demands that Rilke made, but was himself able at best to postulate, of the true orphic poet.[1] What Trakl himself called his "criminal melancholy" is a premise, but it is not the substance, of what he says. As Rilke first pointed out, Trakl's work is affirmative. But what it affirms is a spiritual order of being which may not be at once perceptible in his poems, because he inflects the imagery of this spiritual order so often with an imagery of disintegration. As the poem 'Untergang' shows, Trakl does not exempt himself from this vision of disintegration. Of the poets so far discussed, Trakl had perhaps the most intimate intelligence of the moral and intellectual crisis through which his generation was passing. Thus he is concerned to evaluate freely the crisis of modern man in his relation to death and to evil, whereas Heym, for instance, often excludes crisis by projecting images of death and evil which make them all-pervasive and quite inexorable forces. The same difference exists between Heym's black image of nature and Trakl's variable image which enshrines, even if it does so tonally rather than visually, the changing shadows of a Paradise not irretrievably lost.

The poem 'Klage' shows just this distinctive feature of Trakl's work. For here there is his lamentation, in the language of idyl, for the mortality of the idyl—as if the chant of this language could charm away the idyl's creeping death. This is one of Trakl's last poems, written just before his death in a military hospital in Poland, where he was under observation as a suspected case of schizophrenia. Although he suffered at this time under the delusion that he would be executed as a deserter, for breaking down after the Battle of Grodek, 'Klage' is not Trakl's complaint for himself. It is a complaint for the "golden image of man," or man's true image, which he feared would be lost or obscured in "Eternity's icy wave." As often in Trakl, the image of the boat appears as a symbol of human existence. But that existence is now threatened with extinction. Here too, characteristically, Trakl says "Eternity's icy wave/Would

[1] K. Simon, *Traum und Orpheus*. Salzburg, O. Müller Verlag, 1955.

swallow . . ." He does not say "swallows". The German subjunctive permits a glance into the interior of Trakl's mind—how his vision embraces persistently, or hovers between, the extremes of idyl and anti-idyl. His double vision of a possible redemption of man and of the actual corruption of man, never spills over into a crass statement of either half-truth.

Trakl's rhythms and sound-patterns, too, are as expressive of meaning in his poems as are his recurrent symbols and images. In this respect he realized possibilities which were divined by the Romantic Novalis, sometimes realized by Brentano, and made programmatic by Mallarmé. But since these rhythms and sound-patterns sometimes seem to contradict, and not conventionally to match, the meanings embodied in his images, it might seem that Trakl is less a master than a slave of his ambiguities. Yet it must be realized that his ambiguities derive, firstly, from the tension in his thought between spiritual and temporal orders of being, and secondly, from the tension in his language between the autotelic image and the representational image. Here an analogy exists between Trakl's practice and modern musical harmony, as in Stravinsky's *Sacre du Printemps*, where we are asked to hear two contradictory harmonies at the same time. Also Arnold Schönberg was at this time (1912) developing his dodecaphonic system, which emancipates music from conventional harmony altogether. Kandinsky, the spokesman of abstract painting at the time, whose book *Über das Geistige in der Kunst* also appeared in 1912, was describing the same phenomenon from a painter's standpoint, when he wrote: "The fact that the form may not match the color must not be regarded as something 'unharmonic' . . . but quite the reverse—it must be regarded as a new possibility, as another harmony [*auch eine Harmonie*]."[1]

Sometimes the tension in Trakl's images prevents one from telling whether an image is to be understood descriptively or symbolically. It is true that each of his poems—of which there are about a hundred, excluding the juvenilia—offers a clue to the others. But the meaning of the same words varies according to the degree of literal-

[1] W. Kandinsky. *Über das Geistige in der Kunst*. Munich, R. Piper Verlag, 1912 (3rd ed.), pp. 53–54.

ness involved in each case. The same adjective may be primarily descriptive in one poem (or one line of a poem), synesthetic in another, and symbolic in a third. Yet the expectation of some 'realistic' or 'logical' connection between images presupposes the existence of a common and referable image of reality to which both the poet and his public implicitly assent. And it is precisely the absence of such an image of reality from Trakl's world that constitutes the ground of his poetry. Therefore it is wrong to conclude that he is enigmatic because he deploys images haphazardly, as euphonious formations made up of words that have been rooted away from normal usage, for use as integers in a private fantasy. Certainly, he is a poet of monologue. But not only are the individual words in his poems more often plain than precious (though his feats of association might suggest the opposite); also his laconic image-formations can, if it helps the reader at all, be traced back more frequently than one would expect to some objective source, if not in sense-experience, then in legends, or in the Bible (as in some of the darkest areas of the poem 'Helian'). It is Trakl's genius for deep assimilation which brings a new kind of energy into the language of German poetry, and makes us newly sensitive to the enigma of the familiar world. His poetry is remote; but it is not rarefied. And the more one reads his poems, the more one finds them simultaneously enacting and interpreting sensuous and spiritual experience.

So far, only three years of early Expressionist poetry have been discussed. But it is not too much to say that these three years just before the First World War were some of the most productive in modern German literature. In 1912 also, Rilke began the *Duino Elegies*, and during the next two years wrote some of his best short poems (e.g., 'Wendung' and 'An Hölderlin'). Stefan George was writing *Der Stern des Bundes* (1914); Else Lasker-Schüler was writing her *Hebräische Balladen* (1913); Alfred Mombert published his mythic poem *Äon vor Syrakus* in 1911; and Theodor Däubler was writing his *Der sternhelle Weg* (1915).

The three last-named poets came close enough, in certain poems, to the Expressionist style to be included in most of the anthologies and miscellanies of the period. All three were accounted forerunners, and Däubler and Lasker-Schüler were among the most enthusiastic apologists of the movement. Däubler's poem 'Millionen Nachtigallen schlagen' ('Millions of nightingales are singing') merits special study for its functional sound-effects, its word-conjuring and its central cipher image (the latter kind of image was to be used systematically by Gottfried Benn).

But it is August Stramm, of the same generation as these older poets, who was the most radical experimentalist. His experiments in diction, meter and syntax were of a different order from those of the younger generation, who were concentrating chiefly on the essential image. Stramm's break with the logic of prose and with description —elements retained obdurately by Naturalists and Symbolists—had a strong influence on the development of poetry after Expressionism. Whereas Heym or Trakl composed mythic or symbolic landscapes, Stramm composed only abstract word-patterns. The poem 'Schwermut', for instance, contains no images at all, no adjectives, and only one adverb. The poem voices a state of mind; but it refers to no recognizable objects or symbols. Stramm reverses the usual procedure for objectifying states of mind: he suppresses the world of the object altogether. The poem voices the gesture of the feeling itself which gives the focus. For this reason, verbs and neologisms abound in Stramm's poems. He often arrives at his neologisms by telescoping two or three normal synonyms. In the poem 'Freudenhaus', for instance, the word *schamzerpört* telescopes *schamzerstört* and *empört*, to give a word with the sense, roughly, of "shamesexshattershocked". Gottfried Benn, too, in his poems published in 1917, was like Stramm far more a poet of the provocative single word, the *parole essentielle* of French Symbolism, than of the *image essentielle*. But the new words coined by Stramm were less cerebral than Benn's; at least, they were meant to be emotive. In other poems he invents onomatopœic and pun-like sounds, to voice emotions which he believed could not be rendered by existing words. This was not in itself new: Paul Scheerbart had published the first German sound-poem, 'Kikakoku', in 1897. But Stramm (and before long Hugo Ball in Zürich) used pure sound seriously for the voicing of mental states, just as he had abandoned, in other experiments, normal conjugations and declensions. Although it can be said of Stramm that his mental states, if different at all from those of any average sensual man, are bizarre rather than electric, it should be by now self-evident that the poet here assumes the role of absolute creator. To this role his function as communicator, using lexical and generally intelligible meanings, is strictly subordinated. One sees to what extremes poets at the time could be driven by the despairing scepticism with regard to normal language, of which Hofmannsthal wrote as early as 1902, in his *Brief des Lord Chandos*. It was only one step from Stramm's experiments to the abandonment of the mental state, as an expendable fiction, in certain Dadaist simultaneous poems and bruitist sound-poems which foreshadowed Kurt Schwitters' long and elaborate *Sonata in Basic Sounds*. Hugo Ball, at the end of his Dadaist period in 1917, wrote in his journal: "The safety-valve of an abstract age has burst."[1]

A certain abstractive strain is also found in Gottfried Benn's later poems. But Benn's first published poems, *Morgue* (1912), are realistic expressions of shock: mortuary poems about cancer-effects, about a nest of rats found in the corpse of a drowned girl, and so on. These poems are Expressionistic in their disillusion, aggression and disgust; but not in their form. It is only in such poems as 'Caryatid,' first published in 1916, that Benn emerges as the Expressionist poet of the subliminal. The image of Silenus at the end of stanza 1 in 'Caryatid' shows what kind of distortion enters Benn's subliminal imagery at this stage of his work:

> from his loud blood forever drowned by roars
> shivered by alien music and unique,
> wine drips into his sex.

The distortion creates an image that is deliberately fussed and turbid: the image of the essential Silenus at large in the living soul. This is not the involuntary distortion by bombast which is found in such Phase II Expressionist poems as those of Johannes R. Becher. 'Caryatid' also has other important implications: the poem suggests that only the human imagination can emancipate man from the stony fixity of his actual state; but finally even this belief is put in doubt, for the moment of ecstasy is a *Glück-Lügenstunde* ("moment of joy and lie"). In this typical *parole essentielle*, the ecstasy and the

[1] H. Ball, *Die Flucht aus der Zeit*. Lucerne, Verlag Josef Stocker, 1946, p. 152.

doubt merge and are fixed. Nonetheless, the idea of transcendent imagination underlies the whole of Benn's subsequent work, with its irrationalism strangely consorting with a phrasing so urbane and a diction so near-scientific. It also underlies his attitude to distinctively modernist poetry: its ring-dance of irrationality and intellect. In his later essays Benn often returns to "Nietzsche's assertion . . . that art is the only metaphysical activity to which life still obliges us."[1]

Of the more important early Expressionists, only Gottfried Benn, Franz Werfel and Yvan Goll survived the 1914–18 war. Meanwhile the pioneers had been succeeded by poets whose first concern was not so much a new poetry as a new society. They were the poets whom Thomas Mann, with some justice, stigmatized at the time as "political literati" and against whom he wrote much of his book *Reflections of a Non-Political Man*. It was the literariness as well as the vaguely Utopian political ideas of the post-1914 poets which, in fact, contributed to the expiring, during the first years of the 1920's, of Expressionism as a coherent literary movement. Yet it is necessary to distinguish two phases of Expressionism within the decade 1910–20: the first from 1910 to 1914, and the second from 1914 to 1920. Phase I produced the best poems and the real revolution in poetic language, the impact of which continued during the 1920's, and can still be felt today. Phase II diluted the innovations of Phase I, to the extent of producing work in which mindless feeling and oratory combine to limit, if not to cancel, its value as poetry. Phase I ended early in the war, with the deaths of Lichtenstein, Stadler, Trakl and Stramm, and with the insanity of Jakob van Hoddis. The end of Phase II came during the two fatal years of counter-revolutionary gains which followed the 1920 splitting of the German Independent Socialist Party (USPD), whose policies for a bourgeois republic and for appeasing the masses had coincided broadly with the indecisive Marxism of most Phase II Expressionists. Of course, one can see continuity between the two phases. The earlier flight into the pure poetic image, or into the grotesque, oscillated between morbidity and regeneration no less than the succeeding flight into a political image. But the distinction of these two phases within the decade does at least aid understanding of the shift of accent and the change

[1] G. Benn, *Essays, Reden, Vorträge*. Wiesbaden, Limes Verlag, 1959, p. 249.

of style within Expressionism. It also allows for factors which are not discriminated in two other views of Expressionism: the Marxist view of Georg Lukács, and the *soi-disant* nihilist view of Gottfried Benn. Lukács confines Expressionism almost exclusively to the bourgeois left-wing writers of the 1914–20 period, e.g., Ludwig Rubiner, Karl Otten, Walter Hasenclever and Kurt Hiller; and he attacks these writers from a Leninist standpoint (his views were written down in 1938).[1] Benn, on the other hand, spreads his range of reference wider. He writes of a "Phase II of the Expressionistic style," which presupposes a *pre-Expressionist* Phase I, covering the period from the end of classical antiquity down to Nietzsche.[2] This "Phase II" is not, therefore, a second Phase within Expressionism as a literary movement at all. It relates to Expressionism as a whole, as a manifestation of the intellect and art of modern Western man, as opposed to Western man before Nietzsche, in Benn's own cultural and anthropological perspective.

Much as some English poets used the innovations of the Imagists for quasi-doctrinaire ends in the 1930's, Expressionist poets after 1914 converted early Expressionist innovations and visions into ideological weapons. True, left-wing poets in Phase II believed that they were fighting to defend the status of poetry as a life-shaping force, and that poems could be used as invectives against reaction—the reactionary creeds which they believed to be responsible for the war. For the idealistic humbug of the materialistic society then involved in war they were, however, no less responsible themselves. Accordingly, they were rarely intellectually free or technically skillful enough to wield any weapon more subtle than a sandbag. The tocsin had first been sounded in Phase I by Franz Werfel. But Werfel also wrote some disturbing poems (e.g., 'Der Ritt'); and his message was much less a political than an ethical one. He, no less than the Dadaists, who sat in the Café Odeon in Zürich at a table decisively apart from him and his confederates, was searching for what Hugo Ball called in his journal at this time, in 1916, "the specific rhythm, the buried face, of the epoch." But all too often, as

[1] G. Lukács, *Probleme des Realismus*. Berlin, Aufbau Verlag, 1955, pp. 146–83.

[2] G. Benn, 'Phase II. Interview über Nihilismus, Artistik und Religion', *Merkur* (Stuttgart), Vol. IV, 1950, No. 23.

Ball pointed out, Werfel's poems were a means to this end, not ends in themselves—a feature which relates them unfortunately to some of the more shapeless poems of the period. Werfel was for a time the accepted spokesman of Phase II. But after 1920 his poetry changed its manner, and his novels and plays took most of his attention. What was needed during Phase II was, in any case, less a spokesman than a critic. There was no critic who was sympathetic but ready to curb excesses. Neither was there a critic who had criteria by which to discern, coolly, the relations between the declamatory style and the politics of the Phase II Expressionists. Such a critic might, at least, have followed up the implications of Hugo Ball's penetrating remark: "The force of the modern esthetic consists in this: you can't be an artist and still believe in history."[1]

Documents of the period relating to the aims of its poetry in Phase II have the same buskinading manner as many of the poems. Kurt Pinthus, advocate and anthologist of Expressionism, wrote from the trenches in 1915:

> The common will of the latest poetry is to free reality from the outline of its appearances, to free ourselves from it [reality], to overcome it, not by its own means, not by evading it, but, embracing it all the more fervently, to conquer and master it by intellectual penetration [*des Geistes Bohrkraft*], by suppleness, by a longing for clarity, by intensity of feeling and by explosive force.[2]

Pinthus then went on to say that Expressionist poets were wanting a total image of reality seen from the core, a poetry not of appearances and of ornament, but of "essence, heart and nerve." This theme is taken up by Kasimir Edschmid in his 1917 manifesto, 'On Poetic Expressionism,' in which he is groping, through the jargon of the period, toward an idea of poetry as stark inclusive vision, although, symptomatically, he deplores reality as fact. He dissociates Expressionism from the Naturalist and Impressionist trends which preceded it, and goes on:

[1] H. Ball, *Die Flucht aus der Zeit*, p. 143.
[2] K. Pinthus, 'Die jüngste Dichtung', *Die weissen Blätter*, Vol. II, 1915, No. 12 (p. 1503). Kurt Pinthus' anthology, *Menschheitsdämmerung* (1920) was reprinted in 1959 (Hamburg, Rowohlt Verlag).

Above all, there was now, against the atomistic fragmentation
[*das Atomische, Verstückte*] of the Impressionists, a great embracing
cosmic feeling [*Weltgefühl*—a normal German locution] . . . A
new image of the world had to be created, one that had no share in
the Naturalist image—which could only be grasped in terms of
experience, and no share in the fragmented space given by the
impression; rather an image which had to be *simple*, literal
[*eigentlich*] and therefore beautiful . . . We had to create reality.
The sense of the object had to be rooted out. No longer may one
be satisfied with the believed, supposed, noted fact; the image of
the world must be mirrored pure and unfalsified. But that image
lies only within ourselves. Thus the Expressionist artist's whole
dimension becomes vision. He does not look, he sees. He does not
describe, he has the inner experience. He does not reproduce, he
creates. The chain of facts no longer exists: factories, houses,
sickness, whores, shrieks and hunger. What now exists is the vision
of them.[1]

This statement not only extends Pinthus' views; it is also a crude
attempt to apply to writing the aims of those artists of the time,
notably Hans Arp, who wanted to create an *ab initio* concrete art
which was by definition non-figurative, and the aims of those artists
who practised what Kandinsky had preached about abstract painting
five years earlier. But Arp had rejected existing objects altogether,
and Kandinsky had been defining truth to sensation and to feeling
in an attempt to limit strictly the domain of objects within the free
realm of imagination. What Edschmid does is to generalize both
concretist and abstractist theories into bombast, and to add the
postulate that poetic vision, which to him concerns not particulars
but types, should define truth to objects. In the development of the
modern esthetic, this is a decidedly retrograde step. As for its
relevance to poetry, it divorces the typifying function of language
from its truly creative particularizing function: the same process,
in the name of "vision," is noticeable in the sprawling, jumbled
poems of Johannes R. Becher. What the poets wanted, Robert Musil
thought at the time, was some synthetic procedure. But, he wrote,

---

[1] K. Edschmid, *Frühe Manifeste*. Hamburg, C. Wegner Verlag, 1957, p. 32.

"the Expressionist . . . is looking for the new feeling of life as a chemist looks for synthetic rubber. His limitation is this: there is no exclusively synthetic procedure."[1]

In the 1920's, an Expressionist manner still prevails in many plays and novels, as well as in poems. Expressionist drama, which flourished between 1916 and 1922, now found a model producer in Erwin Piscator. Of the poets active in the 1920's, Yvan Goll, much of whose work is written in French, created an idiom which is both highly idiosyncratic and cosmopolitan enough to incorporate some features of French Surrealist poetry. Goll also avoided the provincialism which limited some other poets (not Rilke), and which marked a reaction against the "cosmic feeling" convention of Phase II. Erich Kästner, with his satiric 'New Realist' poems, represented with Kurt Tucholsky a stronger reaction against the irrationalism and mind-exorcising oratory of Phase II. Goll, however, remained faithful to his early Expressionist beginnings. Though his first poems tend toward Whitmanesque oratory, the poems which he wrote during the long illness before his death in 1950, show a controlled freedom of imagery and rhythm won only from years of careful experiment. These last poems of Goll's *Traumkraut*, mark one possible extreme of the liberation of the image initiated by the early Expressionists. But Goll's last poems are much more overtly personal in tone than any of the early Expressionist poems by poets discussed above. Much of his previous work had an intimacy of voice as well. But the new intimacy of *Traumkraut* is not merely that of a practised symbolist with a natural style, nor is it only consistent with Goll's knowledge that he was to die. It is consistent also with an awareness which has, directly or indirectly, informed much poetry during the last fifteen years, the awareness of the Bomb, about which Goll wrote (in English, while in the United States) one of the first Bomb poems, 'Atom Elegy'.

Oskar Loerke's work never lost density even in the oratorical climate of Phase II, and it retained it in the years which followed

---

[1] R. Musil, *Tagebücher, Aphorismen, Essays und Reden*. Hamburg, Rowohlt Verlag, 1955, p. 207 (diary entry dated 1918). Yet there were three poets in Phase II who did write poems in which the language is particular and concrete: Wilhelm Klemm, Alfred Vagts and Paul Zech. Some of Alfred Vagts' forgotten war-poems are comparable with those of Wilfred Owen.

the collapse of Expressionism as a movement. Loerke was possibly the purest pastoral poet of the post-Expressionist period. It is noticeable that Lichtenstein's 'Die Dämmerung' cadence returns again in Loerke's poem 'Die Vogelstrassen'. Into the pastoral he also brings the identification principle of early Expressionist metaphor. His observation, sharp as it is, is that of the disembodied eye detecting in the smallest natural phenomenon the mythology of the human soul. Wilhelm Lehmann, whose work was not widely known before 1945, is another poet of this quasi-mythopoeic vision into nature. Both Loerke and Lehmann exerted influence on poets after 1945, particularly since 'nature' remained one of the few object-worlds which had not disintegrated when Germany fell.

The Nazi period is a period of inner and outer emigration. Of the poets represented here, few remained in Germany. Of these, three seem to have had typical fates. Lehmann was as hermetic as ever; Loerke was removed from his office as secretary in the Prussian Academy of Arts and withdrew into a suburb; and Benn, after a brief but serious assent to Nazism, suddenly saw through it and "exiled" himself into the medical corps of the army in 1935. A passage from Loerke's diary illustrates the nature of the 1933 crisis: "I stand between the terrorists of the Right and the Left. Perhaps I shall be destroyed. My nerves won't stand any more. The anguish of being confronted with terrible consequences, without having done or even known the least thing."[1]

But it is often forgotten that there were two generations of poets who went into exile during the crisis: older poets, like Wolfskehl, Werfel, Herrmann-Neisse, Becher, Brecht and Else Lasker-Schüler, but also poets of a succeeding generation which reached maturity within the Nazi period. Both Franz Baermann Steiner and Jesse Thoor went to England. Two younger poets, Hans Werner Cohn and Erich Fried, still live there. The debt of Steiner and Thoor to Expressionism, if it exists at all, is infinitesimal. It is no wonder that these poets were far more conscious of racial and family ties than of literary roots. Neither shows, in any case, the kind of consciousness of a literary role to be played, which is blatant among Phase II Expressionists.

[1] O. Loerke, *Tagebücher*. Heidelberg, Verlag Lambert Schneider, 1955, p. 261.

This may seem a slender thread with which to connect them with poets whose work began to appear in Germany after 1948. But it is not so slender. The two generations of poets who became known after 1948, from Günter Eich to the poets born after 1920, are in effect as different as may be from the poets caught in the wash of the First World War. This is, at least, the case in Western Germany. But it is not the reason why we have included, with the exceptions of Brecht and Huchel, only West German poets. Some fine poets have emerged in East Germany during the last five years, notably Johannes Bobrowski (born 1917), as is shown in the selection *Deutsche Lyrik auf der anderen Seite* (Munich 1960). But they are not represented because, when we were choosing and translating poems, we had not read enough of their work to enable us to choose representative poems. Little enough of their work, after all, has been available. So it is not that we have been partial to West German poets; it is simply that we have been ignorant of good East German poets.

The influence, on the post-1948 poets in Western Germany, of Benn's view that poetry transcends history and cannot affect it, was symptomatically ambiguous. On the one hand, recent experience seemed to confirm it. On the other hand, it tended to ascribe to the poet a mandarin remoteness from history which seemed nonsensical after the explosions in 1945. The consequence has been that much recent work (and here Brecht has helped) has a strong sense of commitment—often to a greater extent, even, than some poems from East Germany. There is, in the construction of such poems, a sense of concrete values that was missing from the work of the post-1914 poets. Poems which have this quality do not therefore exhaust themselves in bardic gesture and programmatic assertion. On the contrary, they are poems in which (as in those of Schnurre or Fried) the resources created by the early Expressionists—imagery, rhythms, syntax, diction—are reduced to the simplest means for the indirect expression of a committed view, in language which is no less constructive and exploratory for being matter-of-fact. Paul Celan's 'Fugue of Death' is a poem whose language has the positive signs of this regeneration of style. It is a poem which could not have been written in any other age than the age of genocide. Yet it is a poem of incantation, in which the poet is quarrelling with nobody but himself. It shows that incantatory word-music need not at all sever its taproots in historical realities, and that incantation itself can become the most expressive form that a judgment on history can assume. Out of the quarrel with others, Yeats said, we make rhetoric; but out of the quarrel with ourselves we make poetry. The anti-rhetorical manner in much German poetry today—and the close-grained surface is no longer considered as a sign of missing depth—does offset certain other forms of pretension which persist in the work of poets who are less serious artists than might be desired.

Yeats also believed that "the first flying-fish leaped, not because it sought 'adaptation' to the air, but out of horror of the sea;"[1] and Alexander von Villers, writing at the end of the nineteenth century, believed that "there are more marvellous beasts in syntax than in the depths of the sea."[2] These two statements apply to the new German poetry. For in it one finds an often precarious balance between two views of language, which may conflict with each other: language as a key for the survival of the human, and language as a means of exploratory creation. The dehumanization of the arts, much discussed not so long ago, and the mechanization and animalization of society which jointly consort with it, were certainly reflected in (and probably fostered by) certain aspects of Expressionism. The problem now seems to take this form: how can the language of men, in an age of uncompassion, explore creatively the human mind, or even set value on it. Often contemporary experimental poets seem to explore language as if it were not a creation of the human mind. Other poets, on the other hand, often seem to flinch from confronting the human mind on its own present terms.

Yet everywhere there is diversity and singularity. There is a new sense of delight in the infinitesimal, and in the surreally true, as in the poems of Günter Grass. There is also self-criticism, urbanity and wit—qualities for which German literature has not been much renowned in the past. It may be that such facets of contemporary

[1] W. B. Yeats, *Autobiographies* [1926]. London, Macmillan, 1955, p. 143.

[2] Alexander von Villers, *Briefe eines Unbekannten* (ed. Rudolf Graf Hoyos) Vienna 1887, Vol. II, p. 51.

verse have more purity and impact than fulminations of anger: they hit hidden nerves, while the fulminations fizzle out, Western German society having as it does, like some other Western societies, certain self-sealing devices which convert eruptions on the surface into marketable goods.

Lastly, there is a new cosmopolitan feeling about the new German poetry, which began to take shape soon after 1948 with a spate of travel poems. Once again, this can be understood in terms of Yeats' image of the flying-fish. But perhaps this cosmopolitan feeling will eventually turn out to have been less a flight, made in horror, from the intolerable laral domain, than an exploration of the alien and strange which, as Hölderlin said, must be made if the laral domain is to be discovered at all.

London 1961
MICHAEL HAMBURGER
CHRISTOPHER MIDDLETON

NOTE ON DATES

Normally the dates of poems can be established by reference to the NOTES ON AUTHORS or to the list of ACKNOWLEDGEMENTS. Ascertainable dates of writing which differ significantly from dates of first publication are given in square brackets under the translations of the poems in question. Dates without brackets show the chronological sequence in a poet's work, or a chronological relation between one poem and another within the same period. With these aids, using also the NOTES ON AUTHORS and ACKNOWLEDGEMENTS, the reader can follow from year to year the chronological sequence of all the poems in the book.

MODERN GERMAN POETRY
1910-1960

ELSE LASKER-SCHÜLER

MEIN VOLK

Der Fels wird morsch,
Dem ich entspringe
Und meine Gotteslieder singe . . .
Jäh stürz ich vom Weg
Und riesele ganz in mir
Fernab, allein über Klagegestein
Dem Meer zu.

Hab mich so abgeströmt
Von meines Blutes
Mostvergorenheit.
Und immer, immer noch der Widerhall
In mir,
Wenn schauerlich gen Ost
Das morsche Felsgebein,
Mein Volk,
Zu Gott schreit.

GEORG GROSZ

Manchmal spielen bunte Tränen
In seinen äschernen Augen.

Aber immer begegnen ihm Totenwagen,
Die verscheuchen seine Libellen.

Er ist abergläubig—
—Ward unter einem grossen Stern geboren—

MY PEOPLE

The rock grows brittle
From which I spring,
To which my canticles I sing . . .
Down I rush from the track
And inwardly only ripple
Far off, alone over wailing stones
Toward the sea.

Have flowed so much away
From the wine ferment
Of my blood.
And yet for ever, endlessly the echo
In me,
When eastward, awesomely,
The brittle rock of bone,
My people,
Cries out to God.

1905: *Der siebente Tag*   1913: *Hebräische Balladen*

GEORG GROSZ

Sometimes tears of many colors
Play in his ashen eyes.

But always he encounters hearses;
They scare his dragonflies away.

He is superstitious
—Born under a great star—

Seine Schrift regnet,
Seine Zeichnung: Trüber Buchstabe.

Wie lange im Fluss gelegen,
Blähen seine Menschen sich auf.

Mysteriöse Verlorene mit Quappenmäulern
Und verfaulten Seelen.

Fünf träumende Totenfahrer
Sind seine silbernen Finger.

Aber nirgendwo ein Licht im verirrten Märchen
Und doch ist er ein Kind,

Der Held aus dem Lederstrumpf
Mit dem Indianerstamm auf Duzfuss.

Sonst hasst er alle Menschen,
Sie bringen ihm Unglück.

Aber Georg Grosz liebt sein Missgeschick
Wie einen anhänglichen Feind.

Und seine Traurigkeit ist dionysisch,
Schwarzer Champagner seine Klage.

Er ist ein Meer mit verhängtem Mond,
Sein Gott ist nur scheintot.

His handwriting a downpour,
His drawings: letters of cloud.

As though they'd long lain in the river
His subjects bloat their bodies out.

Mysterious vagrants with tadpole mouths
And putrefied souls.

His silver fingers are
Five dreaming undertakers

But nowhere a light in the stray legend,
And yet he is a child,

The Leatherstocking Saga hero,
On intimate terms with the Redskins.

All others he hates;
They bring him bad luck.

But Georg Grosz loves his misfortune
Like a dear adversary.

And his sadness is dionysian,
Black champagne his lamentation.

He is a sea with a veiled moon.
His God seems dead, but is not so.

1917: *Die gesammelten Gedichte*

AN MEINE FREUNDE

Nicht die tote Ruhe—
Bin nach einer stillen Nacht schon ausgeruht.
Oh, ich atme Geschlafenes aus,
Den Mond noch wiegend
Zwischen meinen Lippen.

Nicht den Todesschlaf—
Schon im Gespräch mit euch
Himmlisch Konzert . . .
Und neu Leben anstimmt
In meinem Herzen.

Nicht der Überlebenden schwarzer Schritt!
Zertretene Schlummer zersplittern den Morgen.
Hinter Wolken verschleierte Sterne
Über Mittag versteckt—
So immer wieder neu uns finden.

In meinem Elternhause nun
Wohnt der Engel Gabriel . . .
Ich möchte innig dort mit euch
Selige Ruhe in einem Fest feiern—
Sich die Liebe mischt mit unserem Wort.

Aus mannigfaltigem Abschied
Steigen aneinandergeschmiegt die goldenen Staubfäden,
Und nicht ein Tag ungesüsst bleibt
Zwischen wehmütigem Kuss
Und Wiedersehn!

Nicht die tote Ruhe—
So ich liebe im Odem sein . . . !
Auf Erden mit euch im Himmel schon.
Allfarbig malen auf blauem Grund
Das ewige Leben.

TO MY FRIENDS

Not the dead calm—
Night was quiet and I am rested now.
O I exhale drowsedness,
Still cradling the moon
Between my lips.

Not the sleep of death—
But in talk with you
Heavenly concert . . .
And new life strikes up
In my heart.

Not the black stride of the survivors!
Trampled slumbers dissever the morning.
Behind clouds veiled stars
Latent over noonday—
Find us this way new and new again.

Now in my family house
Dwells Gabriel the angel . . .
It is my heart's want there with you
To celebrate serene calm in a feast—
Love mingles with our words.

From devious departures
In tight embrace the golden pistils rise,
And no day goes unsweetened
Between the wistful kiss
And meeting again!

Not the dead calm—
So much I love to be in breath . . . !
On earth, with you, it is in heaven.
Paint on a blue ground all kinds of color
The eternal life.

1932: *Konzert*

ÜBER GLITZERNDEN KIES

Könnt ich nach Haus—
Die Lichte gehen aus—
Erlischt ihr letzter Gruss.

Wo soll ich hin?
Oh Mutter mein, weisst du's?
Auch unser Garten ist gestorben! . . .

Es liegt ein grauer Nelkenstrauss
Im Winkel wo im Elternhaus.
Er hatte grosse Sorgfalt sich erworben.

Umkränzte das Willkommen an den Toren
Und gab sich ganz in seiner Farbe aus.
Oh liebe Mutter! . . .

Versprühte Abendrot
Am Morgen weiche Sehnsucht aus
Bevor die Welt in Schmach und Not.

Ich habe keine Schwestern mehr und keine Brüder.
Der Winter spielte mit dem Tode in den Nestern
Und Reif erstarrte alle Liebeslieder.

OVER SHINING SHINGLE

O to go home at last—
The lights fade fast—
Their final greeting gone.

Where lay my head?
Mother, say soon.
Our garden, too, is dead.

A bunch of grey carnations lies
In some lost corner of the house.
Every ounce it took of all our care,

It wreathed the welcome at the door,
And gave itself, in color generous,
O mother dear.

It spread the sunset gold,
And in the morning soft desires,
Before this downfall of the world.

None of my sisters live now and no brothers live.
Winter has played with death in every nest
And frozen cold our every song of love.

1943: *Mein blaues Klavier*

KARL WOLFSKEHL

ICH

Nun muss ich krampfig an den rand geschmiegt
Das andre und mich andren ganz verlieren.
Noch wie ein schütteres flimmern ferner stadt
Noch wie blutwellenschlag abends vorm einschlaf
Noch wie den letzten liebesblick beim abschied
Abdrängen alles, nichts mehr bleibt! Wahn flamme
Versprühn, der kelch birst bittersüssen weins,
Die lippen fasern, nebelbilder, meins
Zerreisst wie todesschrei von tieren.

HINFAHRT

Du bist allein, entrückt, gemieden, sag es
Nur tiefer stets dir in den düstern Sinn.
Du wolltest dich, nur dich, Hiob, ertrag es,
Nun unter andern Sternen wirf dich hin

Ins Ungewisse, das wie Mondlichtnähe,
Wie Mondlichtwolke farbig fahl dir droht,
Droht oder lockt. Die Nacht ist duftwarm. Spähe
Den leeren Himmel aus von deinem Boot.

Hier ein Geleucht. Ist das ein Stern gleich jenen
Die deiner Väter Gang gewiesen und
Den Edlen Halt und Gunst—uns und Hellenen
Gottschimmer, Kairos, Tucht und Ewigen Bund?

I

So as I clutch and cling to the brink I must
Lose what is other and that other, me.
Now like scant flickers of a distant town
Now like bloodwaves lapping before sleep at night
Now like the last adoring glance before farewell
Thrust all away, nothing is left! Delusion flame
Are quenched, the glass of sweet and bitter wine
Breaks, the lips unthread, vague images in vapor, mine
Rends like the death cry of animals.

1919

OUTWARD JOURNEY

Your are alone, distanced and shunned, impress this
Ever more deeply on your darkened soul.
You wanted self, only self, Job: now bear this—
Under new constellations let self fall

Where the Indefinite threatens like the moonlight's
Nearness, like pallid moonlit mass of cloud,
Threatens or draws on. From your ship, in night's
Warm perfume, search the empty heavens out.

A brightness here. Was it just such a star
Lighted your fathers' way, gave help, and sent
Blessing to us and Hellas—shechinah,
Kairos, strength and eternal covenant?

Ein Himmel, sprachst du, hält uns allumfangen.
Ist dem so, Hiob? Neues Firmament,
Abweisend, einsam. Bist zu dir gegangen
In eine Ferne da kein Gott dich kennt.

Weisst du nun, spürst du nun, Hiob, dich selber?
Hast furchtbarn Ringens Preis du dir erbracht?
Schleier und Schlacken schmelzen. Abendgelber,
Wie Sonnenrüste brennst du vor der Nacht.

Umbreite dich als deinen Mantel, innen
Du selbst dir Herzpunkt, rings von dir umwallt,
Und willig einzugehn. Doch nicht verrinnen
Wie Höhnrauch sollst: sink in dich, Nam', Gestalt

Völlig bewahrend, und der Mantel fahre
Spät erst dir nach, den Späten ein Gesicht,
Zeugnis und Abbild langer Leidensjahre,
Bis blauer Meerwind seinen Glimmer bricht.

One heaven, you said, holds all in its embrace.
Is that still so, Job? New empyrean,
Rebuffing, lonely. You have come to face
Yourself in a far-off no god can span.

Then is the sense of knowing self the prize
That your titanic struggle, Job, has won?
Veils and dross melt. You, fulvid day-star, rise
Burning before the night like the setting sun.

Spread yourself round as your own cloak. Revolve
About your own heart's center, self-walled, willing
To make surrender; and yet not dissolve
Like smoke on heights: plunge in yourself, preserving

Your name and essence whole. Let the cloak wait
And follow then, a vision for the late,
Witness and image of long years of pain,
Till the blue sea-wind breaks its gleam again.

1950: *Sang aus dem Exil*

CHRISTIAN MORGENSTERN

GEISS UND SCHLEICHE

Die Schleiche singt ihr Nachtgebet,
die Waldgeiss staunend vor ihr steht.

Die Waldgeiss schüttelt ihren Bart,
wie ein Magister hochgelahrt.

Sie weiss nicht, was die Schleiche singt,
sie hört nur, dass es lieblich klingt.

Die Schleiche fällt in Schlaf alsbald.
Die Geiss geht sinnend durch den Wald.

ANT-OLOGIE

Im Anfang lebte, wie bekannt,
als grösster Säuger der Gig-ant.

Wobei gig eine Zahl ist, die
es nicht mehr gibt,—so gross war sie!

Doch jene Grösse schwand wie Rauch.
Zeit gab's genug—und Zahlen auch.

Bis eines Tags, ein winzig Ding,
der Zwölef-ant das Reich empfing.

Wo blieb sein Reich? Wo blieb er selb?—
Sein Bein wird im Museum gelb.

SHE-GOAT AND SLOW-WORM

The slow-worm sings her bed-time prayers.
The woodland she-goat, marvelling, stares.

The she-goat wags her beard, as though
she knew all that there is to know.

She finds the slow-worm's song unclear,
but very sweet upon the ear.

The slow-worm soon takes her repose.
The goat through woodland thoughtful goes.

1905: *Galgenlieder*

ANT-OLOGY

The hugest mammal in the land
in days gone by was the Gigant.

But now this category 'Gig'
no more exists—it was so big.

That bigness vanished like a puff.
Numbers there were and time enough.

Until one day a tiny mite,
the Twelefant, beheld the light.

Where is he now? Sing his Te Deums!
His bones grow yellow in museums.

Zwar gab die gütige Natur
den Elef-anten uns dafur.

Doch ach, der Pulverpavian,
der Mensch, voll Gier nach seinem Zahn,

erschiesst ihn, statt ihm Zeit zu lassen,
zum Zehen-anten zu verblassen.

O „Klub zum Schutz der wilden Tiere",
hilf, dass der Mensch nicht ruiniere

die Sprossen dieser Riesenleiter,
die stets noch weiter führt und weiter!

Wie dankbar wird der Ant dir sein,
lässt du ihn wachsen und gedeihn,—

bis er dereinst im Nebel hinten
als Nulel-ant wird stumm verschwinden.

Yet Mother Nature kindly bred
the elefants for us instead.

But Man, that murderous baboon,
desirous of his capture, soon

dispatched the beast before it could
diminish into ten-ant-hood!

Up, R.S.P.C.A., make haste
or Man will utterly lay waste

that monster breed whose scions climb
on to the furthest peaks of time!

How much the Ant will thank you if
you let him flourish on and live

until, lost in the mists in front,
he fades out as the Nilefant!

1905: *Galgenlieder*

DER TRÄUMER

Palmström stellt ein Bündel Kerzen
auf des Nachttischs Marmorplatte
und verfolgt es beim Zerschmelzen.

Seltsam formt es ein Gebirge
aus herabgeflossner Lava,
bildet Zotteln, Zungen, Schnecken.

Schwankend über dem Gerinne
Stehn die Dochte mit den Flammen
gleichwie goldene Zypressen.

Auf den weissen Märchenfelsen
schaut des Träumers Auge Scharen
unverzagter Sonnenpilger.

THE DREAMER

Palmström sets a bunch of candles
on the table by his bedside
and observes them slowly melting.

Wondrously they fashion mountains
out of downward-dripping lava,
fashion tongues, and toads, and tassels.

Swaying o'er the guttering candles
stand the wicks with flames aspiring,
each one like a golden cypress.

On the pearly fairy boulders
soon the dreamer's eyes see hosts of
dauntless pilgrims of the sun.

1910: *Palmström*

AUGUST STRAMM

BEGEGNUNG

Dein Gehen lächelt in mich über
und
reisst das Herz.
Das Nicken hakt und spannt.
Im Schatten deines Rocks
verhaspelt
schlingern
schleudert
klatscht!
Du wiegst und wiegst
mein Greifen haschet blind.
Die Sonne lacht!
Und
blödes Zagen lahmet fort
beraubt beraubt!

ENCOUNTER

Your walking smiles across to me
and
jerks the heart.
Your nodding hooks and tenses.
In the shadow of your skirt
entangled
flinging
fillips
flaps!
You sway and sway.
My grasping blindly snatches.
The sun laughs!
And
timid wavering limps away
bereft bereft!

November, 1914

SCHWERMUT

Schreiten Streben
Leben sehnt
Schauern Stehen
Blicke suchen
Sterben wächst
das Kommen
schreit!
Tief
stummen
wir.

SCHLACHTFELD

Schollenmürbe schläfert ein das Eisen
Blute filzen Sickerflecke
Roste Krumen
Fleische schleimen
Saugen brünstet um Zerfallen
Mordesmorde
blinzen
Kinderblicke

MELANCHOLY

Striding striving
living longs
shuddering standing
glances look for
dying grows
the coming
screams!
Deeply
we
dumb.

December, 1914

BATTLEFIELD

Yielding clod lulls iron off to sleep
bloods clot the patches where they oozed
rusts crumble
fleshes slime
sucking lusts around decay.
Murder on murder
blinks
in childish eyes.

January, 1915

RAINER MARIA RILKE

WENDUNG

Der Weg von der Innigkeit zur Grösse geht durch das
Opfer.

Rudolf Kassner

Lange errang ers im Anschaun.
Sterne brachen ins Knie
unter dem ringenden Aufblick.
Oder er anschaute knieend,
und seines Instands Duft
machte ein Göttliches müd,
dass es ihm lächelte schlafend.

Türme schaute er so,
dass sie erschraken:
wieder sie bauend, hinan, plötzlich, in Einem!
Aber wie oft, die vom Tag
überladene Landschaft
ruhete hin in sein stilles Gewahren, abends.

Tiere traten getrost
in den offenen Blick, weidende,
und die gefangenen Löwen
starrten hinein wie in unbegreifliche Freiheit;
Vögel durchflogen ihn grad,
den gemütigen; Blumen
wiederschauten in ihn
gross wie in Kinder.

TURNING-POINT

The way from intense inwardness to greatness leads through sacrifice.

Rudolf Kassner

Long he attained it by looking.
Stars would fall on their knees
under his strenuous up-glance.
Or he would look at it kneeling,
and his urgency's odor
made a divine being tired
so that it smiled at him, sleeping.

Towers he would gaze at so
that they were startled:
building them up again, suddenly, sweeping them up!
But how often the landscape
overburdened by day
ebbed to rest in his quiet perceiving, at nightfall.

Animals trustingly stepped
into his open glance, grazing ones,
even the captive lions
stared into it, as at incomprehensible freedom;
birds flew through it unswerving,
it that could feel them; and flowers
met and returned his gaze,
great as in children.

Und das Gerücht, dass ein Schauender sei,
rührte die minder,
fraglicher Sichtbaren,
rührte die Frauen.

Schauend wie lang?
Seit wie lange schon innig entbehrend,
flehend im Grunde des Blicks?

Wenn er, ein Wartender, sass in der Fremde; des Gasthofs
zerstreutes, abgewendetes Zimmer
mürrisch um sich, und im vermiedenen Spiegel
wieder das Zimmer
und später vom quälenden Bett aus
wieder:
da beriets in der Luft,
unfassbar beriet es
über sein fühlbares Herz,
über sein durch den schmerzhaft verschütteten Körper
dennoch fühlbares Herz
beriet es und richtete:
dass es der Liebe nicht habe.

(Und verwehrte ihm weitere Weihen.)

Denn des Anschauns, siehe, ist eine Grenze.
Und die geschautere Welt
will in der Liebe gedeihn.

Werk des Gesichts ist getan,
tue nun Herz-Werk
an den Bildern in dir, jenen gefangenen; denn du
überwältigtest sie: aber nun kennst du sie nicht.
Siehe, innerer Mann, dein inneres Mädchen,
dieses errungene aus
tausend Naturen, dieses
erst nur errungene, nie
noch geliebte Geschöpf.

And the rumor that here was a seeing man
moved the more faintly,
dubiously visible,
moved the women.

Seeing how long?
How long now profoundly deprived,
beseeching deep down in his glance?

When he, a waiting one, sat in strange towns; the hotel's
distracted, preoccupied bedroom
morose about him, and in the avoided mirror
that room once more
and later, from the tormenting bedstead
once more:
then in the air it pronounced
beyond his grasping pronounced
on his heart that was still to be felt
through his painfully buried body,
on his heart nonetheless to be felt
something pronounced then, and judged:
that it was lacking in love.

(And forbade him further communions.)

For looking, you see, has a limit.
And the more looked-at world
wants to be nourished by love.

Work of seeing is done,
now practise heart-work
upon those images captive within you; for you
overpowered them only: but now do not know them.
Look, inward man, look at your inward maiden,
her the laboriously wrested
from a thousand natures, at her the
creature till now only
wrested, never yet loved.

[June, 1914]

KLAGE

Wem willst du klagen, Herz? Immer gemiedener
ringt sich dein Weg durch die unbegreiflichen
Menschen. Mehr noch vergebens vielleicht,
da er die Richtung behält,
Richtung zur Zukunft behält,
zu der verlorenen.

Früher. Klagtest? Was wars? Eine gefallene
Beere des Jubels, unreife.
Jetzt aber bricht mir mein Jubel-Baum,
bricht mir im Sturme mein langsamer
Jubel-Baum.
Schönster in meiner unsichtbaren
Landschaft, der du mich kenntlicher
machtest Engeln, unsichtbaren.

AN HÖLDERLIN

Verweilung, auch am Vertrautesten nicht,
ist uns gegeben; aus den erfüllten
Bildern stürzt der Geist zu plötzlich zu füllenden; Seen
sind erst im Ewigen. Hier ist Fallen
das Tüchtigste. Aus dem gekonnten Gefühl
überfallen hinab ins geahndete, weiter.

Dir, du Herrlicher, war, dir war, du Beschwörer, ein ganzes
Leben das dringende Bild, wenn du es aussprachst,
die Zeile schloss sich wie Schicksal, ein Tod war
selbst in der lindesten, und du betratest ihn; aber
der vorgehende Gott führte dich drüben hervor.

COMPLAINT

To whom, heart, would you complain? Ever more unfrequented
does your way grapple on through incomprehensible
human kind. All the more vainly perhaps
for keeping to its direction,
direction toward the future,
the future that's lost.

Before. You complained? What was it? A fallen
berry of joy, an unripe one.
But now it is my tree of joy that breaks,
what breaks in the gale is my slow
tree of joy.
Loveliest in my invisible
landscape, you that brought me more close to the
ken of angels, invisible.

[July, 1914]

TO HÖLDERLIN

We may not abide, even with what is most
familiar; from images already fulfilled
the spirit pours down to others that suddenly demand fulfilment;
there are no lakes till eternity. Here
it is best to fall. Fall over and down,
on from the emotion learnt to the emotion dreamt of.

To you, O splendid enchanter, to you the compelling image
was a life complete in itself, once uttered: the line
closed like destiny, even the gentlest
ended in death, and you entered it; but the god
who walked ahead led you out into freedom beyond it.

O du wandelnder Geist, du wandelndster! Wie sie doch alle
wohnen im warmen Gedicht, häuslich, und lang
bleiben im schmalen Vergleich. Teilnehmende. Du nur
ziehst wie der Mond. Und unten hellt und verdunkelt
deine nächtliche sich, die heilig erschrockene Landschaft,
die du in Abschieden fühlst. Keiner
gab sie erhabener hin, gab sie ans Ganze
heiler zurück, unbedürftiger. So auch
spieltest du heilig durch nicht mehr gerechnete Jahre
mit dem unendlichen Glück, als wär es nicht innen, läge
keinem gehörend im sanften
Rasen der Erde umher, von göttlichen Kindern verlassen.
Ach, was die Höchsten begehren, du legtest es wunschlos
Baustein auf Baustein: es stand. Doch selber sein Umsturz
irrte dich nicht.

Was, da ein solcher, Ewiger, war, misstraun wir
immer dem Irdischen noch? Statt am Vorläufigen ernst
die Gefühle zu lernen für welche
Neigung, künftig im Raum?

O restless spirit, most restless of all! How smugly
the others all live in their well-heated poems; and linger
long and with interest in narrow comparisons. Only
you move like the moon. And the nocturnal landscape below you,
your holy terrified landscape brightens and darkens
and in farewells you feel it. No other
ever gave it more grandly away, gave it back to the Whole
more completely, ungraspingly. Thus you also
spent sacred years you no longer counted, playing
with infinite joy, as if it were not an inner possession,
but lay, belonging to no one,
around on the earth's gentle greensward, where children of gods
   had left it.
O wishless you laid what the loftiest souls have craved for,
stone upon stone, till it stood: but not even the fall
of the building could trouble you.

Why, with such predecessors as these, so timeless,
do we still lack faith in the earth? and not reverently learn
from these precursory things the emotions for
what future attachment, in space?

[September, 1914]

IRRLICHTER

Wir haben einen alten Verkehr
mit den Lichtern im Moor.
Sie kommen mir wie Grosstanten vor . . .
Ich entdecke mehr und mehr

zwischen ihnen und mir den Familienzug,
den keine Gewalt unterdrückt:
diesen Schwung, diesen Sprung, diesen Ruck, diesen Bug,
der den andern nicht glückt.

Auch ich bin dort, wo die Wege nicht gehn,
im Schwaden, den mancher mied,
und ich habe mich oft verlöschen sehn
unter dem Augenlid.

JACKOLANTERNS

They've been for ages in our mind,
the jackolanterns we see.
Like great-aunts they seem to me . . .
More and more I find

between them and myself the family trait
that no dominion smothers:
this dance, curve, twirl, float
—impossible for others.

In swaths of mist that bar most men,
I too am there, where no pathways lead,
and I've seen myself, time and again,
quenched under my eyelid.

[February, 1924]

MAUSOLEUM

Königsherz. Kern eines hohen
Herrscherbaums. Balsamfrucht.
Goldene Herznuss. Urnen-Mohn
mitten im Mittelbau,
(wo der Widerhall abspringt,
wie ein Splitter der Stille,
wenn du dich rührst,
weil es dir scheint,
dass deine vorige
Haltung zu laut war . . .)
Völkern entzogenes,
sterngesinnt,
im unsichtbaren Kreisen
kreisendes Königsherz.

Wo ist, wohin,
jenes der leichten
Lieblingin?
: Lächeln, von aussen,
auf die zögernde Ründung
heiterer Früchte gelegt;
oder der Motte, vielleicht,
Kostbarkeit, Florflügel, Fühler . . .

Wo aber, wo, das sie sang,
das sie in Eins sang,
das Dichterherz?
: Wind,
unsichtbar,
Windinnres.

MAUSOLEUM

King-heart. Seed of a lofty
monarch-tree. Balm fruit.
Golden heartnut. Urn poppy
in mid-nave's midst
(where the echo ricochets
like a splinter of silence
when you move,
because you feel
your former
posture was over-loud . . .)
drawn away from peoples,
starminded,
in the invisible circle
circling king-heart.

Where is, where is it gone,
that of the light in-
amorata?
: Smile, from without,
laid on the hesitant
curve of calm fruits,
or else a precious thing
of moth, lace wing, feeler . . .

But where, where, that sang them,
sang them to union,
the poet-heart?
: Wind,
invisible,
wind-innermost.

[October, 1924]

THEODOR DÄUBLER

KATZEN

Es silbern Mondflocken durchs Fenster nieder.
Auf bleichem Teppich spielen weisse Katzen,
Mit silberblauen Augen, Seidentatzen.
Beinah gebrechlich sind die feinen Glieder.

Ich klatsche, lache, schliesse meine Lider.
Doch bleibt das nahe Katzenhaschen, Kratzen.
Auf einmal raschelt es in den Matratzen,
Und blasse Kleider gibt der Spiegel wider.

Ich wusste wohl, sie würden lautlos spielen.
Wie sind die Katzen und die Kinder zierlich.
Sie balgen sich auf den beglänzten Dielen.

Das grosse Kind ist nackt und doch manierlich,
Die Kleinen tragen blaue Mondlichthemden.
Wie mich die Augen und ihr Schmuck befremden.

CATS

Silvering through the window moonflakes fall.
Upon a faded carpet white cats play,
With silken paws and eyes of silver blue.
Their delicate limbs are almost breakable.

I clap my hands, and laugh, and shut my eyes.
The same cat-catchings and the scratchings stay.
A something in the matresses flits through.
The looking-glass reflects faint fineries.

I knew that they would play without a sound.
Upon the shining boards they romp around.
How graceful cats and children too must be.

The big child is quite naked, but polite.
The small ones wear blue blouses of moonlight.
How strange their eyes and fineries are to me.

1915: *Der sternhelle Weg*

WILHELM LEHMANN

NACH DER ZWEITEN SINTFLUT

Geschieden wieder Wasser, Erde;
Doch keine Arche legte an.
Die Wege steinigen und sanden,
Da alle Menschenzeit verrann.

Die Ammer schüttet dünne Strophe,
Ein Hier entstieg dem Nirgendwo—
Der Menschenstimme überdrüssig,
Spricht sich das Schweigen lieber so.

Wo Bomber stürzte, rostet Eisen,
Vergesslich hüllt das Gras den Platz.
Die Lüfte zucken drachenschweifig,
Kein Lindwurm hütet solchen Schatz.

Der Himmel glüht, die Steine beben,
Die Ammer bleibt bei ihrem Ton.
Die zweite Sintflut überleben
Nicht Pyrrha, nicht Deukalion.

FEBRUARMOND

Ich seh den Mond des Februar sich lagern
Auf reinen Himmel, türkisblauen.
In wintergelben Gräsern, magern,
Gehn Schafe, ruhen, kauen.

Dem schönsten folgt der Widder, hingerissen.
Die Wolle glänzt, gebadete Koralle.
Ich weiss das Wort, den Mond zu hissen,
Ich bin im Paradiese vor dem Falle.

AFTER THE SECOND FLOOD

Waters and earth once more are parted,
But no bow's token overhead.
Roads choke on sands and stony deserts,
Since what was human time has fled.

From Nowhere rose a Here—the strophes
The yellowhammer drops are weak.
By human voices overwearied,
Silence prefers this way to speak.

Where bombs once tumbled, iron is rusting,
With mindless grass the place is floored.
Like dragontails the breezes flicker,
No dragon guards this kind of hoard.

The heavens glow, the stones are trembling,
The yellowhammer still sings on.
The second flood has for survivor
Not Pyrrha, not Deucalion.

1950: *Noch nicht genug*

FEBRUARY MOON

I see the February moon lie down
On a pure heaven, turquoise-blue.
In winter grasses, yellow-brown,
Sheep ramble, rest and chew.

The loveliest has drawn the ram's desire.
Their fleeces gleam, sea-clean as coral.
I know the word to make the moon rise higher,
I am in Paradise before the Fall.

1954: *Überlebender Tag*

JOACHIM RINGELNATZ

CASSEL (DIE KARPFEN IN DER WILHELMSTRASSE 15)

Man hat sie in den Laden
In ein intimes Bassin gesetzt.
Dort dürfen sie baden.
Äusserlich etwas ausgefranst, abgewetzt—
Scheinen sie inwendig
Doch recht lebendig.
Sie murmeln Formeln wie die Zauberer,
Als würde dadurch ihr Wasser sauberer.
Sie kauen Mayonnaise stumm im Rüssel
Und träumen sich gegen den Strich rasiert,
Sodann geläutert, getötet, erwärmt und garniert
Auf eine silberne Schüssel.
Sie enden in Kommerzienräten,
Senden die witzigste von ihren Gräten
In eine falsche Kehle.
Und ich denke mir ihre Seele
Wie eine Kellerassel,
Die Kniebeuge übt.—
Ja und sonst hat mich in Cassel
Nichts weiter erregt oder betrübt.

CASSEL (CARPS AT WILHELMSTRASSE 15)

In the shop they've been put
Into a tank, so intimate.
To swim in this is their privilege.
A bit frazzled outside—not much edge—
Inside they're
Altogether livelier.
Mumbling spells like wizards is part of their demeanor,
As if this made the water cleaner.
Dumbly in their probosces mayonnaise they munch,
And dream of being shaved against the grain,
Of being gutted, killed, warmed, or, again,
Garnished on a silver plate for lunch.
Inside tycoons they end,
Their funniest bone they send
The wrong way down the larynx.
And picturing their souls one thinks
Of wood lice
Doing knee-bends for exercise.
In Cassel there wasn't, let me confess,
Much else besides to captivate or depress.

1927: *Reisebriefe eines Artisten*

EHRGEIZ

Ich habe meinen Soldaten aus Blei
Als Kind Verdienstkreuzchen eingeritzt.
Mir selber ging alle Ehre vorbei,
Bis auf zwei Orden, die jeder besitzt.

Und ich pfeife durchaus nicht auf Ehre.
Im Gegenteil. Mein Ideal wäre,
Dass man nach meinem Tod (grano salis)
Ein Gässchen nach mir benennt, ein ganz schmales
Und krummes Gässchen, mit niedrigen Türchen,
Mit steilen Treppchen und feilen Hürchen,
Mit Schatten und schiefen Fensterluken.

Dort würde ich spuken.

AMBITION

I used to scratch medals, when I was a lad,
On my tin soldiers with a knife.
Except for the two that everyone had,
I got no other honors myself in all my life.

That is not to say that to me it is all the same.
In fact, my *Ideal* is
That after my death (cum grano salis)
A little street should be given my name,
A narrow twisty street with lowdown doors,
Steep stairways and cheap little whores,
Shadows and sloping roof-windows I want.

It would be my haunt.

1932 : *Gedichte dreier Jahre*

ERNST STADLER

FAHRT ÜBER DIE KÖLNER RHEINBRÜCKE
BEI NACHT

Der Schnellzug tastet sich und stösst die Dunkelheit entlang.
Kein Stern will vor. Die ganze Welt ist nur ein enger, nachtum-
    schienter Minengang,
Darein zuweilen Förderstellen blauen Lichtes jähe Horizonte reissen:
    Feuerkreis
Von Kugellampen, Dächern, Schloten, dampfend, strömend . . nur
    sekundenweis . .
Und wieder alles schwarz. Als führen wir ins Eingeweid der Nacht
    zur Schicht.
Nun taumeln Lichter her . . verirrt, trostlos vereinsamt . . mehr . .
    und sammeln sich . . und werden dicht.
Gerippe grauer Häuserfronten liegen bloss, im Zwielicht bleichend,
    tot—etwas muss kommen . . o, ich fühl es schwer
Im Hirn. Eine Beklemmung singt im Blut. Dann dröhnt der Boden
    plötzlich wie ein Meer:
Wir fliegen, aufgehoben, königlich durch nachtentrissne Luft, hoch
    übern Strom. O Biegung der Millionen Lichter, stumme
    Wacht,
Vor deren blitzender Parade schwer die Wasser abwärts rollen.
    Endloses Spalier, zum Gruss gestellt bei Nacht!
Wie Fackeln stürmend! Freudiges! Salut von Schiffen über blauer
    See! Bestirntes Fest!
Wimmelnd, mit hellen Augen hingedrängt! Bis wo die Stadt mit
    letzten Häusern ihren Gast entlässt.
Und dann die langen Einsamkeiten. Nackte Ufer. Stille. Nacht.
    Besinnung. Einkehr. Kommunion. Und Glut und Drang
Zum Letzten, Segnenden. Zum Zeugungsfest. Zur Wollust. Zum
    Gebet. Zum Meer. Zum Untergang.

ON CROSSING THE RHINE BRIDGE AT
COLOGNE BY NIGHT

The express train gropes and thrusts its way through darkness. Not
a star is out.

The whole world's nothing but a mine-road the night has railed
about

In which at times conveyors of blue light tear sudden horizons:
fiery sphere

Of arc-lamps, roofs and chimneys, steaming, streaming—for seconds
only clear,

And all is black again. As though we drove into Night's entrails to
the seam.

Now lights reel into view . . . astray, disconsolate and lonely . . .
more . : . and gather . . . and densely gleam.

Skeletons of grey housefronts are laid bare, grown pale in the
twilight, dead—something must happen . . . O heavily

I feel it weigh on my brain. An oppression sings in the blood. Then
all at once the ground resounds like the sea:

And royally upborne we fly through air from darkness wrested,
high up above the river. O curve of the million lights, mute
guard at the sight

Of whose flashing parade the waters go roaring down. Endless line
presenting arms by night!

Surging on like torches! Joyful! Salute of ships over the blue sea!
Star-jewelled, festive array!

Teeming, bright-eyed urged on! Till where the town with its last
houses sees its guest away.

And then the long solitudes. Bare banks. And Silence. Night.
Reflection. Self-questioning. Communion. And ardor out-
ward-flowing.

To the end that blesses. To conception's rite. To pleasure's consum-
mation. To prayer. To the sea. To self's undoing.

1914: *Der Aufbruch*

KLEINE STADT

Die vielen kleinen Gassen, die die langgestreckte
  Hauptstrasse überqueren
Laufen alle ins Grüne.
  Überall fängt Land an.
Überall strömt Himmel ein und Geruch von Bäumen
  und der starke Duft der Äcker.
Überall erlischt die Stadt
  in einer feuchten Herrlichkeit von Wiesen,

Und durch den grauen Ausschnitt
  niederer Dächer schwankt
Gebirge, über das die Reben klettern,
  die mit hellen Stützen in die Sonne leuchten.
Darüber aber schliesst sich Kiefernwald : der stösst
Wie eine breite dunkle Mauer an die rote Fröhlichkeit
  der Sandsteinkirche.

Am Abend, wenn die Fabriken schliessen,
  ist die grosse Strasse mit Menschen gefüllt.
Sie gehen langsam
  oder bleiben mitten auf der Gasse stehn.
Sie sind geschwärzt von Arbeit und Maschinenruss.
  Aber ihre Augen tragen
Noch Scholle, zähe Kraft des Bodens
  und das feierliche Licht der Felder.

SMALL TOWN

The many narrow alleys that cut across
   the long through mainstreet
All run into the country.
   Everywhere the green begins.
Everywhere the sky pours in and fragrance of trees
   and the strong scent of ploughland.
Everywhere the town stops
   in a moist magnificence of pastures,

And through the grey slit between
   low roofs hills lean
With vines that climb over them and shine
   with bright supporting poles in the sunlight.
Still higher the pinewood closes in: like a thick dark
   Wall to border on the red rejoicing
of the sandstone church.

At nightfall when the factories close
   the mainstreet is filled with people.
They walk slowly
   or in the middle of an alley they stop and stand.
They are blackened with work and engine soot.
   But their eyes uphold
Earth still, the tough power of the soil
   and the festive light of the fields.

1914: *Der Aufbruch*

JAKOB VAN HODDIS

WELTENDE

Dem Bürger fliegt vom spitzen Kopf der Hut,
in allen Lüften hallt es wie Geschrei.
Dachdecker stürzen ab und gehn entzwei,
und an den Küsten—liest man—steigt die Flut.

Der Sturm ist da, die wilden Meere hupfen
an Land, um dicke Dämme zu zerdrücken.
Die meisten Menschen haben einen Schnupfen.
Die Eisenbahnen fallen von den Brücken.

END OF THE WORLD

The bourgeois' hat flies off his pointed head,
the air re-echoes with a screaming sound.
Tilers plunge from roofs and hit the ground,
and seas are rising round the coasts (you read).

The storm is here, crushed dams no longer hold,
the savage seas come inland with a hop.
The greater part of people have a cold.
Off bridges everywhere the railroads drop.

1911: '*Die Aktion*'

HYMNE

O Traum, Verdauung meiner Seele!
Elendes ,,combination" womit ich vor Frost mich schütze
Zerstörer aller Dinge die mir Feind sind;
Aller Nachttöpfe,
Kochlöffel und Litfasssäulen
O du mein Schiessgewehr!
In purpurne Finsternis tauchst du die Tage
Alle Nächte bekommen violette Horizonte
Meine Grossmama Pauline erscheint als Astralleib.
Und sogar ein Herr Sanitätsrat
Ein braver, aber etwas zu gebildeter
Sanitätsrat
Wird mir wieder amüsant.
Er taucht auf aus seiner efeuumwobenen Ruhestätte
—War es nicht soeben ein himmelblauer Ofenschirm?
[He, Sie da!]
Und gackt: ,,Sogar—— "
Frei nach Friedrich von Schiller.
O Traum, Verdauung meiner Seele
O du mein Schiessgewehr!
Gick! Gack!

HYMN

O dream, digestion of my soul!
Wretched combination with which I shield myself from frost
Destroyer of all things that are my enemies;
All chamber pots
Kitchen ladles and poster pillars,
My fire arm!
You plunge the days in purple darkness
All nights acquire violet horizons
My Grandma Pauline appears as an astral body.
And even a Physician Extraordinary,
An honest, but somewhat too cultivated
Physician Extraordinary,
Amuses me once again.
He emerges from his ivytwined resting place
—Wasn't it just now a skyblue fire screen?
[Hi! You there!]
And cackles: "Even . . ."
Freely adapting from Friedrich von Schiller.
O dream, digestion of my soul,
My fire arm!
Cack! Cack!

1916: *'Cabaret Voltaire'*

OSKAR LOERKE

HINTER DEM HORIZONT

Mein Schiff fährt langsam, sein Alter ist gross,
Algen, Muscheln, Moos,
Der Kot des Meeres hat sich angesetzt.
Eine bunte Insel, fast steht es zuletzt.

Soll ich noch fahren? Ich fahre nicht mehr.
Aber alle Dinge kommen,
Kontinente, frachtenschwer
Nun wie fremde Schiffe zu mir geschwommen.

Vorbei ist der Menschen feste Küste
Wie der Donner im Winter;
Übriggeblieben im Gewölke
Der prophetische Vogelflug.

Steigender, stürzender Völker beharrendes Bild!
Soviel Blut und soviel Leid!
Und alles, was da gilt,
Geschieht doch in der Einsamkeit.

BEYOND THE HORIZON

My ship moves slowly, vast is its age;
The whole ocean sludge,
Barnacle, weed, moss, clings to its keel.
A motley island, it stands almost still.

Should I sail further? I'll not sail hence.
Yet all things are coming—
See the full-fraught continents
Like foreign vessels now towards me swimming.

Gone is the solid coast of men,
Like thunder in winter;
In cloud overhead
Prophetic birdflight remains.

Immutable image of nations that rise and fall!
So much sorrow, and so much blood!
Yet nothing there is meaningful
But it is done in the solitude.

1926: *Der längste Tag*

DIE VOGELSTRASSEN

Vor vielen tausend Jahren auferbaut,
Ziehn hoch durch Luft die grossen Vogelstrassen.
Den Erdball, wie ihn Ferndampf drunten blaut,
Ermassen Flügel nur mit Himmelsmassen.

Sie sind verboten aller Menschenlast,
Verwehrt dem zwiegespaltnen Huf, der Klaue.
Kein Stäubchen lagert dort, kein Blatt vom Ast
Und, gibt es Gott, kein Haar von seiner Braue.

Von einer solchen Strasse überbrückt,
Sahst du ums Haupt dir ihren Schatten stürzen.
Das Licht, das jemals unter ihr gerückt,
Sahst du erscheinen und zum Blitz sich kürzen.

Du hast die magische Figur befragt:
Als Donner schlug sie sich in träge Stücke!
Dein Magisches, dein Vogel-Leichtes jagt
Entlang die unsichtbare lange Brücke.

Des einen Endes Pfeiler steht in Frost,
Wo Moorpech quillt und Sumpfohreulen kreisen
Und Federschwänze klatschen, rot von Rost,
Entrafft der Flut voll aufgelöstem Eisen.

Des andern Endes Pfeiler hüllt Geschmeiss,
Zum Frass gesellt, im Neide sich Gehilfe—
Doch dort ertönt ein Strom in seinem Fleiss,
Dort senkt die Vogelstrasse sich zum Schilfe.

Nicht fern besteigt den klaren Bergvulkan
Ein Elefant, schaut einsam in den Krater.
Darüber sinnt der Himmel, aufgetan,
Sein Alter aus, und er weiss keinen Vater.

THE BIRD CAUSEWAYS

Constructed many thousand years ago,
Through air aloft the great bird causeways fly.
The earth's far orb, blue in the mist below,
Wings measured only to a scale of sky.

These ways are shut to cloven hoof and claw;
No human load is shouldered there, none shed.
No dust can settle, and no leafage, nor,
If God is there, can one hair of his head.

When such a causeway arched high over you,
You saw how round your brow its shadow broke.
The light you saw, drawn close beneath it, grew
And flashed compacted in the lightning-stroke.

And then you catechized the magic trace:
Its thunder boomed, the heavy fragments fell!
But your bird-levity and magic race
Across the long and unseen arch as well.

Its one extremity stands firm in frost
Where marshblack flows and hawk-owls fly around
And feathered tails are flapping, red with rust,
Rapt off the molten iron flooded ground.

Thick vermin hide the other end from view,
Each envious aiding each and munching sludge—
But there a busy stream makes music too;
And there the causeway dips into the sedge.

A lonely elephant ascends nearby
The clear volcano, at the top it peers
Into the crater, while the open sky,
No father found, excogitates its years.

Un Bild um Bild erbangt nach einem Sinn
Ob Worten, die wir sonst im Sinne hatten.
Auch dies scheint Donnerrufen her und hin,
Dem Blitz vorweggenommen als sein Schatten.

Zu reisen, ist der Vögel Winterschlaf,
Der schwere Frösche, Schlangen oder Bären
Im Schwebetraume nur mitschwebend traf.
O dass wir alle Vogelseelen wären!

And image after puzzled image so
Fears meaning lost, for other words were meant.
This too seems thunder passing to and fro—
Like shadows lightning casts before descent.

For birds a journey is their winter sleep
Which heavy frogs, and snakes, or bears arrest
Only as airy into airy dream they creep.
O that we all with souls of birds were blest!

1926: *Der längste Tag*

DER STEINPFAD (19)

Mich presst ein Traum. Der Frost ist schwerer Groll,
Der Himmel eine fahle niedre Stirn,
Der weisse Weg wie eine Windung Hirn—
Das Weltall weiss nicht, wo es bleiben soll.

Es schwirrt heran im Weltlauf ohne Lauf
Der schwarze Vogel Rok. Er späht nach Saat
Und lässt sich nieder auf dem Steinquadrat.
Er schluckt. Ich sah nicht, was. Er schluckt es auf.

Das All füllt nun ein Vogelaugen-Rund.
Sein Sinnen ist der Paarung fern und starr.
Im Schnabelkeil verstarb das Brunstgequarr;
Mit schiefem Schlag behackt er bös den Grund.

Es scheint, der Fels zieht in das Auge ein,
Die Härte wächst, die Lebensglut verschlackt.
Nichts ist mehr da als nur des Hornkeils Takt
Und, der ihm nicht barmherzig ist, der Stein.

Wie Laster, die uns nicht barmherzig sind,
Berauben mir die Schläge das Gehirn—
Bis es erwacht ist.—Draussen schneits gelind.
Es glänzt der Weg, ein unberührter Firn,
In einer lauen Weihnacht ohne Wind.

From THE STONE PATH

A dream's my burden, leaden frost my foe;
The sky bows down its bare low brow again.
The white path coils and is a whorl of brain.
The world goes ignorant of where to go.

Over the world's unmoving course my way
The black Orc whistles, hunting seed, descends
And perches on the square of stone. He stands,
He pecks, then swallows, what, I cannot say.

Now fills the world his eyes' bird-flighted round.
His mind is set, all thought of mating fled.
In his beak's axe the cry of rut is dead.
In wrath diagonal he hacks the ground.

Into his eye the very rock seems gone;
The hardness grows, the glow of living wanes.
Only the beat of his horned axe remains
And, giving him no mercy now, the stone.

Like vices, and as merciless, the sheer
Blows batter down. They rob me of my mind
Till it awakens. And then outside I hear
The snow fall soft. A virgin glacier, with no wind
This warm and Christmas night, my path shines clear.

[1938]

HUGO BALL

DIE SONNE

Zwischen meinen Augenlidern fährt ein Kinderwagen.
Zwischen meinen Augenlidern geht ein Mann mit einem Pudel.
Eine Baumgruppe wird zum Schlangenbündel und zischt in den
Himmel.
Ein Stein hält eine Rede. Bäume in Grünbrand. Fliehende Inseln.
Schwanken und Muschelgeklingel und Fischkopf wie auf dem
Meeresboden.

Meine Beine strecken sich aus bis zum Horizont. Ein Hofkutsche
knackt
drüber weg. Meine Stiefel ragen am Horizont empor wie die Türme
einer
versinkenden Stadt. Ich bin der Riese Goliath. Ich verdaue Ziegen-
käse.
Ich bin ein Mammutkälbchen. Grüne Grasigel schnüffeln an mir.
Gras spannt grüne Säbel und Brücken und Regenbögen über
meinen Bauch.

Meine Ohren sind rosa Riesenmuschel, ganz offen. Mein Körper
schwillt an
von Geräuschen, die sich gefangen haben darin. Ich höre das
Meckern
des grossen Pan. Ich höre die zinnoberrote Musik der Sonne. Sie
steht
links oben. Zinnoberrot sprühen die Fetzen hinaus in die Weltnacht.
Wenn sie herunterfällt, zerquetscht sie die Stadt und die Kirch-
türme
und alle Vorgärten voll Krokus und Hyazinthen, und wird einen
Schall geben
wie Blech von Kindertrompeten.

THE SUN

Through the slits of my eyes a perambulator passes.
Through the slits of my eyes walks a man with a poodle.
A treeclump turns into a cluster of snakes and hisses heavenward.
A stone makes a speech. Trees in Greenbrand. Escaping islands.
A swaying and a shell-tinkling and fish-head as on the floor of the
        ocean.

My legs stretch out right to the horizon. A carriage bangs
away over them. My boots soar on the horizon like the towers
of a sinking town. I am the Giant Goliath. I digest goat cheese.
I am a mammoth's calf. Green grassbugs snuffle me.
Grass spans green sabers and bridges and rainbows over my belly.

My ears are giant pink shells, open wide. My body swells
with the sounds that are trapped in it. I hear the bleating
of great Pan. I hear the vermilion music of the sun. It stands
up on the left. Its wisps flash vermilion into the world's night.
When it falls it will crush the town and the church towers
and all the front gardens full of crocus and hyacinth and will blare
like the tin of children's trumpets.

Aber es ist in der Luft ein Gegeneinanderwehen von Purpur und
    Eigelb
und Flaschengrün: Schaukeln, die eine orangene Faust festhält an
    langen Fäden,
und ist ein Singen von Vogelhälsen, die über die Zweige hüpfen.
Ein sehr zartes Gestänge von Kinderfahnen.

Morgen wird man die Sonne auf einen grossrädrigen Wagen laden
und in die Kunsthandlung Caspari fahren. Ein viehköpfiger Neger
mit wulstigem Nacken, Blähnase und breitem Schritt wird fünfzig
    weiss-
juckende Esel halten, die vor den Wagen gespannt sind beim
    Pyramidenbau.

Eine Menge blutbunten Volks wird sich stauen: Kindsbetterinen
    und Ammen,
Kranke im Fahrstuhl, ein stelzender Kranich, zwei Vietstänzerinnen,
ein Herr mit einer Ripsschleifenkrawatte und ein rotduftender
    Schutzmann.

Ich kann mich nicht halten: Ich bin voller Seligkeit. Die Fenster-
    kreuze
zerplatzen. Ein Kinderfräulein hängt bis zum Nabel aus einem
    Fenster heraus.
Ich kann mir nicht helfen: Die Dome zerplatzen mit Orgelfugen.
    Ich will
eine neue Sonne schaffen. Ich will zwei gegeneinanderschlagen
wie Zymbeln, und meiner Dame die Hand hinreichen. Wir werden
    entschweben
in einer violetten Sänfte über die Dächer euerer
hellgelben Stadt wie Lampenschirme aus Seidenpapier im Zugwind.

But in the air there is a counterblowing of crimson and egg-yellow
and bottle-green: swings that an orange fist holds on long threads,
and there is a singing from birdthroats that hop over branches.
A very fragile fencing of children's banners.

Tomorrow the sun will be loaded on a big-wheeled wagon
and taken to Caspari's art gallery. A beast-headed negro
with bulging neck, bladder nose and a long stride will hold fifty
      white
bucking asses like those yoked to wagons at the building of pyramids.

A crowd of bloodbright people will clot the street: midwives and
            wetnurses,
invalids in wheel chairs, a stilting crane, two female St. Vitus dancers,
a man with a ribbed silk tie and a red-smelling policeman.

I can't stop myself: I'm full of joy. The window crossbars
shatter. A children's nurse hangs to her navel from a window.
I can't help myself: the cathedrals burst with organ-fugues. I want
to make a new sun. I want to strike two together
like cymbals, and to hold my hand to my lady. Away we shall float
in a violet sedan over the roofs of your
bright yellow town in the breeze like lampshades of tissue paper.

1914: '*Die Aktion*'

GOTTFRIED BENN

KARYATIDE

Entrücke dich dem Stein! Zerbirst
die Höhle, die dich knechtet! Rausche
doch in die Flur! Verhöhne die Gesimse—
sieh: Durch den Bart des trunkenen Silen
aus seinem ewig überrauschten
lauten einmaligen durchdröhnten Blut
träuft Wein in seine Scham!

Bespei die Säulensucht: toderschlagene
greisige Hände bebten sie
verhangenen Himmeln zu. Stürze
die Tempel vor die Sehnsucht deines Knies,
in dem der Tanz begehrt!

Breite dich hin, zerblühe dich, oh, blute
dein weiches Beet aus grossen Wunden hin:
Sieh, Venus mit den Tauben gürtet
sich Rosen um der Hüften Liebestor—
sieh dieses Sommers letzten blauen Hauch
auf Astermeeren an die fernen
baumbraunen Ufer treiben; tagen
sieh diese letzte Glück-Lügenstunde
unserer Südlichkeit
hochgewölbt.

CARYATID

Leave stone behind, rise higher! Burst
the socket that enslaves you! Rush
out of the meadows! Mock the cornices—
Look at the drunk Silenus: through his beard
from his loud blood forever drowned in roars,
shivered by alien music and unique,
wine drips into his sex!

Spit on this column mania: done to death
mere senile hands they trembled
toward cloud-covered heavens. Tear down
the temples to the longing of your knee
which prisoned dance desires!

Spread out your limbs, O bloom to death and bleed
your gentle bed away through gaping wounds:
Look, Venus with her doves is twining
roses around the love-gate of her hips—
Look how the summer's last and hazy blue
drifts over seas of asters to the far
fall-foliage-colored shores: and look:
now dawns the last glad lying hour
of our southernness,
vaulted high.

1916: *'Die weissen Blätter'*

NACHTCAFÉ

824: Der Frauen Liebe und Leben.
Das Cello trinkt rasch mal. Die Flöte
rülpst tief drei Takte lang: das schöne Abendbrot.
Die Trommel liest den Kriminalroman zu Ende.

Grüne Zähne, Pickel im Gesicht
winkt einer Lidrandentzündung.

Fett im Haar
spricht zu offenem Mund mit Rachenmandel
Glaube Liebe Hoffnung um den Hals.

Junger Kropf ist Sattelnase gut.
Er bezahlt für sie drei Biere.

Bartflechte kauft Nelken,
Doppelkinn zu erweichen.

B-moll: die 35. Sonate.
Zwei Augen brüllen auf:
Spritzt nicht das Blut von Chopin in den Saal,
damit das Pack drauf rumlatscht!
Schluss! He, Gigi!—

Die Tür fliesst hin: ein Weib.
Wüste ausgedörrt. Kanaanitisch braun.
Keusch. Höhlenreich. Ein Duft kommt mit. Kaum Duft.
Es ist nur eine süsse Vorwölbung der Luft
gegen mein Gehirn.

Eine Fettleibigkeit trippelt hinterher.

NIGHT CAFÉ

824: The Love and Life of Women.
The 'cello has a quick drink. The flute
belches throughout three beats: his tasty evening snack.
The drum reads on to the end of the thriller.

Green teeth, pimples on his face,
waves to conjunctivitis.

Grease in his hair
talks to open mouth with swollen tonsils,
faith hope and charity round his neck.

Young goiter is sweet on saddle-nose.
He stands her three half pints.

Sycosis buys carnations
to mollify double chin.

B flat minor: sonata op. 35.
A pair of eyes roars out:
Don't splash the blood of Chopin round the place
for this lot to slouch about in!
Hey, Gigi! Stop!

The door dissolves: a woman.
Desert dried out. Canaanite brown.
Chaste. Full of caves. A scent comes with her. Hardly scent.
It's only a sweet leaning forward of the air
against my brain.

A paunched obesity waddles after her.

1917: *Fleisch*

IKARUS

I

O Mittag, der mit heissem Heu mein Hirn
zu Wiese, flachem Land und Hirten schwächt,
dass ich hinrinne und, den Arm im Bach,
den Mohn an meine Schläfe ziehe—
o du Weithingewölbter, enthirne doch
stillflügelnd über Fluch und Gram
des Werdens und Geschehns
mein Auge.
Noch durch Geröll der Halde, noch durch Land-aas,
verstaubendes, durch bettelhaft Gezack
der Felsen—überall
das tiefe Mutterblut, die strömende
entstirnte
matte
Getragenheit.

Das Tier lebt Tag um Tag
und hat an seinem Euter kein Erinnern,
der Hang schweigt seine Blume in das Licht
und wird zerstört.

Nur ich, mit Wächter zwischen Blut und Pranke,
ein hirnzerfressenes Aas, mit Flüchen
im Nichts zergellend, bespien mit Worten,
veräfft vom Licht—
o du Weithingewölbter,
träuf meinen Augen eine Stunde
des guten frühen Voraugenlichts—
schmilz hin den Trug der Farben, schwinge
die kotbedrängten Höhlen in das Rauschen
gebäumter Sonnen, Sturz der Sonnen-sonnen,
o aller Sonnen ewiges Gefälle—

ICARUS

I

O noon that with hot hay reduce
my brain to meadow, shepherds and flat land,
so that I flow away, my arm immersed
in the stream's water, and to my brow
draw down the poppies—noon that's vaulted wide,
now mutely winging above the curse and grief
of all that is and will be,
unbrain my eye.
Still through the hillside boulders, still through land-carrion,
turning to dust, through beggarly sharp shapes
of rocks—still everywhere
deep mother-blood, this streaming
deforeheaded
weary
drifting away.

The animal lives only for the day
and in its udder has no memory,
the slope in silence brings its flower to light
and is destroyed.

I only, with a sentry between blood and claw,
mere brain-devoured carrion, shrieking and cursing plunged
into annihilation, bespat with words,
guyed by the light—
O noon that's vaulted wide,
but for one hour infuse my eyes
with that good light which was before eyes were—
melt down the lie of colors, hurl
these cavities pressed by filth into the roar
of rearing suns, whirl of the sun of suns,
O everlasting fall of all the suns—

II

Das Hirn frisst Staub. Die Füsse fressen Staub.
Wäre das Auge rund und abgeschlossen,
dann bräche durch die Lider süsse Nacht,
Gebüsch und Liebe.
Aus dir, du süsses Tierisches,
aus euern Schatten, Schlaf und Haar,
muss ich mein Hirn besteigen,
alle Windungen,
das letzte Zwiegespräch—

III

So sehr am Strand, so sehr schon in der Barke,
im krokosfarbnen Kleide der Geweihten
und um die Glieder schon den leichten Flaum—
ausrauschst du aus den Falten, Sonne,
allnächtlich Welten in den Raum—
o eine der vergesslich hingesprühten
mit junger Glut die Schläfe mir zerschmelzend,
auftrinkend das entstirnte Blut—

II

The brain eats dust. Our feet devour the dust.
If but the eye were round and self-contained
then through the lids sweet night would enter in,
brushwood and love.
From you, the sweetly bestial,
from out your shadows, sleep and hair,
I must bestride my brain,
all loops and turns,
the ultimate duologue—

III

So near the beach, so much embarked already,
dressed in the victim's crocus-colored garment,
and round your limbs the light and delicate down—
O sun, you rustle forth from out your folds
each night new universes into space—
O, one of these, obliviously scattered here
with its young glow is melting down my temples,
drinks my deforeheaded blood.

[*c.* 1920]
1922: *Gesammelte Schriften*

UNTERGRUNDBAHN

Die weichen Schauer. Blütenfrühe. Wie
aus warmen Fellen kommt es aus den Wäldern.
Ein Rot schwärmt auf. Das grosse Blut steigt an.

Durch all den Frühling kommt die fremde Frau.
Der Strumpf am Spann ist da. Doch, wo er endet,
ist weit von mir. Ich schluchze auf der Schwelle:
laues Geblühe, fremde Feuchtigkeiten.

Oh, wie ihr Mund die laue Luft verprasst!
Du Rosenhirn, Meer-Blut, du Götter-Zwielicht,
du Erdenbeet, wie strömen deine Hüften
so kühl den Gang hervor, in dem du gehst!

Dunkel: Nun lebt es unter ihren Kleidern:
nur weisses Tier, gelöst und stummer Duft.

Ein armer Hirnhund, schwer mit Gott behangen.
Ich bin der Stirn so satt. Oh, ein Gerüste
von Blütenkolben löste sanft sie ab
und schwölle mit und schauerte und triefte.

So losgelöst. So müde. Ich will wandern.
Blutlos die Wege. Lieder aus den Gärten.
Schatten und Sintflut. Fernes Glück: ein Sterben
hin in des Meeres erlösend tiefes Blau.

SUBWAY TRAIN

Lascivious shivers. Early bloom. As if
from warm furred skins it wafted from the woods.
A red swarms up. The great strong blood ascends.

Through all of Spring the alien woman walks.
The stocking, stretched, is there. But where it ends
is far from me. I sob upon the threshold:
sultry luxuriance, alien moistures teeming.

O how her mouth squanders the sultry air!
You brain of roses, sea-blood, goddess-twilight,
you bed of earth, how coolly from your hips
your stride flows out, the glide that is in your walking.

Dark: underneath her garments now it lives:
white animal only, loosed, and silent scent.

A wretched braindog, laden down with God.
My forehead wearies me. O that a frame
of clustered blooms would gently take its place,
to swell in unison and stream and shudder.

So lax, adrift. So tired. I long to wander.
The ways all bloodless. Songs that blow from gardens.
Shadows and Flood. Far joys: a languid dying
down into ocean's deep redeeming blue.

1922: *Gesammelte Schriften*

PALAU

„Rot ist der Abend auf der Insel von Palau
und die Schatten sinken—"
singe, auch aus den Kelchen der Frau
lässt es sich trinken,
Totenvögel schrein
und die Totenuhren
pochen, bald wird es sein
Nacht und Lemuren.

Heisse Riffe. Aus Eukalypten geht
Tropik und Palmung,
was sich noch hält und steht,
will auch Zermalmung
bis in das Gliederlos,
bis in die Leere,
tief in den Schöpfungsschoss
dämmernder Meere.

Rot ist der Abend auf der Insel von Palau
und im Schattenschimmer
hebt sich steigend aus Dämmer und Tau:
„niemals und immer",
alle Tode der Welt
sind Fähren und Furten,
und von Fremdem umstellt
auch deine Geburten—

Einmal mit Opferfett
auf dem Piniengerüste
trägt sich dein Flammenbett
wie Wein zur Küste,
Megalithen zuhauf
und die Gräber und Hallen,
Hammer des Thor im Lauf
zu den Asen zerfallen—

PALAU

"Evening is red on the island of Palau
and the shadows sink—"
sing, from woman's chalices too
it is good to drink,
deathly the little owls cry
and the death-watch ticks out,
very soon it will be
Lemurs and night.

Hot these reefs. From eucalypti there flows
a tropical palm concoction,
all that still holds and stays
also longs for destruction
down to the limbless stage,
down to the vacuum,
back to the primal age,
dark ocean's womb.

Evening is red on the island of Palau
in the gleam of these shadows
there issues rising from twilight and dew:
"Never and Always,"
all the deaths of the earth
are fords and ferries,
what to you owes its birth
surrounded with strangeness—

once with sacrificial
fat on the pinewood floor
your bed of flames would travel
like wine to the shore,
megaliths heaped around
and the graves and the halls,
hammer of Thor that's bound
for the Aesir, crumbled, falls—

Wie die Götter vergehn
und die grossen Cäsaren,
von der Wange des Zeus
emporgefahren—
singe, wandert die Welt
schon in fremdestem Schwunge,
schmeckt uns das Charonsgeld
längst unter der Zunge.

Paarung. Dein Meer belebt
Sepien, Korallen,
was sich noch hält und hebt,
will auch zerfallen,
rot ist der Abend auf der Insel von Palau,
Eukalyptenschimmer
hebt in Runen aus Dämmer und Tau:
niemals und immer.

WER BIST DU—

Wer bist du—alle Mythen
zerrinnen. Was geschah,
Chimären, Leda-iten
sind einen Kniefall da,

gemalt mit Blut der Beeren
der Trunkenen Schläfe rot,
und die—des Manns Erwehren—
die nun als Lorbeer loht,

mit Schlangenhaar die Lende
an Zweig und Thyrsenstab,
in Trunkenheit und Ende
und um ein Göttergrab—

as the gods surcease,
the great Caesars decline,
from the cheek of Zeus
once raised up to reign—
sing, already the world
to the strangest rhythm is swung,
Charon's coin if not curled
long tasted under the tongue.

Coupling. Sepias your seas
and coral animate,
all that still holds and sways
also longs to disintegrate,
evening is red on the island of Palau,
eucalyptus glaze
raises in runes from twilight and dew:
Never and Always.

1924: *Schutt*

WHO ARE YOU

Who are you—all the legends
are vanishing. What was—
chimeras, Leda's kindred
in genuflecting pass,

painted with blood of berries,
the scarlet drunkards, she—
the masculine-defying—
a fiery laurel tree,

with serpent hair the haunches,
by branch and thyrsus staff,
in drunken fit, finale,
and round a holy grave—

Was ist, sind hohle Leichen,
die Wand aus Tang und Stein,
was scheint, ist ewiges Zeichen
und spielt die Tiefe rein—

in Schattenflur, in Malen,
das sich der Form entwand—:
Ulyss, der nach den Qualen
schlafend die Heimat fand.

AUS FERNEN, AUS REICHEN

Was dann nach jener Stunde
sein wird, wenn dies geschah,
weiss niemand, keine Kunde
kam je von da,
von den erstickten Schlünden
von dem gebrochnen Licht,
wird es sich neu entzünden,
ich meine nicht.

Doch sehe ich ein Zeichen:
über das Schattenland
aus Fernen, aus Reichen
eine grosse, schöne Hand,
die wird mich nicht berühren,
das lässt der Raum nicht zu:
doch werde ich sie spüren,
und das bist du.

Und du wirst niedergleiten
am Strand, am Meer,
aus Fernen, aus Weiten:
,,—erlöst auch er; "

What is, are hollow corpses,
the rock and seawrack screen,
what seems, eternal token
that plays the whole depth clean—

in phantom fields, portrayal
inhabiting no form—:
Odysseus past affliction
who sleeping found his home.

1925 : *Spaltung*

FROM FAR SHORES, FROM KINGDOMS

What were that moment over
shall be, and were this done,
cannot be told, no message
came thence, not one,
from breathless gorges can it,
from rays that, broken, slant,
can it be resurrected,
I think it can't.

Yet I discern a token:
over the shadow-land
from far shores, from kingdoms
a large, a beauteous hand,
it cannot touch me ever,
no space will let it through:
yet feel it I shall surely,
and it is you.

And you will come down gliding
borne landward by the wave
from far shores, from distances:
"—him too I save";

ich kannte deine Blicke
und in des tiefsten Schoss
sammelst du unsere Glücke,
den Traum, das Los.

Ein Tag ist zu Ende,
die Reifen fortgebracht,
dann spielen noch zwei Hände
das Lied der Nacht,
vom Zimmer, wo die Tasten
den dunklen Laut verwehn,
sieht man das Meer und die Masten
hoch nach Norden gehn.

Wenn die Nacht wird weichen,
wenn der Tag begann,
trägst du Zeichen,
die niemand deuten kann,
geheime Male
von fernen Stunden krank
und leerst die Schale
aus der ich vor dir trank.

SEPTEMBER

I

Du, über den Zaun gebeugt mit Phlox
(vom Regenguss zerspalten,
seltsamen Wildgeruchs),
der gern auf Stoppeln geht,
zu alten Leuten tritt,
die Balsaminen pflücken,
Rauch auf Feldern
mit Lust und Trauer atmet—

your eyes I knew, their glancings
deepest where gathered are,
gathered by you, our gladness,
vision, and star.

A day is now ended,
the children's hoops are gone,
the song of night
two hands play on, play on,
and from the room where fading
dark chords from keys resound,
watch now how mast and ocean
move northward bound.

When the night shall vanish,
and come the day,
tokens you bring with
meanings that none can say,
cryptic, stigmata
of distant time's disease,
the cup I drank you drink
and drain the lees.

[After 1925, before 1927]

SEPTEMBER

I

You leaning there over the fence with phlox
(splintered by rainstorm,
with a strange animal smell),
who are pleased to walk over stubble
and to accost old folk
gathering balm apples,
breathe with joy and sadness
smoke over ploughland—

aufsteigenden Gemäuers,
das noch sein Dach vor Schnee und Winter will,
kalklöschenden Gesellen
ein: „ ach, vergebens " zuzurufen
nur zögernd sich verhält—

gedrungen eher als hochgebaut,
auch unflätigen Kürbis nackt am Schuh,
fett und gesichtslos, dies Krötengewächs—

Ebenen-entstiegener,
Endmond aller Flammen,
aus Frucht-und Fieberschwellungen
abfallend, schon verdunkelten Gesichts—
Narr oder Täufer,
des Sommers Narr, Nachplapperer, Nachruf
oder der Gletscher Vorlied,
jedenfalls Nussknacker,
Schilfmäher,
Beschäftigter mit Binsenwahrheiten—

vor dir der Schnee,
Hochschweigen, unfruchtbar
die Unbesambarkeit der Weite:
Da langt dein Arm hin,
doch über den Zaun gebeugt
die Kraut-und Käferdränge,
das Lebenwollende,
Spinnen und Feldmäuse—

rising walls want there
a roof before the snow and winter come,
to shout a "You're wasting your time"
at lime-slaking laborers,
but, hesitant, restrain yourself,

thickset rather than tall in build,
with dirty pumpkin also bare at your shoe,
fat and faceless this toady growth—

Risen from the plains,
ultimate moon of all flames,
from tumescences of fruit and fever
dropping, darkened your face already—
fool or baptist,
summer's fool, echoer, necrologue,
or foresong of glaciers,
anyway nutcracker,
sedge-cutter,
ponderer of platitudes—

Snowfall ahead of you,
high silence, barren
the far unplantable distance:
that far your reach extends,
but, leaning over the fence,
throngs of beetles and plants now,
all life-desiring things,
spiders and field mice—

II

Du, ebereschenverhangen
von Frühherbst,
Stoppelgespinst,
Kohlweisslinge im Atem,
lass viele Zeiger laufen,
Kuckucksuhren schlagen,
lärme mit Vespergeläut,
gonge
die Stunde, die so golden feststeht,
so bestimmt dahinbräunt,
in ein zitternd Herz!

Du:—anderes!
So ruhn nur Götter
oder Gewänder
unstürzbarer Titanen
langgeschaffener,
so tief eingestickt
Falter und Blumen
in die Bahnen!

Oder ein Schlummer früher Art,
als kein Erwachen war,
nur goldene Wärme und Purpurbeeren,
benagt von Schwalben, ewigen,
die nie von dannen ziehn—
Dies schlage, gonge,
diese Stunde,
denn
wenn du schweigst,
drängen die Säume herab
pappelbestanden und schon kühler.

II

You, rowan-veiled
by early autumn,
stubblephantom,
cabbage-whites in your breath,
let many clock-hands turn,
cuckoo-clocks call,
clamor with vesper bells,
gong
the golden persistent hour
that so firmly continues to tan,
into a trembling heart!

You:—world of difference!
Only gods rest thus
or the robes
of untoppleable Titans
long-created,
so deeply embroidered
the butterflies and flowers
into their orbits!

Or a slumber of pristine kind,
when no awakening was,
only golden warmth and purple berries,
nibbled by swallows, eternal ones,
that never fly away—
This note strike, gong
this hour,
for
when you fall silent,
downward the forest-edges press,
thick with poplars, already cooler.

1948: *Statische Gedichte* (1937–47)

WENN ETWAS LEICHT

Wenn etwas leicht und rauschend um dich ist
wie die Glyzinienpracht an dieser Mauer,
dann ist die Stunde jener Trauer,
dass du nicht reich und unerschöpflich bist,

nicht wie die Blüte oder wie das Licht:
in Strahlen kommend, sich verwandelnd,
an ähnlichen Gebilden handelnd,
die alle nur der eine Rausch verflicht,

der eine Samt, auf dem die Dinge ruhn
so strömend und so unzerspalten,
die Grenze ziehn, die Stunden halten
und nichts in jener Trauer tun.

NACHZEICHNUNG

I

O jene Jahre! Der Morgen grünes Licht,
auch die noch nicht gefegten Lusttrottoire—
der Sommer schrie von Ebenen in der Stadt
und sog an einem Horn,
das sich von oben füllte.

Lautlose Stunde. Wässrige Farben
eines hellgrünen Aug's verdünnten Strahls,
Bilder aus diesem Zaubergrün, gläserne Reigen:
Hirten und Weiher, eine Kuppel, Tauben—
gewoben und gesandt, erglänzt, erklungen—,
verwandelbare Wolken eines Glücks!

A WEIGHTLESS ELEMENT

When like wistaria against this wall
around you rings a weightless element,
then is the time that you lament
being not rich and inexhaustible,

not like the blossom or not like the light:
in rays arriving, changing its design,
acting on forms akin to it
that ringed in single ecstasy entwine,

the single velvet ground where things repose,
so lush, so undivided, and
with time according, self-confined,
go not the way lamenting goes.

1948: *Statische Gedichte* (1937–47)

RETROSPECTIVE SKETCH

I

O the green light, the mornings of those years,
the pleasure pavements before the sweepers came—
the summer cried of plains within the city
and sucked a horn of plenty
replenished from above.

Hour without sound. Watery colors
of a pale-green eye's diluted ray,
images out of this magical green, dances in glass:
shepherds and ponds, a cupola, pigeons—
woven and vouchsafed, flashed out or intuned—,
mutable clouds of a happiness!

So standest du vor Tag: die Springbrunnen noch ohne Perlen, tatenlos
Gebautes und die Steige; die Häuser
verschlossen, du *erschufst*
den Morgen, jasminene Frühe,
sein Jauchzen, uranfänglich
sein Strahl—noch ohne Ende—o jene Jahre!

Ein Unauslöschliches im Herzen,
Ergänzungen vom Himmel und der Erde;
Zuströmendes aus Schilf und Gärten,
Gewitter abends
tränkten die Dolden ehern,
die barsten dunkel, gespannt von ihren Seimen;
und Meer und Strände,
bewimpelte mit Zelten,
glühenden Sandes trächtig,
bräunende Wochen, gerbend alles
zu Fell für Küsse, die niedergingen
achtlos und schnell verflogen
wie Wolkenbrüche!

Darüber hing die Schwere
auch jetzt—doch Trauben
aus ihr,

die Zweige niederziehend und wieder hochlassend,
nur einige Beeren,
wenn du mochtest,
erst—

noch nicht so drängend und überhangen
von kolbengrossen Fruchtfladen,
altem schwerem Traubenfleisch—

O jene Jahre!

So you stood before daybreak: the fountains
still without pearls, constructions
raised without effort, the stairways; the houses
still locked, it was you that *created*
the morning, syringa time of the day,
its jubilation, pristine
its beam—without end as yet—O those years!

A sense of inextinguishable things,
completions of heaven and earth;
encroachments from reeds and gardens,
thunderstorms nightly
watered the umbels to brass
that darkly burst, held taut by their sap;
and sea and beaches
with their streamers, their tents,
pregnant with glowing sand,
sunburning weeks tanning all
to fur for kisses that descended
heedless and briefly felt
as summer cloudbursts.

Over it all hung the sadness
even then—but grapes
out of it,

dragging the tendrils down and releasing them,
only a berry or two
when you wanted it,
then—

not yet so urgent and overhung
with bunches of fruit as big as clubs,
heavy old grape-flesh—

O those years!

II

Dunkle Tage des Frühlings,
nicht weichender Dämmer um Laub;
Fliederblüte gebeugt, kaum hochblickend
narzissenfarben und starken Todesgeruchs,
Glückausfälle,
sieglose Trauer des Unerfüllten.

Und in den Regen hinein,
der auf das Laub fällt,
höre ich ein altes Wälderlied,
von Wäldern, die ich einst durchfuhr
und wiedersah, doch ich ging nicht
in die Halle, wo das Lied erklungen war,
die Tasten schwiegen längst,
die Hände ruhten irgendwo,
gelöst von jenen Armen, die mich hielten,
zu Tränen rührten,
Hände aus den Oststeppen,
blutig zertretenen längst—
nur noch ihr Wälderlied
in den Regen hinein
an dunklen Tagen des Frühlings
den ewigen Steppen zu.

II

Dark days of Spring,
half-light clinging to foliage;
lilac blossom that dropped, hardly glancing upward
narcissus-colored and strongly scented with death,
cessations of gladness,
unavailing gloom of the unfulfilled.

And into the rain
that falls on leaves
I hear an old woodland song
about woods I once drove through
and revisited, but I did not go
to the hall where the song had sounded,
the keyboard had long been still,
the hands were resting somewhere,
detached from those arms that held me,
moved me to tears,
hands out of the Eastern steppes,
long ago bloodily trampled—
only her woodland song
into the rain
in the dark days of Spring
toward the undying steppes.

1948: *Statische Gedichte* (1937–47)

GEWISSE LEBENSABENDE

I

Du brauchst nicht immer die Kacheln zu scheuern, Hendrickje,
mein Auge trinkt sich selbst,
trinkt sich zu Ende—
aber an anderen Getränken mangelt es—
dort die Buddhastatue,
chinesischen Haingott,
gegen eine Kelle Hulstkamp,
bitte!

Nie etwas gemalt
in Frostweiss oder Schlittschuhläuferblau
oder dem irischen Grün,
aus dem der Purpur schimmert—
immer nur meine Eintönigkeit,
mein Schattenzwang—
nicht angenehm,
diesen Weg so deutlich zu verfolgen.

Grösse—wo?
Ich nehme den Griffel
und gewisse Dinge stehn dann da
auf Papier, Leinwand
oder ähnlichem Zunder—
Resultat: Buddhabronze gegen Sprit—
aber Huldigungen unter Blattpflanzen,
Bankett der Pinselgilde— :
was fürs Genre—!

... Knarren,
Schäfchen, die quietschen,
Abziehbilder
flämisch, rubenisch
für die Enkelchen—!
(ebensolche Idioten—!)

THE EVENINGS OF CERTAIN LIVES

I

You needn't always be scrubbing the tiles, Hendrickje,
my eye drinks itself,
drinks itself dry—
but then it has no other liquor—
the statue of Buddha over there,
Chinese god of the bosk,
as against a good tot of Hulstkamp,
I ask you!

Never painted a thing
in frost-white or skater's blue
or in Irish green
with the purple flickering out of it—
only my own monotony always—
my coactive shadows—
it's not pleasant
to follow this bent with such distinctness.

Greatness—where?
I take my pencil
and certain things emerge, stand there
on paper, canvas
or similar things—
result: bronze Buddha as against hooch—
all those obeisances under indoor plants,
banquet of the dimwit daubers' guild—:
give it to the genre painter!

Rattles,
lambs bleating,
transfers,
Flemish, rubenesque,
for small grandchildren—
(likewise idiots—!)

Ah—Hulstkamp—
Wärmezentrum,
Farbenmittelpunkt,
mein Schattenbraun—
Bartstoppelfluidum um Herz und Auge—

II

Der Kamin raucht
—schneuzt sich der Schwan vom Avon—,
die Stubben sind nass,
klamme Nacht, Leere vermählt mit Zugluft—
Schluss mit den Gestalten,
übervölkert die Erde
reichlicher Pfirsichfall, vier Rosenblüten
pro anno—
ausgestreut,
auf die Bretter geschoben
von dieser Hand,
faltig geworden
und mit erschlafften Adern!

Alle die Ophelias, Julias,
bekränzt, silbern, auch mörderisch—
alle die weichen Münder, die Seufzer,
die ich aus ihnen herausmanipulierte—
die ersten Aktricen längst Qualm,
Rost, ausgelaugt, Rattenpudding—
auch Herzens-Ariel bei den Elementen.

Die Epoche zieht sich den Bratenrock aus.
Diese Lord- und Lauseschädel,
ihre Gedankengänge,
die ich ins Extrem trieb—
meine Herren Geschichtsproduzenten
alles Kronen- und Szepteranalphabeten,
Grossmächte des Weltraums
wie Fledermaus oder Papierdrachen!

Ah—Hulstkamp—
midpoint of warmth,
center of colors,
my shadow brown—
aura of unshaved bristle round heart and eye—

II

The fire is smoking
—the Swan of Avon blows his nose—
the tree-stumps are wet,
clammy night, emptiness suffused with draughts—
have done with characters,
earth overpopulated
by copious fall of peach, four rosebuds
pro anno—
strewn far and wide,
thrust on the boards
by this hand,
with its wrinkles now,
and its exhausted veins.

All the Ophelias, Juliets
wreathed, silvery, also murderous—
all the soft mouths, the sighs
I manipulated out of them—
the first actresses long since vapor,
rust, lixiviated, rats' pudding—
even the heart's Ariel off to the elements.

The age takes off its Sunday best.
These duke and desperado skulls,
their trains of thought
I drove to the extreme—
my history-making gentlemen
all illiterates of crown and scepter,
major powers of space,
like flittermouse or paper kite!

Sir Goon schrieb neulich an mich:
„Der Rest ist Schweigen":—
Ich glaube, das ist von mir,
kann nur von mir sein,
Dante tot—eine grosse Leere
zwischen den Jahrhunderten
bis zu meinen Wortschatzzitaten—

aber wenn sie fehlten,
der Plunder nie aufgeschlagen,
die Buden, die Schafotte, die Schellen
nie geklungen hätten—:
Lücken—?? Vielleicht Zahnlücken,
aber das grosse Affengebiss
mahlte weiter
seine Leere, vermählt mit Zugluft—
die Stubben sind nass
und der Butler schnarcht in Porterträumen.

Sir Goon recently wrote to me:
"The rest is silence."
I think I said that myself,
nobody else could have said it,
Dante dead,—a great emptiness
between the centuries
up to the quotations from my vocabulary—

but if they were missing,
if all that stuff had never been turned out,
the booths and the gallowtrees, if the bells
had never jingled—:
gaps then—?? Gaps possibly in the teeth,
but the ape's great jaws
would go on grinding
their emptiness the draughts suffuse—
the tree-stumps are wet,
and the butler snores in his porter dreams.

1949: *Statische Gedichte* (2nd. ed.)

MAX HERRMANN-NEISSE

DU MEINER BEETE STILLE GÄRTNERIN

Wo deine Füsse wandeln, blüht Vergissmeinnicht,
du meiner Beete stille Gärtnerin.

Du öffnest deine Hand und wirfst die weissen Wellen
wippender Sätze über meinen Geist.

—Gedanken gehn in Waffen . . . Glied an Glied . . .

Im Mond sind Mühlen, winterlich verwaist,
so braun wie ausgebrannt, umzäunt von Nervenlicht.

—Schläfst du? Träumst du von mir? Entstellen
dein Atmen Ängste? Fühlst du, wie ich bei dir bin?

Stumm singt die Nacht ihr namenloses Lied.

LEGENDE VOM ZAUBER DER ZÄRTLICHEN ZELLEN

Die Nonnen nächtigten in ihren Gärten,
denn Angst stieg plötzlich aus den schwülen Zellen;
sie beteten zum kühlen Gott der Quellen,
und Stern und Springbrunn wurden Traumgefährten.

YOU QUIET ATTENDER TO MY GARDEN

Where you tread, forget-me-nots come into flower,
you quiet attender to my garden.

You open your hand, and throw the white waves
of seesawing phrases over my mind.

—Thoughts walk armed . . . rank upon rank . . .

In the moon are mills, wintrily orphaned,
as brown as burned, fenced by nerve-light.

—You are asleep? You dream of me? Do fears
trouble your breathing? You feel how I am near?

The night dumbly sings its nameless song.

1918

LEGEND OF THE BEWITCHED NUNNERY

The nuns kept to their garden all night long,
for sudden fear stirred in the sultry cells;
they prayed to the cool God of silver wells,
and through their dreams stars leapt and well-springs flung.

—Die Morgenmühle klappert. Hunde bellen—
Als sie mit rührend zagen, unbeschwerten
Schritten zurück in ihre Räume kehrten,
begannen sich die Dinge zu entstellen.

Und Altarschmuck und Kranz und Buch und Bild
sind schamlos wie in Liebeskampf verflochten.
Aus steilen Kerzen brünstig Brodem quillt.

Und eh die Fraun zu flüchten noch vermochten,
fühlten sie plötzlich hüllenlos sich schweben,
süss einem Unsichtbaren hingegeben.

—The morning mill claps loudly. Hounds give tongue.
And as with timid steps at matin-bells
they slowly moved back to their cubicles,
things started into change, alluring, wrong.

For altar-piece and image, book and dove
were tangled as in shameless sweet embrace.
Tall tapers breathed sharp fragrances of love.

And lo, before the nuns could flee the place,
they felt themselves unveiled; they swayed and quivered,
to the Unseen deliciously delivered.

1921

ALBERT EHRENSTEIN

DER DICHTER UND DER KRIEG

Ich sang die Gesänge der rotaufgeschlitzten Rache,
Und ich sang die Stille des waldumbuchteten Sees;
Aber zu mir gesellte sich niemand,
Steil, einsam
Wie die Zikade sich singt,
Sang ich mein Lied für mich.
Schon vergeht mein Schritt ermattend
Im Sand der Mühe.
Vor Müdigkeit entfallen mir die Augen,
Müde bin ich der trostlosen Furten,
Des Überschreitens der Gewässer, Mädchen und Strassen.
Am Abgrund gedenke ich nicht
Des Schildes und Speeres.
Von Birken umweht,
Vom Winde umschattet.
Entschlaf' ich zum Klange der Harfe
Anderer,
Denen sie freudig trieft.
Ich rege mich nicht,
Denn alle Gedanken und Taten
Trüben die Reinheit der Welt.

THE POET AND WAR

I sang the songs of red ripped-up vengeance,
And I sang the stillness of the lake with wooded bays,
But none came to join me,
Steep, lonely
As the cicada singing,
I sang my song for myself.
My footsteps fade already, slackening
In the sand of travail.
With weariness my eyes drop from me,
I am weary of comfortless fords,
Of crossing waters, girls and streets.
In the abyss I do not remember
The shield and the spear.
Round me the whispering birches,
Round me the wind's shadow.
I fall asleep to the sound of the harp
Of other men
For whom it joyfully spills.
I do not stir,
For every thought and deed
Darkens the purity of the world.

1917: *Die rote Zeit*

AUTOFAHRT

Mögen Steinklopfer abends
Keine Steine zerklopfen—
Rasch wie Helfer durcheilen wir Nacht.
Schon liegt, was ferne prangte im Mond,
Begraben unter unsern Rädern.
Staub frass die Zeit,
Wir sind schneller,
Sehen Geländer einander die Hände reichen,
Bäume heben und senken verärgert die Zweige,
Hasen wirbelt's in den Lichtkreis,
Geknirsch steil gradauslaufender Strassen,
Ohnmächtiger Wind,
Den blutigen Mond verwehen die Wolken—
Uns leuchten
Johanniskäfer und Sterne.

CAR JOURNEY

Even if stonebreakers do not want
To break any stones in the evening—
Quickly like helpers we rush through night.
What shone far off in the moon lies
Now buried under our wheels.
Dust ate time,
We are faster,
See railings that clasp hands,
Trees lift and drop their branches, peeved,
Hares are whirled into the circle of light,
Crunching of steep roads that rise straight,
Impotent wind,
The clouds blow over the bloody moon—
Our way is lit
By glow-worms and stars.

1931

GEORG TRAKL

HELIAN

I

In den einsamen Stunden des Geistes
Ist es schön in der Sonne zu gehn
An den gelben Mauern des Sommers hin.
Leise klingen die Schritte im Gras; doch immer schläft
Der Sohn des Pan im grauen Marmor.

Abends auf der Terrasse betranken wir uns mit braunem Wein.
Rötlich glüht der Pfirsich im Laub;
Sanfte Sonate, frohes Lachen.

Schön ist die Stille der Nacht.
Auf dunklem Plan
Begegnen wir uns mit Hirten und weissen Sternen.

Wenn es Herbst geworden ist,
Zeigt sich nüchterne Klarheit im Hain.
Besänftigte wandeln wir an roten Mauern hin
Und die runden Augen folgen dem Flug der Vögel.
Am Abend sinkt das weisse Wasser in Graburnen.

In kahlen Gezweigen feiert der Himmel.
In reinen Händen trägt der Landmann Brot und Wein
Und friedlich reifen die Früchte in sonniger Kammer.

O wie ernst ist das Antlitz der teueren Toten.
Doch die Seele erfreut gerechtes Anschaun.

HELIAN

I

In the lonely hours of the spirit
Beautiful it is to walk in the sun,
Beside the yellow walls of the summer.
Softly the footfalls ring in the grass; but always
The son of Pan sleeps in the gray marble.

Evenings on the terrace we got drunk with brown wine.
Reddish the peach glows in the leaves;
Gentle sonata, happy laughing.

Beautiful is the quiet of the night.
On a dark plain
We meet with shepherds and white stars.

When Autumn has come
Sober clearness enters the grove.
Calmed we wander beside red walls
And the round eyes follow the flight of birds.
At nightfall the white water sinks in funeral jars.

In bare branches heaven celebrates.
In pure hands the countryman carries bread and wine
And the fruits ripen peacefully in the sunny larder.

O how earnest is the countenance of the dear dead.
Yet a just regard delights the soul.

II

Gewaltig ist das Schweigen des verwüsteten Gartens,
Da der junge Novize die Stirne mit braunem Laub bekränzt,
Sein Odem eisiges Gold trinkt.

Die Hände rühren das Alter bläulicher Wasser
Oder in kalter Nacht die weissen Wangen der Schwestern.

Leise und harmonisch ist ein Gang an freundlichen Zimmern hin,
Wo Einsamkeit ist und das Rauschen des Ahorns,
Wo vielleicht noch die Drossel singt.

Schön ist der Mensch und erscheinend im Dunkel,
Wenn er staunend Arme and Beine bewegt,
Und in purpurnen Höhlen stille die Augen rollen.

Zur Vesper verliert sich der Fremdling in schwarzer November-
    zerstörung,
Unter morschem Geäst, an Mauern voll Aussatz hin,
Wo vordem der heilige Bruder gegangen,
Versunken in das sanfte Saitenspiel seines Wahnsinns.

O wie einsam endet der Abendwind.
Ersterbend neigt sich das Haupt im Dunkel des Ölbaums.

III

Erschütternd ist der Untergang des Geschlechts.
In dieser Stunde füllen sich die Augen des Schauenden
Mit dem Gold seiner Sterne.

Am Abend versinkt ein Glockenspiel, das nicht mehr tönt,
Verfallen die schwarzen Mauern am Platz,
Ruft der tote Soldat zum Gebet.

Ein bleicher Engel
Tritt der Sohn ins leere Haus seiner Väter.

II

Immense is the silence of the ravaged garden
When the young novice garlands his temples with brown leaves,
His breath drinks icy gold.

The hands stir the age of bluish waters
Or in cold night the white cheeks of the sisters.

Soft and harmonious is a walk past friendly rooms,
Where solitude is, and the rustling of the maple tree,
Where still perhaps the thrush is singing.

Beautiful is man and evident in the darkness,
When marveling he moves his arms and legs
And silent in purple caves the eyes roll.

At vespers the stranger is lost in black November destruction,
Under rotted boughs, beside leprous walls
Where earlier the holy brother walked,
Sunk in the faint thrumming of his madness.

O how lonely the evening wind desists.
Fading, the head bows in the dark of the olive tree.

III

Overwhelming is the generation's decline,
At this hour the eyes of him who gazes
Fill with the gold of his stars.

At nightfall bells die that will chime no more,
The black walls on the square decay,
To prayer the dead soldier calls.

A pale angel,
The son steps into the empty house of his fathers.

Die Schwestern sind ferne zu weissen Greisen gegangen.
Nachts fand sie der Schläfer unter den Säulen im Hausflur,
Zurückgekehrt von traurigen Pilgerschaften.

O wie starrt von Kot und Würmern ihr Haar,
Da er darein mit silbernen Füssen steht,
Und jene verstorben aus kahlen Zimmern treten.

O ihr Psalmen in feurigen Mitternachtsregen,
Da die Knechte mit Nesseln die sanften Augen schlugen,
Die kindlichen Früchte des Holunders
Sich staunend neigen über ein leeres Grab.

Leise rollen vergilbte Monde
Über die Fieberlinnen des Jünglings,
Eh dem Schweigen des Winters folgt.

IV

Ein erhabenes Schicksal sinnt den Kidron hinab,
Wo die Zeder, ein weiches Geschöpf,
Sich unter den blauen Brauen des Vaters entfaltet,
Über die Weide nachts ein Schläfer seine Herde führt.
Oder es sind Schreie im Schlaf,
Wenn ein eherner Engel im Hain den Menschen antritt,
Das Fleisch des Heiligen auf glühendem Rost hinschmilzt.

Um die Lehmhütten rankt purpurner Wein,
Tönende Bündel vergilbten Korns,
Das Summen der Bienen, der Flug des Kranichs.
Am Abend begegnen sich Auferstandene auf Felsenpfaden.

In schwarzen Wassern spiegeln sich Aussätzige;
Oder sie öffnen die kotbefleckten Gewänder
Weinend dem balsamischen Wind, der vom rosigen Hügel weht.

The sisters have gone far away to white old men,
At night the sleeper found them under the columns in the hall,
Returned from their sorrowful pilgrimages.

O how their hair curds with filth and worms
When he plants his silver feet therein,
And from bare rooms they move with dead steps.

O you psalms in fiery midnight rains,
When the servants with nettles thrashed the gentle eyes,
The childlike fruits of the elder tree
Marveling stoop over an empty grave.

Softly yellowed moons roll
Over the fever sheets of the young man,
Before he follows the silence of the winter.

IV

A high destiny ponders down Kidron passing,
Where the cedar, tender being,
Unfolds beneath the blue brows of the father,
Over the meadow at night a shepherd leads his flock.
Or there are cries in sleep
When in the grove a brazen angel advances on man
And the saint's flesh melts on the glowing grill.

Round the clay huts purple vines abound,
Sonorous sheaves of yellowed corn,
The hum of bees, the flight of the crane.
At nightfall the resurrected meet on mountain paths.

Lepers are mirrored in black waters
Or they part their filth-bespattered robes,
Weeping to the wind that blows with balm from the rosy hill.

Schlanke Mägde tasten durch die Gassen der Nacht,
Ob sie den liebenden Hirten fänden.
Sonnabends tönt in den Hütten sanfter Gesang.

Lasset das Lied auch des Knaben gedenken,
Seines Wahnsinns, und weisser Brauen und seines Hingangs,
Des Verwesten, der bläulich die Augen aufschlägt.
O wie traurig ist dieses Wiedersehn.

V

Die Stufen des Wahnsinns in schwarzen Zimmern,
Die Schatten der Alten unter der offenen Tür,
Da Helians Seele sich im rosigen Spiegel beschaut
Und Schnee und Aussatz von seiner Stirne sinken.

An den Wänden sind die Sterne erloschen
Und die weissen Gestalten des Lichts.

Dem Teppich entsteigt Gebein der Gräber,
Das Schweigen verfallener Kreuze am Hügel,
Des Weihrauchs Süsse im purpurnen Nachtwind.

O ihr zerbrochenen Augen in schwarzen Mündern,
Da der Enkel in sanfter Umnachtung
Einsam dem dunkleren Ende nachsinnt,
Der stille Gott die blauen Lider über ihn senkt.

UNTERGANG

An Karl Borromäus Heinrich

Über den weissen Weiher
Sind die wilden Vögel fortgezogen.
Am Abend weht von unseren Sternen ein eisiger Wind.

Slim girls grope through the alleys of night,
Who seek to find the loving shepherd.
On Saturdays quiet singing sounds in the huts.

Let the song also remember the boy,
His madness, and white temples and his departing,
The mouldered boy, who opens bluish his eyes.
O how sorrowful is this meeting again.

V

The stairs of madness in black rooms,
The shadows of the old men under the open door,
When Helian's soul regards itself in the rosy mirror
And snow and leprosy slide from his temples.

On the walls the stars have been extinguished
And the white forms of the light.

From the tapestry bones of the graves descend,
The silence of decayed crosses on the hill,
Sweetness of incense in the purple night wind.

O you crushed eyes in black mouths,
When the grandson in his mind's gentle night,
Lonely, ponders the darker ending,
The quiet god closes his blue eyelids over him.

[Winter 1912–13]

DECLINE

(to Karl Borromäus Heinrich)

Over the white pond
The wild birds have travelled on.
In the evening an icy wind blows from our stars.

Über unsere Gräber
Beugt sich die zerbrochene Stirne der Nacht.
Unter Eichen schaukeln wir auf einem silbernen Kahn.

Immer klingen die weissen Mauern der Stadt.
Unter Dornenbogen
O mein Bruder klimmen wir blinde Zeiger gen Mitternacht.

UNTERWEGS

Am Abend trugen sie den Fremden in die Totenkammer;
Ein Duft von Teer; das leise Rauschen roter Platanen;
Der dunkle Flug der Dohlen; am Platz zog eine Wache auf.
Die Sonne ist in schwarze Linnen gesunken; immer wieder kehrt
    dieser vergangene Abend.
Im Nebenzimmer spielt die Schwester eine Sonate von Schubert.
Sehr leise sinkt ihr Lächeln in den verfallenen Brunnen,
Der bläulich in der Dämmerung rauscht. O, wie alt ist unser
    Geschlecht.
Jemand flüstert drunten im Garten; jemand hat diesen schwarzen
    Himmel verlassen.
Auf der Kommode duften Äpfel. Grossmutter zündet goldene
    Kerzen an.

O, wie mild ist der Herbst. Leise klingen unsere Schritte im alten Park
Unter hohen Bäumen. O, wie ernst ist das hyazinthene Antlitz der
    Dämmerung.
Der blaue Quell zu deinen Füssen, geheimnisvoll die rote Stille
    deines Munds,
Umdüstert vom Schlummer des Laubs, dem dunklen Gold ver-
    fallener Sonnenblumen.
Deine Lider sind schwer von Mohn und träumen leise auf meiner
    Stirne.
Sanfte Glocken durchzittern die Brust. Eine blaue Wolke
Ist dein Antlitz auf mich gesunken in der Dämmerung.

Over our graves
The broken brow of the night inclines.
Under oak-trees we sway in a silver boat.

Always the town's white walls resound.
Under arches of thorns,
O my brother, blind minute-hands,
We climb towards midnight.

[1913]

WAYFARING

At nightfall they carried the stranger dead into the house;
An odor of tar; the red plane-trees' soft rustling;
The dark flutter of jackdaws; the guard paraded on the square.
The sun has sunk in black linen; time and again this bygone evening
    returns.
In the next room my sister is playing a Schubert sonata.
Very softly her smile sinks into the decayed fountain,
Which murmurs blue in the twilight. O how old our family is.
Someone whispers down in the garden; someone has left this black
    heaven.
The scent of apples up on the cupboard. Grandmother is lighting
    golden candles.

O how mild the autumn is. Soft our footsteps in the old park
Sound under lofty trees. O how earnest is the hyacinthine face of
    twilight.
The blue spring at your feet, mysterious your mouth's red stillness,
Shrouded by the slumber of leaves, by the dark gold of decayed sun-
    flowers.
Your eyelids are heavy with poppy and dream softly against my
    forehead.
Gentle bells tremble through the heart. A blue cloud,
Your face has sunk over me in the twilight.

Ein Lied zur Gitarre, das in einer fremden Schenke erklingt,
Die wilden Holunderbüsche dort, ein lang vergangener Novem-
   bertag,
Vertraute Schritte auf der dämmernden Stiege, der Anblick
   gebräunter Balken,
Ein offenes Fenster, an dem ein süsses Hoffen zurückblieb—
Unsäglich ist das alles, o Gott, das man erschüttert ins Knie bricht.

O, wie dunkel ist diese Nacht. Eine purpurne Flamme
Erlosch an meinem Mund. In der Stille
Erstirbt der bangen Seele einsames Saitenspiel.
Lass, wenn trunken von Wein das Haupt in die Gosse sinkt.

A song for the guitar, sounding in a strange tavern,
Wild elderbushes there, a long bygone day in November,
Familiar steps on the dusky stair, the sight of beams tanned brown,
An open window, at which a sweet hope stayed behind—
Unspeakable it all is, O God, one is overwhelmed and falls on one's
   knees.

O how dark this night is. A purple flame
Failed at my mouth. In the stillness
The alarmed soul's lonely music fades and dies.
No more, when the wine-drunk head sinks down to the gutter.

[1913]

KINDHEIT

Voll Früchten der Holunder; ruhig wohnte die Kindheit
In blauer Höhle. Über vergangenen Pfad,
Wo nun bräunlich das wilde Gras saust,
Sinnt das stille Geäst; das Rauschen des Laubs.

Ein gleiches, wenn das blaue Wasser im Felsen tönt.
Sanft ist der Amsel Klage. Ein Hirt
Folgt sprachlos der Sonne, die vom herbstlichen Hügel rollt.

Ein blauer Anblick ist nur mehr Seele.
Am Waldsaum zeigt sich ein scheues Wild und friedlich
Ruhn im Grund die alten Glocken und finsteren Weiler.

Frömmer kennst du den Sinn der dunklen Jahre,
Kühle und Herbst in einsamen Zimmern;
Und in heiliger Bläue läuten leuchtende Schritte fort.

Leise klirrt ein offenes Fenster; zu Tränen
Rührt der Anblick des verfallenen Friedhofs am Hügel,
Erinnerung an erzählte Legenden; doch manchmal erhellt sich die
        Seele,
Wenn sie frohe Menschen denkt, dunkelgoldene Frühlingstage.

CHILDHOOD

Full-berried the elderbush: tranquilly childhood lived
In a blue cave. Over the bygone path
Where now pale brown the wild grasses hiss,
Calm branches ponder; the rustling of leaves.

This too when blue waters sound under the crags.
Gentle the blackbird's plaint. A shepherd
Follows unspeaking the sun that rolls from the autumn hill.

A blue moment is purely and simply soul.
At the forest edge a shy deer shows itself, at peace
Below in the vale the old bells and somber hamlets rest.

Now more devout, you know the meaning of the dark years,
Coolness and autumn in solitary rooms;
And still in holy azure shining footfalls ring.

An open window quietly rasps; tears come
At the sight of the decayed graveyard on the hill,
Memory of told legends; yet the soul sometimes brightens
When she thinks of the glad folk, the dark gold Springtime days.

[1913]

SEBASTIAN IM TRAUM

Für Adolf Loos

Mutter trug das Kindlein im weissen Mond,
Im Schatten des Nussbaums, uralten Holunders,
Trunken vom Safte des Mohns, der Klage der Drossel;
Und stille
Neigte in Mitleid sich über jene ein bärtiges Antlitz,

Leise im Dunkel des Fensters; und altes Hausgerät
Der Väter
Lag im Verfall; Liebe und herbstliche Träumerei.

Also dunkel der Tag des Jahrs, traurige Kindheit,
Da der Knabe leise zu kühlen Wassern, silbernen Fischen hinabstieg,
Ruh und Antlitz;
Da er steinern sich vor rasende Rappen warf,
In grauer Nacht sein Stern über ihn kam;

Oder wenn er an der frierenden Hand der Mutter
Abends über Sankt Peters herbstlichen Friedhof ging,
Ein zarter Leichnam stille im Dunkel der Kammer lag
Und jener die kalten Lider über ihn aufhob.

Er aber war ein kleiner Vogel im kahlen Geäst,
Die Glocke klang im Abendnovember,
Des Vaters Stille, da er im Schlaf die dämmernde Wendeltreppe
    hinabstieg.

*

Frieden der Seele. Einsamer Winterabend,
Die dunklen Gestalten der Hirten am alten Weiher;
Kindlein in der Hütte von Stroh; o wie leise
Sank in schwarzem Fieber das Antlitz hin.
Heilige Nacht.

SEBASTIAN IN DREAM

(for Adolf Loos)

Mother bore this infant in the white moon,
In the nut-tree's shade, in the ancient elder's,
Drunk with the poppy's juice, the thrush's lament;
And mute
With compassion a bearded face bowed down to that woman,

Quiet in the window's darkness; and ancestral heirlooms,
Old household goods,
Lay rotting there; love and autumnal reverie.

So dark was the day of the year, desolate childhood,
When softly the boy to cool waters, to silver fishes walked down,
Calm and countenance;
When stony he cast himself down where black horses raced,
In the gray of the night his star possessed him;

Or holding his mother's icy hand
He walked at nightfall across St. Peter's autumnal churchyard,
While a delicate corpse lay still in the bedroom's gloom
And he raised cold eyelids towards it.

But he was a bird in leafless boughs,
All the churchbells long in dusking November,
His father's stillness, when asleep he descended the dark of the
    winding stair.

*

Peace of the soul. A lonely winter evening.
The dark shapes of shepherds by the ancient pond;
Little child in the hut of straw; O how softly
Into black fever his face sank down.
Holy night.

Oder wenn er an der harten Hand des Vaters
Stille den finstern Kalvarienberg hinanstieg
Und in dämmernden Felsennischen
Die blaue Gestalt des Menschen durch seine Legende ging,
Aus der Wunde unter dem Herzen purpurn das Blut rann.
O wie leise stand in dunkler Seele das Kreuz auf.

Liebe; da in schwarzen Winkeln der Schnee schmolz,
Ein blaues Lüftchen sich heiter im alten Holunder fing,
In dem Schattengewölbe des Nussbaums;
Und dem Knaben leise sein rosiger Engel erschien;

Freude; da in kühlen Zimmern eine Abendsonate erklang,
Im braunen Holzgebälk
Ein blauer Falter aus der silbernen Puppe kroch.

O die Nähe des Todes. In steinerner Mauer
Neigte sich ein gelbes Haupt, schweigend das Kind,
Da in jenem März der Mond verfiel.

*

Rosige Osterglocke im Grabgewölbe der Nacht
Und die Silberstimmen der Sterne,
Dass in Schauern ein dunkler Wahnsinn von der Stirne des Schläfers
    sank.

O wie stille ein Gang den blauen Fluss hinab
Vergessenes sinnend, da im grünen Geäst
Die Drossel ein Fremdes in den Untergang rief.

Oder wenn er an der knöchernen Hand des Greisen
Abends vor die verfallene Mauer der Stadt ging
Und jener in schwarzem Mantel ein rosiges Kindlein trug,
Im Schatten des Nussbaums der Geist des Bösen erschien.

Or holding his father's horny hand
In silence he walked up Calvary Hill
And in dusky rock recesses
The blue shape of Man would pass through His legend,
Blood run purple from the wound beneath His heart.
O how softly the Cross rose up in the dark of his soul.

Love; when in black corners the snow was melting,
Gaily a little blue breeze was caught in the ancient elder,
In the nut-tree's vault of shade;
And in silence a rosy angel appeared to that boy;

Gladness; when in cool rooms a sonata sounded at nightfall,
Among dark brown beams
A blue butterfly crept from its silver chrysalis.

O the nearness of death. From the stony wall
A yellow head bowed down, silent that child,
Since in that month the moon decayed.

*

Rose-colored Easter bells in the burial vault of the night,
And the silver voices of the stars,
So that madness, dark and shuddering, ebbed from the sleeper's
    brow.

O how quiet to ramble along the blue river's bank,
To ponder forgotten things when in leafy boughs
The thrush's call brought strangeness into a world's decline.

Or holding an old man's bony hand
In the evening he walked to the crumbling city walls,
And in his black greatcoat carried a rosy child,
In the nut-tree's shade the spirit of evil appeared.

Tasten über die grünen Stufen des Sommers. O wie leise
Verfiel der Garten in der braunen Stille des Herbstes,
Duft und Schwermut des alten Holunders,
Da in Sebastians Schatten die Silberstimme des Engels erstarb.

Groping his way over the green steps of summer. O how softly
In autumn's brown stillness the garden decayed,
Scent and sadness of the ancient elder,
When in Sebastian's shadow the angel's silver voice subsided.

[1913]

KASPAR HAUSER LIED

Für Bessie Loos

Er wahrlich liebte die Sonne, die purpurn den Hügel hinabstieg,
Die Wege des Waldes, den singenden Schwarzvogel
Und die Freude des Grüns.

Ernsthaft war sein Wohnen im Schatten des Baums
Und rein sein Antlitz.
Gott sprach eine sanfte Flamme zu seinem Herzen:
O Mensch!

Stille fand sein Schritt die Stadt am Abend;
Die dunkle Klage seines Munds:
Ich will ein Reiter werden.

Ihm aber folgte Busch und Tier,
Haus und Dämmergarten weisser Menschen
Und sein Mörder suchte nach ihm.

Frühling und Sommer und schön der Herbst
Des Gerechten, sein leiser Schritt
An den dunklen Zimmern Träumender hin.
Nachts blieb er mit seinem Stern allein;

Sah, dass Schnee fiel in kahles Gezweig
Und im dämmernden Hausflur den Schatten des Mörders.

Silbern sank des Ungebornen Haupt hin.

CASPAR HAUSER SONG

(for Bessie Loos)

He truly adored the sun, as crimson it sank from the hill-top,
The paths of the forest, the blackbird singing
And the joy of green.

Serious was his habitation in the tree-shade
And pure his face.
God spoke a gentle flame into his heart:
O man!

His silent footstep found the city at evening;
The dark lament of his mouth:
I want to be a horseman.

But bush and beast pursued him,
House and pallid garden of pallid men
And his murderer sought him.

Beautifully the spring and summer and the autumn
Of the righteous man, his soft footfall
Beside the dark rooms of dreamers.
By night he stayed alone with his star;

Saw snow falling through bare branches
And in the dusking hall his murderer's shadow.

Silver it fell, the head of the not-yet-born.

November, 1913: '*Der Brenner*'

AN EINEN FRÜHVERSTORBENEN

O, der schwarze Engel, der leise aus dem Innern des Baums trat,
Da wir sanfte Gespielen am Abend waren,
Am Rand des bläulichen Brunnens.
Ruhig war unser Schritt, die runden Augen in der braunen Kühle
    des Herbstes,
O, die purpurne Süsse der Sterne.

Jener aber ging die steinernen Stufen des Mönchsbergs hinab,
Ein blaues Lächeln im Antlitz und seltsam verpuppt
In seine stillere Kindheit und starb;
Und im Garten blieb das silberne Antlitz des Freundes zurück,
Lauschend im Laub oder im alten Gestein.

Seele sang den Tod, die grüne Verwesung des Fleisches
Und es war das Rauschen des Walds,
Die inbrünstige Klage des Wildes.
Immer klangen von dämmernden Türmen die blauen Glocken des
    Abends.

Stunde kam, da jener die Schatten in purpurner Sonne sah,
Die Schatten der Fäulnis in kahlem Geäst;
Abend, da an dämmernder Mauer die Amsel sang,
Der Geist des Frühverstorbenen stille im Zimmer erschien.

O, das Blut, das aus der Kehle des Tönenden rinnt,
Blaue Blume; o die feurige Träne
Geweint in die Nacht.

Goldene Wolke und Zeit. In einsamer Kammer
Lädst du öfter den Toten zu Gast,
Wandelst in trautem Gespräch unter Ulmen den grünen Fluss hinab.

TO ONE WHO DIED YOUNG

O the black angel who softly stepped from the heart of the tree
When we were gentle playmates in the evening,
By the edge of the pale blue fountain.
Our step was easy, the round eyes in autumn's brown coolness,
O the purple sweetness of the stars.

But the other descended the stone steps of the Mönchsberg,
A blue smile on his face, and strangely ensheathed
In his quieter childhood, and died;
And the silver face of his friend stayed behind in the garden,
Listening in the leaves or in the ancient stones.

Soul sang of death, the green decay of the flesh,
And it was the murmur of the forest,
The fervid lament of the animals.
Always from dusky towers rang the blue evening bells.

Times came when the other saw shadows in the purple sun,
The shadows of putrescence in the bare branches;
At nightfall, when by the dusky wall the blackbird sang,
His ghost quietly appeared there in the room.

O the blood that runs from the throat of the musical one,
Blue flower; O the fiery tear
Wept into the night.

Golden cloud and time. In a lonely room
You ask the dead child to visit you more often,
You walk and talk together under elms by the green riverside.

[1913]

DIE SONNE

Täglich kommt die gelbe Sonne über den Hügel.
Schön ist der Wald, das dunkle Tier,
Der Mensch; Jäger oder Hirt.

Rötlich steigt im grünen Weiher der Fisch.
Unter dem runden Himmel
Fährt der Fischer leise im blauen Kahn.

Langsam reift die Traube, das Korn.
Wenn sich stille der Tag neigt,
Ist ein Gutes und Böses bereitet.

Wenn es Nacht wird,
Hebt der Wanderer leise die schweren Lider;
Sonne aus finsterer Schlucht bricht.

THE SUN

Daily the yellow sun comes over the hill.
Lovely the forest is, the dark deer
And man: huntsman or shepherd.

Ruddy the fish rises in the green pond.
Under the rounded heaven
The fisherman softly moves in a blue boat.

Grape ripens slowly, and the corn.
As day in stillness ends,
A good work and an evil is prepared.

When night comes,
The wanderer softly lifts his heavy eyelids.
Sun breaks from a somber abyss.

[1913]

FÖHN

Blinde Klage im Wind, mondene Wintertage,
Kindheit, leise verhallen die Schritte an schwarzer Hecke,
Langes Abendgeläut.
Leise kommt die weisse Nacht gezogen,

Verwandelt in purpurne Träume Schmerz und Plage
Des steinigen Lebens,
Dass nimmer der dornige Stachel ablasse vom verwesenden Leib.

Tief im Schlummer aufseufzt die bange Seele,

Tief der Wind in zerbrochenen Bäumen,
Und es schwankt die Klagegestalt
Der Mutter durch den einsamen Wald

Dieser schweigenden Trauer; Nächte,
Erfüllt von Tränen, feurigen Engeln.
Silbern zerschellt an kahler Mauer ein kindlich Gerippe.

FRÜHLING DER SEELE

Aufschrei im Schlaf; durch schwarze Gassen stürzt der Wind,
Das Blau des Frühlings winkt durch brechendes Geäst,
Purpurner Nachttau und es erlöschen rings die Sterne.
Grünlich dämmert der Fluss, silbern die alten Alleen
Und die Türme der Stadt. O sanfte Trunkenheit
Im gleitenden Kahn und die dunklen Rufe der Amsel
In kindlichen Gärten. Schon lichtet sich der rosige Flor.

SOUTH WIND

Blind lamentation in the wind, moon-days of winter,
Childhood, softly footsteps fade by the dark hedge,
The long peal of bells in the evening.
Softly the pallid night approaches,

Transforms into purple dreams the pain and affliction
Of stony life,
That without abatement the thorn may goad the decaying body.

From the depths of its sleep the fear-stricken soul moans suddenly,

And the wind in the depths of broken trees,
And swaying, a shape of lamentation,
The mother moves through the lonely wood

Of this speechless grief; nights
Full of tears, nights full of fiery angels.
Silver, against a bare wall, a child's skeleton smashes.

[1913]

THE SOUL'S SPRINGTIME

A sudden cry in sleep; wind rushes through dark streets,
Azure of spring beckons through breaking branches,
Night's dew is purple, stars all round the sky are fading.
The river gleams green in the dusk, and silver the old avenues
And the spires of the city. O gentle drunkenness
In the gliding boat, O the dark calls of blackbirds
In childlike gardens. The rose-red veil disperses.

Feierlich rauschen die Wasser. O die feuchten Schatten der Au,
Das schreitende Tier; Grünendes, Blütengezweig
Rührt die kristallene Stirne; schimmernder Schaukelkahn.
Leise tönt die Sonne im Rosengewölk am Hügel.
Gross ist die Stille des Tannewalds, die ernsten Schatten am Fluss.

Reinheit! Reinheit! Wo sind die furchtbaren Pfade des Todes,
Des grauen steinernen Schweigens, die Felsen der Nacht
Und die friedlosen Schatten? Strahlender Sonnenabgrund.

Schwester, da ich dich fand an einsamer Lichtung
Des Waldes und Mittag war und gross das Schweigen des Tiers;
Weisse unter wilder Eiche, und es blühte silbern der Dorn.
Gewaltiges Sterben und die singende Flamme im Herzen.

Dunkler umfliessen die Wasser die schönen Spiele der Fische.
Stunde der Trauer, schweigender Anblick der Sonne;
Es ist die Seele ein Fremdes auf Erden. Geistlich dämmert
Bläue über dem verhauenen Wald und es läutet
Lange eine dunkle Glocke im Dorf; friedlich Geleit.
Stille blüht die Myrthe über den weissen Lidern des Toten.

Leise tönen die Wasser im sinkenden Nachmittag
Und es grünet dunkler die Wildnis am Ufer, Freude im rosigen
        Wind;
Der sanfte Gesang des Bruders am Abendhügel.

Solemnly the waters murmur. O the moist shadows on the meadow,
The animals walking; green things, a spray of blossoms
Touching the crystal brow; shimmering rocking boat;
Softly the sun sings through the rose-red clouds on the hill.
Great is the stillness of the pine-wood, grave the shadows by the
    river.

Purity! Purity! Where are the terrible pathways of death,
Of gray stony silence, the rocks of the night
And the unquiet shades? A radiant pit of sunlight.

O my sister, when I found you by the lonely clearing
In the wood, at noon, in a great silence of all animals,
You were white under the wild oak, and the silver thorn bush
    blossomed.
A mighty dying, and the singing flame in the heart.

Darker the waters flow round the fishes gracefully playing.
O hour of grief, O speechless gaze of the sun.
The soul is an alien thing upon earth. A dim religious
Azure descends on the mishewn forest, and a bell
Tolls from the village dark and long; they lead him to rest.
Silent the myrtle blooms over his dead white eyelids.

Softly the waters murmur in the declining afternoon.
On the river bank the green wilderness darkens, the rose-red wind
    rejoices;
A brother's gentle song on the evening hill.

[1913]

ABENDLAND

Else Lasker-Schüler in Verehrung

I

Mond, als träte ein Totes
Aus blauer Höhle,
Und es fallen der Blüten
Viele über den Felsenpfad.

Silbern weint ein Krankes
Am Abendweiher,
Auf schwarzem Kahn
Hinüberstarben Liebende.

Oder es läuten die Schritte
Elis' durch den Hain
Den hyazinthenen
Wieder verhallend unter Eichen.
O des Knaben Gestalt
Geformt aus kristallnen Tränen,
Nächtigen Schatten.
Zackige Blitze erhellen die Schläfe
Die immerkühle,
Wenn am grünenden Hügel
Frühlingsgewitter ertönt.

II

So leise sind die grünen Wälder
Unserer Heimat,
Die kristallne Woge
Hinsterbend an verfallner Mauer
Und wir haben im Schlaf geweint;
Wandern mit zögernden Schritten
An der dornigen Hecke hin
Singende im Abendsommer
In heiliger Ruh
Des fern verstrahlenden Weinbergs;

OCCIDENT

(for Else Lasker-Schüler)

I

Moon, as if a dead thing
Stepped from a blue cave,
And many blossoms fall
Across the rocky path.
Silver a sick thing weeps
By the evening pond,
In a black boat
Lovers crossed over to death.

Or the footsteps of Elis
Ring through the grove
The hyacinthine
To fade again under oaks.
O the shape of that boy
Formed out of crystal tears,
Nocturnal shadows.
Jagged lightning illumines his temples
The ever-cool,
When on the verdant hill
Springtime thunder resounds.

II

So quiet are the green woods
Of our homeland,
The crystal wave
That dies against a perished wall
And we have wept in our sleep;
Wander with hesitant steps
Along the thorny hedge
Singers in the evening summer
In holy peace
Of the vineyards distantly gleaming;

Schatten nur im kühlen Schoss
Der Nacht, trauernde Adler.
So leise schliesst ein mondener Strahl
Die purpurne Male der Schwermut.

III
Ihr grossen Städte
steinern aufgebaut
in der Ebene!
So sprachlos folgt
der Heimatlose
mit dunkler Stirne dem Wind,
kahlen Bäumen am Hügel.
Ihr weithin dämmernden Ströme!
Gewaltig ängstet
schaurige Abendröte
im Sturmgewölk.
Ihr sterbenden Völker!
Bleiche Woge
zerschellend am Strande der Nacht,
fallende Sterne.

Shadows now in the cool lap
Of night, eagles that mourn.
So quietly does a moonbeam close
The purple wounds of sadness.

III
You mighty cities
stone on stone raised up
in the plain!
So quietly
with darkened forehead
the outcast follows the wind,
bare trees on the hillside.
You rivers distantly fading!
Gruesome sunset red
is breeding fear
in the thunder clouds.
You dying peoples!
Pallid billow
that breaks on the beaches of Night,
stars that are falling.

[1914]

DAS HERZ

Das wilde Herz ward weiss am Wald;
O dunkle Angst
Des Todes, so das Gold
In grauer Wolke starb.
Novemberabend.
Am kahlen Tor am Schlachthaus stand
Der armen Frauen Schar;
In jeden Korb
Fiel faules Fleisch und Eingeweid;
Verfluchte Kost!

Des Abends blaue Taube
Brachte nicht Versöhnung.
Dunkler Trompetenruf
Durchfuhr der Ulmen
Nasses Goldlaub,
Eine zerfetzte Fahne
Vom Blute rauchend,
Dass in wilder Schwermut
Hinlauscht ein Mann.
O! ihr ehernen Zeiten
Begraben dort im Abendrot.

Aus dunklem Hausflur trat
Die goldne Gestalt
Der Jünglingin
Umgeben von bleichen Monden,
Herbstlicher Hofstaat,
Zerknickten schwarze Tannen
Im Nachtsturm,
Die steile Festung.
O Herz
Hinüberschimmernd in schneeige Kühle.

THE HEART

The wild heart turned white in the wood;
O the dark fear
Of death, when the gold
Died in a gray cloud.
November evening.
By the bare gate of the slaughterhouse there stood
The crowd of poor women.
Into every basket
Rank flesh and entrails fell;
Accursed fare!

The blue dove of nightfall
Brought no atonement.
Dark trumpet call
Rang through the elm trees'
Damp golden leaves,
A tattered banner
Steaming with blood,
So that wild in his sadness
A man gives heed.
O brazen ages
Buried there in the sunset red.

From the house's dark hall there stepped
The golden shape
Of the maiden-youth
Surrounded with pale moons
Of autumnal courtliness,
Black pine-trees snapped
In the night gale,
The steep-walled fortress.
O heart
Glistening away into snowy coolness.

[1914] 1915: '*Der Brenner*'

KLAGE

Schlaf und Tod, die düstern Adler
Umrauschen nachtlang dieses Haupt:
Des Menschen goldnes Bildnis
Verschlänge die eisige Woge
Der Ewigkeit. An schaurigen Riffen
Zerschellt der purpurne Leib.
Und es klagt die dunkle Stimme
Über dem Meer.
Schwester stürmischer Schwermut
Sieh ein ängstlicher Kahn versinkt
Unter Sternen,
Dem schweigenden Antlitz der Nacht.

LAMENT

Sleep and death, the dusky eagles
Around this head swoop all night long:
Eternity's icy wave
Would swallow the golden image
Of man; on horrible reefs
His purple body is shattered.
And the dark voice laments
Over the sea.
Sister of stormy sadness,
Look a timid boat is sinking
Under the stars,
The silent face of the night.

[1914]

HANS ARP

SCHWARZE EIER

die flüsse springen wie böcke in ihr zelt. es ist silbern von silbernen
wellen umsäumt.
peitschen knallen und aus den bergen kommen die schlechtge-
scheitelten schatten der hirten.
schwarze eier und narrenschellen stürzen von den bäumen.
gewitter pauken und trommeln bespringen die ohren des esels.
flügel streifen blumen.
quellen regen sich in den augen der eber.

KASPAR IST TOT

weh unser guter kaspar ist tot.
wer verbirgt nun die brennende fahne im wolkenzopf und schlägt
täglich ein schwarzes schnippchen.
wer dreht nun die kaffeemühle im urfass.
wer lockt nun das idyllische reh aus der versteinerten tüte.
wer schneuzt nun die schiffe parapluis windeuter bienenväter
ozonspindeln und entgrätet die pyramiden.
weh weh weh unser guter kaspar ist tot. heiliger bimbam kaspar
ist tot.
die heufische klappern herzzerreissend vor leid in den glocken-
scheunen wenn man seinen vornamen ausspricht. darum seufze ich
weiter seinen familiennamen kaspar kaspar kaspar.
warum hast du uns verlassen. in welche gestalt ist nun deine
schöne grosse seele gewandert. bist du ein stern geworden oder eine
kette aus wasser an einem heissen wirbelwind oder ein euter aus
schwarzem licht oder ein durchsichtiger ziegel an der stöhnenden
trommel des felsigen wesens.

BLACK EGGS

the rivers buck like goats in their tent. silver-rimmed it is by silver
　　billows.
whips crack and out of the hills emerge the ill-combed shadows of
　　the shepherds.
black eggs and fool's bells drop from the trees.
storms rant and drums mount the ass's ears.
wings skim flowers.
sources stir in the wild boar's eyes.

1920: *Der Vogel Selbdritt, 1911–5*

KASPAR IS DEAD

alas our good kaspar is dead.

who'll now hide the burning flag in the cloudpigtail and every
day cock a black snook.

who'll now turn the coffeegrinder in the primeval tub.

who'll now lure the idyllic doe from the petrified paperbag.

who'll now blow the noses of ships parapluis windudders bee-
fathers ozonespindles and who'll bone the pyramids.

alas alas alas our good kaspar is dead. saint dingdong kaspar is
dead.

the grass-shark rattles his teeth heartrendingly in the bellbarns
when his forename is spoken. therefore I shall go on sighing his
familyname kaspar kaspar kaspar.

why hast thou forsaken us. into what form has thy great beautiful
soul migrated. hast thou become a star or a chain of water hanging
from a hot whirlwind or an udder of black light or a transparent
tile on the groaning drum of the rocky essence.

jetzt vertrocknen unsere scheitel und sohlen und die feen liegen
halbverkohlt auf dem scheiterhaufen.

jetzt donnert hinter der sonne die schwarze kegelbahn und
keiner zieht mehr die kompasse und die räder der schiebkarren auf.

wer isst nun mit der phosphoreszierenden ratte am einsamen
barfüssigen tisch.

wer verjagt nun den sirokkoko teufel wenn er die pferde ver-
führen will.

wer erklärt uns nun die monogramme in den sternen.

seine büste wird die kamine aller wahrhaft edlen menschen zieren
doch ist das kein trost und schnupftabak für einen totenkopf.

now our tops and toes go dry and the fairies are lying halfcharred on the funeral pyre.

now the black skittle alley thunders behind the sun and nobody winds up the compasses and the pushcart wheels any more.

who'll now eat with the phosphorescent rat at the lonely barefoot table.

who'll now shoo away the siroccoco devil when he tries to ravish the horses.

who'll now elucidate for us the monograms in the stars.

his bust will grace the mantelpieces of all truly noble men but that's no consolation and snuff for a death's head.

1920: *Die Wolkenpumpe*

DIE UNAUSSPRIESSLICHE AU

Herr von So-und-So
zerstampft seinen Papageien,
bis sich der Papa von der Mama scheidet,
bis sich der Papa von der Mama scheidet,
sagte ich,
und die Geien als Saft frei werden.
Die reifen Monokel fallen aus den Fleischwolken.
Die grauen Springbrunnen humpeln auf Krücken fort.
In den Krallen fasst etwas festen Fuss,
und von den Hüten bis hinab in die Schuhe
trocknen die self-made Euter ein.
Auf den Quecksilberwiesen
tanzen Quasten Troddeln Haare Knochen Federn
um ein elektrisches Herz.
Langsam werden die Gliederpuppen schweigsamer und schweig-
        samer,
kälter und kälter.
Die steinalten Steine und die blutjungen Steine
spazieren zwischen dem Hintergrund und dem Vordergrund
pflichtgemäss hin und her.
Es knackt in dem Busen der Luft.
Die mutierenden Stimmen der Pyramiden versiegen.
Aus den Knopflöchern der Wolken
fallen die galvanisierten Hasenpfoten.
Unvermittelt springt Herr von So-und-So
mit einem schneidigen „Qui-vive"
in das Bodenlose.
Da aber das Bodenlose doch einen Boden hat,
sehen wir Herrn von So-und-So
resigniert wieder zu seinem Gähnstühlchen zurückkehren,
Papa, Mama und Papagei lallen
und einschlummern.

THE INEFFERTILE LEA

Sire So-and-So
pulverizes his parakeet,
till Pa divorces Ma,
till Pa divorces Ma,
I said,
and the rakeets are spunk and free.
Ripe monocles fall from the flesh clouds.
The gray fountains hobble away on crutches.
Something gets a foothold in the claws,
and from the hats to the shoes
the selfmade udders run dry.
On meadows of quicksilver
tassels tufts hairs bones feathers dance
round an electrical heart.
The manikins slowly grow more and more taciturn,
frigider and frigider.
The palaeostones and the callow stones
saunter between the background and the foreground
dutifully to and fro.
Something cracks in the bust of air.
The pyramids' breaking voices fade away.
From the buttonholes of the clouds
the galvanized fungi descend.
Suddenly Sire So-and-So jumps
with a cutting "qui vive"
into the bottomless pit.
But since in fact the bottomless pit is not bottomless,
we see Sire So-and-So
return again resigned to his yawning-chair,
mutter Pa, Ma and parakeet,
and fall asleep.

1927: *Der gestiefelte Stern* (1924–27)

BAOBAB

Und sie genas eines gesunden kräftigen Jungen
welcher den Namen Baobab erhielt.
Der Junge wuchs und wuchs
und hörte nicht auf zu wachsen
und wuchs bis an das Blau des Himmels.
Das Volk dem Baobab angehörte wollte beim Sprechen
seinem Gegenüber in die Augen sehen können.
Dies war aber bei einem so Langen wie Baobab
nicht mehr möglich.
Sie huben darum Erde aus
und gruben ein abgrundtiefes Loch
in das Baobab willig stieg
denn auch ihm war es unausstehlich
seinem Gegenüber beim Sprechen
nicht in die Augen sehen zu können.
Die Erde die sie aushuben
warfen sie über den Rand ihres Sternleins
in das Bodenlose.
Nachdem Baobab hundert Jahre
in diesem Loch zugebracht hatte
fing er an zu schwinden.
Er wurde täglich kleiner und kleiner
bis er schliesslich verschwand.
Nun sassen die Bewohner des Sternleins da
mit nichts anderem mehr
als mit einem abgrundtiefen Loch
und einem schmalen Landstreifen um das Loch
und schauten
bald in das abgrundtiefe Loch ihres Sternleins
bald über den Rand ihres Sternleins in das Bodenlose.

BAOBAB

And she gave birth to a strong healthy boy
who was named Baobab.
The boy grew and grew,
and did not stop growing
and grew as high as the blue of the sky itself.
Baobab's compatriots liked to look into the eyes
of whomsoever they might be talking to.
But this was no longer possible in the case
of a person as tall as Baobab was.
So they lifted a lot of earth
and dug a chasmic hole,
into which Baobab willingly inserted himself,
for he too found it unbearable
not to be able to look into the eyes
of whomsoever he might be talking to.
The earth they lifted
they threw over the edge of their small star
into the emptiness.
After Baobab had spent
a hundred years in this hole,
he began to disappear.
Every day he grew smaller and smaller,
till at length he disappeared altogether.
Now the inhabitants of the small star
were left with nothing but a chasmic hole
and a narrow strip of land around the hole,
and they looked alternately
into the chasmic hole on their small star
and over the edge of their small star into the emptiness.

1955

GEORG HEYM

UND DIE HÖRNER DES SOMMERS VERSTUMMTEN

Und die Hörner des Sommers verstummten im Tode der Fluren,
In das Dunkel flog Wolke auf Wolke dahin.
Aber am Rande schrumpften die Wälder verloren,
Wie Gefolge der Särge in Trauer vermummt.

Laut sang der Sturm im Schrecken der bleichenden Felder,
Er fuhr in die Pappeln und bog einen weissen Turm.
Und wie der Kehricht des Windes lag in der Leere
Drunten ein Dorf, aus grauen Dächern gehäuft.

Aber hinaus bis unten am Grauen des Himmels
Waren aus Korn des Herbstes Zelte gebaut,
Unzählige Städte, doch leer und vergessen.
Und niemand ging in den Gassen herum.

Und es sang der Schatten der Nacht. Nur die Raben noch irrten
Unter den drückenden Wolken im Regen hin,
Einsam im Wind, wie im Dunkel der Schläfen
Schwarze Gedanken in trostloser Stunde fliehn.

AND THE HORNS OF SUMMER FELL SILENT

And the horns of summer fell silent in the death of the meadows,
Into the darkness cloud upon cloud floated off.
But remotely the bordering forests were shrinking,
Muffled in mourning like men that follow a hearse.

Loud sang the gale in the terror of fields that were fading;
It drove into poplars to shape a white tower between boughs.
And like the sweepings of winds there lay in the waste land
Below, a village, drab roofs in a huddle of gray.

But on and on, as far as the pallid horizon
The tents of autumn extended their fabric of corn,
The numberless cities, but empty, forgotten.
And no one was walking about in the streets.

And the shade of the night sang. Only the ravens still drifted
Here and there under leaden clouds in the rain,
Alone in the wind, as down in the dark of our foreheads
Black thoughts abate in disconsolate hours.

[Before 1912.] 1922 : *Dichtungen*

O WEITER, WEITER ABEND

O weiter, weiter Abend. Da verglühen
Die langen Hügel an dem Horizont,
Wie klarer Träume Landschaft bunt besonnt.
O weiter Abend, wo die Saaten sprühen
Des Tages Licht zurück in goldnem Schein.
Hoch oben singen Schwalben, winzig klein.
Auf allen Feldern glitzert ihre Jagd,
Im Wald des Rohres und in hellen Buchten,
Wo hohe Masten stehn. Doch in den Schluchten
Der Hügel hinten nistet schon die Nacht.

UMBRA VITAE

Die Menschen stehen vorwärts in den Strassen
Und sehen auf die grossen Himmelszeichen,
Wo die Kometen mit den Feuernasen
Um die gezackten Türme drohend schleichen.

Und alle Dächer sind voll Sternedeuter,
Die in den Himmel stecken grosse Röhren,
Und Zauberer, wachsend aus den Bodenlöchern,
Im Dunkel schräg, die ein Gestirn beschwören.

Selbstmörder gehen nachts in grossen Horden,
Die suchen vor sich ihr verlornes Wesen,
Gebückt in Süd und West und Ost und Norden,
Den Staub zerfegend mit den Armen-Besen.

Sie sind wie Staub, der hält noch eine Weile.
Die Haare fallen schon auf ihren Wegen.
Sie springen, dass sie sterben, und in Eile,
Und sind mit totem Haupt im Feld gelegen,

O BOUNDLESS, BOUNDLESS EVENING

O boundless, boundless evening. Soon the glow
Of long hills on the skyline will be gone,
Like clear dream country now, rich-hued by sun.
O boundless evening where the cornfields throw
The scattered daylight back in an aureole.
Swallows high up are singing, very small.
On every meadow glitters their swift flight,
In woods of rushes and where tall masts stand
In brilliant bays. Yet in ravines beyond
Between the hills already nests the night.

[Before 1912.] 1922: *Dichtungen*

UMBRA VITAE

The people on the streets draw up and stare,
While overhead huge portents cross the sky;
Round fanglike towers threatening comets flare,
Death-bearing, fiery-snouted where they fly.

On every roof astrologers abound,
Enormous tubes thrust heavenward; there are
Magicians springing up from underground,
Aslant in darkness, conjuring to a star.

Through night great hordes of suicides are hurled,
Men seeking on their way the selves they've lost;
Crook-backed they haunt all corners of the world,
And with their arms for brooms they sweep the dust.

They are as dust, keep but a little while;
And as they move their hair drops out. They run,
To hasten their slow dying. Then they fall,
And in the open fields lie prone,

Noch manchmal zappelnd. Und der Felder Tiere
Stehn um sie blind und stossen mit dem Horne
In ihren Bauch. Sie strecken alle Viere,
Begraben unter Salbei und dem Dorne.

Die Meere aber stocken. In den Wogen
Die Schiffe hängen modernd und verdrossen,
Zerstreut, und keine Strömung wird gezogen,
Und aller Himmel Höfe sind verschlossen.

Die Bäume wechseln nicht die Zeiten
Und bleiben ewig tot in ihrem Ende,
Und über die verfallnen Wege spreiten
Sie hölzern ihre langen Fingerhände.

Wer stirbt, der setzt sich auf, sich zu erheben,
Und eben hat er noch ein Wort gesprochen,
Auf einmal ist er fort. Wo ist sein Leben?
Und seine Augen sind wie Glas zerbrochen.

Schatten sind viele. Trübe und verborgen.
Und Träume, die an stummen Türen schleifen,
Und der erwacht, bedrückt vom Licht der Morgen,
Muss schweren Schlaf von grauen Lidern streifen.

PILATUS

Ein Lächeln schiefen Grames, das verschwindet
Hinein in seiner Stirne weisses Tor.
Er sitzt auf seinem Stuhl. Seine Hände erhoben
Brechen den Stab und fallen von oben.

But twitch a little still. Beasts of the field
Stand blindly round them, prod with horns
Their sprawling bodies till at last they yield,
Lie buried by the sage-bush, by the thorns.

But all the seas are stopped. Among the waves
The ships hang rotting, scattered, beyond hope.
No current through the water moves,
And all the courts of heaven are locked up.

Trees do not change, the seasons do not change.
Enclosed in dead finality each stands,
And over broken roads lets frigid range
Its palmless thousand-fingered hands.

The dying man sits up, as if to stand,
Just one more word a moment since he cries,
All at once he's gone. Can life so end?
And crushed to fragments are his glassy eyes.

The secret shadows thicken, darkness breaks;
Behind the speechless doors dreams watch and creep.
Burdened by light of dawn the man that wakes
Must rub from grayish eyelids leaden sleep.

[1912]

PILATE

A smile of grief askance that vanishes,
Gone through the white gate of his brow.
He sits upon his chair. His hands uplifted
Break the staff, and have fallen now.

Aber wie eine Blume voll grüner Helle
Leuchtet im Dunkel der Höfe der König der Juden,
Und die Stirn, die sie schattig mit Dornen beluden,
Brennt wie ein Stein in fahler Grelle.

Und der Gott steigt hinauf, von den Schultern gehoben
Riesiger Engel. Er singet, ein Schwan,
Leicht und klein fährt er auf, in strahlender Bahn,
Und der Vater im Glanze wartet sein droben.

Aber der Richter am blauen Gebirge
Hänget im riesigen Mantel wie faltige Frucht.
Wilder kommt der Abend über die hallenden Öden,
Schweigsame Wasser fallen in grüner Schlucht.

JUDAS

Die Locke der Qual springt über der Stirne,
Drin wispern Winde und viele Stimmen,
Die wie Wasser vorüberschwimmen.

Doch er rennet bei Ihm gleich einem Hunde.
Und er picket die Worte hervor in dem Kote.
Und er wieget sie schwer. Sie werden tote.

Ah, der Herr ging über die Felder weiss
Sanft hinab am schwebenden Abendtag,
Und die Ähren sangen zum Preis,
Seine Füsse waren wie Fliegen klein
In goldener Himmel gellem Schein.

But in the bailey dark the King of the Jews
Shines like a flower full of green effulgence,
And like a gem in livid lustre burns
The brow they cumbered with thorns and shadows.

And the god ascends, mounted on giant
Angel shoulders. Small, buoyant,
Swanlike singing he flies his bright path home,
And in upper light his father prepares his welcome.

But the judge down on the blue mountain below
Hangs like a wrinkled fruit in his giant mantle.
Savager sundown comes over deserts of echo,
Mute in a green gorge plunging waters fall.

[1912]

JUDAS

Torment's curl leaps above his brow,
In which winds and many voices whispering
Swim by like waters flowing.

Yet he runs by his side just like a dog.
And in the mire he pecks up every saying said.
And he weighs it heavily. And it is dead.

Ah gently in the swaying eventide
The Lord walked down over the white fields.
It was him the corn-ears glorified.
His feet were small as flies
In the shrill gleam of golden skies.

[1912]

WAS KOMMT IHR, WEISSE FALTER,
SOOFT ZU MIR?

Was kommt ihr, weisse Falter, sooft zu mir?
Ihr toten Seelen, was flattert ihr also oft
Auf meine Hand, von eurem Flügel,
Haftet dann oft ein wenig Asche.

Die ihr bei Urnen wohnt, dort, wo die Träume ruhn,
In ewigen Schatten gebückt, in dem dämmrigen Raum,
Wie in den Grüften Fledermäuse,
Die nachts entschwirren mit Gelärme.

Ich höre oft im Schlaf der Vampire Gebell
Aus trüben Mondes Waben wie Gelächter,
Und sehe tief in leeren Höhlen
Der heimatlosen Schatten Lichter.

Was ist das Leben? Eine kurze Fackel,
Umgrinst von Fratzen aus dem schwarzen Dunkel,
Und manche kommen schon und strecken
Die magren Hände nach der Flamme.

Was ist das Leben? Kleines Schiff in Schluchten
Vergessner Meere. Starrer Himmel Grauen.
Oder wie nachts auf kahlen Feldern
Verlornes Mondlicht wandert und verschwindet.

Weh dem, der jemals einen sterben sah,
Da unsichtbar in Herbstes kühler Stille
Der Tod trat an des Kranken feuchtes Bette
Und einen scheiden hiess, da seine Gurgel

Wie einer rostigen Orgel Frost und Pfeifen
Die letzte Luft mit Rasseln stiess von dannen.
Weh dem, der sterben sah! Er trägt für immer
Die weisse Blume bleiernen Entsetzens.

WHY DO YOU VISIT ME, WHITE MOTHS, SO OFTEN?

Why do you visit me, white moths, so often?
You dead souls, why should you often flutter
Down to my hand, so that a little
Ash from your wings is often left there?

You who dwell among urns, there, where dreams rest,
Bowed among eternal shades, in the twilit place,
Like bats in sepulchres,
Swirling out by night with much sound.

Often in sleep I hear the barking of vampires,
Like laughter from the dull moon's honeycombs,
And see deep down in empty caverns
The tapers of the homeless shades.

What is life? A brief torchlight,
Grimaces grinning from black gloom around it,
And some approach and stretch
Their thin hands toward the flame.

What is life? A small ship in the gulfs
Of forgotten seas. Pallor of frozen skies.
Or the way lost moonlight on bare fields
Wanders in the night and vanishes.

Alas for him who ever saw a man die,
When in cool autumn's quiet, invisible,
Death walked to the sick man's damp bed
And told him he must go, when the throat

Blew with a rattle the last air out
Like the frost and whistling of a rusty organ.
Alas for him who has seen death! Evermore
He wears the white flower of leaden horror.

Wer schliesst uns auf die Länder nach dem Tod,
Und wer das Tor der ungeheuren Rune?
Was sehn die Sterbenden, dass sie so schrecklich
Verkehren ihrer Augen blinde Weisse?

Who opens the countries to us after death?
And who the gateway of the monstrous rune?
What do the dying see, that makes them turn
Their eyes' blind whiteness round so terribly?

[1912]

ALFRED LICHTENSTEIN

RÜCKKEHR DES DORFJUNGEN

In meiner Jugend war die Welt ein kleiner Teich
Grossmutterchen und rotes Dach, Gebrüll
Von Ochsen und ein Busch aus Bäumen.
Und ringsumher die grosse grüne Wiese.

Wie schön war dieses In-die-Weite-Träumen.
Dies Garnichtssein als helle Luft und Wind
Und Vogelruf und Feenmärchenbuch.
Fern pfiff die fabelhafte Eisenschlange—

DIE GUMMISCHUHE

Der Dicke dachte:
Am Abend geh ich gern in Gummischuhen,
Auch wenn die Strassen fromm und flecklos sind.
In Gummischuhen bin ich nie ganz nüchtern . . .

Ich halte in der Hand die Zigarette.
Auf schmalen Rhythmen tänzelt meine Seele.
Und alle Zentner meines Leibes tänzeln.

DER LACKSCHUH

Der Dichter dachte:
Ach was, ich hab den Plunder satt!

RETURN OF THE VILLAGE LAD

When I was young the world was a little pond
Grandmother and red roof, the lowing
Of oxen and a bush made up of trees.
And all around was the great green meadow.

Lovely it was, this dreaming-into-the-distance,
This being nothing at all but air and wind
And bird-call and fairy-tale book.
Far off the fabulous iron serpent whistled—

1913

THE GALOSHES

The fat man thought:
At night I like to walk in my galoshes,
Even through pious and immaculate streets.
I'm not quite sober when I wear galoshes . . .

I hold my cigarette in one gloved hand.
On tightrope rhythms then my soul goes tripping.
And all the hundredweights of my body dance.

1913

THE PATENT LEATHER SHOE

The poet thought:
Enough. I'm sick of the whole lot!

Die Dirnen, das Theater und den Stadtmond,
Die Oberhemden, Strassen und Gerüche,
Die Nächte und die Kutscher und die Fenster,
Das Lachen, die Laternen und die Morde—
Den ganzen Dreck hab ich nun wirklich satt,
Beim Teufel!
Mag werden, was da will . . . mir ist es gleich:
Der Lackschuh drückt mich. Und ich zieh ihn aus—

Die Leute mögen sich verwundert wenden.
Nur schade ists um meinen seidnen Strumpf . . .

PROPHEZEIUNG

Einmal kommt—ich habe Zeichen—
Sterbesturm aus fernem Norden.
Überall stinkt es nach Leichen.
Es beginnt das grosse Morden.

Finster wird der Himmelsklumpen,
Sturmtod hebt die Klauentatzen.
Nieder stürzen alle Lumpen.
Mimen bersten. Mädchen platzen.

Polternd fallen Pferdeställe.
Keine Fliege kann sich retten.
Schöne homosexuelle
Männer kullern aus den Betten.

Rissig werden Häuserwände.
Fische faulen in dem Flusse.
Alles nimmt sein ekles Ende.
Krächzend kippen Omnibusse.

The whores, the theatre and the city moon,
The streets, the laundered shirtfronts and the smells,
The nights, the coachmen and the curtained windows,
The laughter and the streetlamps and the murders—
To hell with it!
Happen what may . . . it's all the same to me:
This black shoe pinches me. I'll take it off—

Let people turn their heads for all I care.
A pity, though, about my new silk sock.

1913

PROPHECY

Soon there'll come—the signs are fair—
A death-storm from the distant north.
Stink of corpses everywhere,
Mass assassins marching forth.

The clump of sky in dark eclipse,
Storm-death lifts his clawpaws first.
All the scallywags collapse.
Mimics split and virgins burst.

With a crash a stable falls.
Insects vainly duck their heads.
Handsome homosexuals
Tumble rolling from their beds.

Walls in houses crack and bend.
Fishes rot in every burn.
All things reach a sticky end.
Buses, screeching, overturn.

1913

ASCHERMITTWOCH

Gestern noch ging ich gepudert und süchtig
In der vielbunten tönenden Welt.
Heute ist alles schon lange ersoffen.

Hier ist ein Ding.
Dort ist ein Ding.
Etwas sieht so aus.
Etwas sieht anders aus.
Wie leicht pustet einer die ganze
Blühende Erde aus.

Der Himmel ist kalt und blau.
Oder der Mond ist gelb und platt.
Ein Wald hat viele einzelne Bäume.

Ist nichts mehr zum Weinen.
Ist nichts mehr zum Schreien.
Wo bin ich—

ASH WEDNESDAY

Only yesterday powdered and lustful I walked
In this various and resonant world.
Today how long ago the lot was drowned.

Here is a thing.
There is a thing.
Something looks like this.
Something else looks different.
How easily one can blow out
The whole blossoming earth.

The sky is cold and blue.
Or the moon is yellow and flat.
A wood contains many single trees.

Nothing now worth weeping for.
Nothing now worth screaming for.
Where am I—

1913

DER MORGEN

... Und alle Strassen liegen glatt und glänzend da.
Nur selten hastet über sie ein fester Mann.
Ein fesches Mädchen haut sich heftig mit Papa.
Ein Bäcker sieht sich mal den schönen Himmel an.

Die tote Sonne hängt an Häusern, breit und dick.
Vier fette Weiber quietschen spitz vor einer Bar.
Ein Droschkenkutscher fällt und bricht sich das Genick.
Und alles ist langweilig hell, gesund und klar.

Ein Herr mit weisen Augen schwebt verrückt, voll Nacht,
Ein siecher Gott ... in diesem Bild, das er vergass,
Vielleicht nicht merkte—Murmelt manches. Stirbt. Und lacht.
Träumt von Gehirnschlag, Paralyse, Knochenfrass.

MORNING

And all the streets lie snug there, clean and regular.
Only at times some brawny fellow hurries by.
A very smart young girl fights fiercely with Papa.
A baker, for a change, looks at the lovely sky.

The dead sun hangs on houses, broad as it is thick.
Four bulging women shrilly squeak outside a bar.
The driver of a cab falls down and breaks his neck.
And all is boringly bright, salubrious and clear.

A wise-eyed gentleman floats madly, full of night,
An ailing god . . . within this scene, which he forgot
Or failed to notice—Mutters something. Dies. And laughs.
Dreams of a cerebral stroke, paralysis, bone-rot.

1913

FRANZ WERFEL

ELEVATION

Welchen Weg bist du gegangen
Dass du kamst hier heran?

    Keinen Weg bin ich gegangen.
    Ich sprang ich sprang von Traum zu Traum.

Und du hast dich verirrt nicht
Dort in Fels Wald Schilf Moor?

    Herr, ich nahm doch den Weiser
    Am Kreuzweg den Weiser nicht wahr.

Und es würgten den Fuss dir
Nicht viel Meilen Gestrüpps?

    Ich folg auf dem Sturm her
    Ein Weinen ein einziges Weinen lang.

Sag, was hat dich gerettet
Aus der Sandflut der Nacht?

    Mir im Haar glomm beständig
    Ein Nest ein Nest blauen Lichts.

ELEVATION

Which way can you have traveled
To have come up this far?

     No way at all it was I traveled.
     I leapt I leapt from dream to dream.

And did you not get lost
There mid crag wood sedge moor?

     The signpost, Lord, at the crossroads,
     I missed the signpost there.

And your feet were not throttled
By undergrowth, mile upon mile?

     I follow hither the storm
     For the fall fall of a single tear.

Tell me, what brought you safely
Through all the nightseas of sand?

     In my hair shone unfailing
     A nest a nest of blue light.

1923: *Beschwörungen*

KLABUND

ENZIAN

I

Schluchze, Enzianblau!
Die Felsen tosen.
Das Wasser schmeckt eisen,
Himmel helmt mein Haupt.

Her weint der letzte Schnee
ins Moos.
Hier beben die Knie
im Niedersturz.

Der Wind singt
im Abendrauh
und ein Kind
hinter Häusern.

II

Wenn ich wüsste warum—
ich wüsste weniges.
Wenn ich wüsste woher—
ich wüsste viel.

Der Anker auf dem Matrosenarm
fasst Fleisch.
Dein Gesang aus den Fenstern
verstummt.

Dorthin segelt die Jacht,
die Jähe.
Weisse Brust
atmet die Salzsee.

GENTIAN

I

Sob, gentian blue!
The crags re-echo.
Water tastes iron,
heaven helmets my head.

The last snow weeps away
into moss.
Knees tremble here
in sharp descent.

Wind sings
in evenchill
and a child
behind houses.

II

If I knew why
I would know a little.
If I knew from where
I would know much.

The anchor on the sailor's arm
grasps flesh.
Your song floating from windows
is hushed.

That way the yacht sails,
the Rapid.
Salt lake breathes,
a white breast.

Die grossen Meere! Aber die kleine Quelle
sah niemand im Alpendickicht.
Nur ein sterbendes Murmeltier
netzte die Lefzen.

III

Es werden Tage kommen,
sonnenlose ohne Gelächter.
Brachfelder.
Kein Korn glänzt.

Leichen rollen in den Flüssen,
die Eisenbahnen sind voll toller Fahrgäste,
wer ein Herz hat, weint,
hingebückt über das Jaucheloch.

Kahlkopf und Kohlkopf
wechseln wie Wild.
Der Sieg ist versiegt,
viel Teppiche zerfasert.

Eine Tanne
steht noch—vielleicht.
Das Gehörn einer Gemse
hängt am Abgrund.

IV

Ein alter Berg,
ein altes Weib.
Das Hospiz
bröckelt.

Eis und Felsen
schlafen.
Nur ein Windstoss
wacht.

The huge seas! But no one saw
the tiny source in the alpine thicket.
Only a dying beaver
moistened its flews.

III

Days will come,
sunless without laughter.
Fields fallow.
No corn shines.

Corpses roll in the rivers,
trains are packed with mad passengers,
whoever has a heart weeps,
stooping over the cesspit.

Baldhead and blockhead
alternate like wild game.
The victory vanishes,
many carpets are worn thin.

A firtree
still stands—perhaps.
A chamois' horns hang
on the chasm's brink.

IV

An old mountain,
an old woman.
The hostel
is crumbling.

Ice and crags
are asleep.
Only a gust of wind
wakes.

Aus dem Tale die Tiefe
steigt lodernd.
Schon brennt ein Blumenbusch
am Abhang.

Schon weht ein Glockenruf,
ein Ziegenbock.
Ein kleines Mädchen
lächelt aufwärts.

Out of the valley the depths
rise glowing.
A bush of flowers burns now
on the slope.

Now bells waft over,
and a billygoat.
A little girl
smiles upward.

1917: *Die Himmelsleiter*

JOHANNES R. BECHER

BRÜLLTE ICH

Brüllte ich
Visionen schwangerer Stier,
—mit einem Bauch prall von der Bespringung eines Dämon
aufgetriebenen
Zerstörerischen Blitz aus den Hörnern schleudernd gegen die triste
Endlichkeit euerer alltäglichen Landschaft—
Gefrässig würgend Frucht Saat Baum und an der elegischen Quelle
den unschuldigen Leib eines Gotts . . .
Riss ich, zerstampfte und malmte und boxte—
Sintflut und unbarmherziger Wüterich—
Barbarischer Eroberer, ausschreitend über die verseuchten Gründe
und unfruchtbaren Äcker euerer armseligen Erde—
Kroch ich schnaubend herauf durch die Lorbeerbäume und
Limonenwälder der antiken Gezeiten
Zwischen Latschen-Wildnis und Giessbach hindurch
Heran die trostlosen, die spärlich mit den Blau-Sternen des En-
zians durchsetzten beizenden Geröll-Felder
Empor zum erlösenden Schoss-Trichter des Ätna—
Empedokles fiebernd vor tödlichem Lava-Sprung—
Geätzt von Schweiss und den dicken Wut-Brei ohnmächtiger
Empörung ums zerbissene Maul—
Mich verzweifeltst aufbäumend hilflos brutal und wie zu einem
letzten Mal gegen den frechen Ausschlag der Sonne—
Immer wieder meiner Tierheit Härte
In Asphodelen-Milde verzauberte sich—
Immer wieder meines Wahnsinns Schwerter
Mit seraphischem Kindheits-Lächeln belaubten sich.
Immer wieder niederbog mich,
Wehrlos und gebändigt
In des Lichtes letzten Rest
Auf den kargen Schlaf der Herden,
Würze euerer Flöten-Frucht, o Knaben.

IF I ROARED (from the cycle 'Ecstasy Dream Grace')

If I roared
vision-gravid bull
—belly plump from a demon's mounting me
Hurling deadly lightning from my horns at the triste finitude of
        your workaday landscape—
Throttling greedily fruit seed tree and the innocent body of a god
        beside the elegiac spring . . .
If I ripped, stamped and crushed and boxed—
Diluvial and ruthless rager—
Barbaric conqueror, striding vast over the infested valleys and arid
        fields of your wretched earth—
If I crawled up gasping through the laurel trees and lemon groves
        of antique seasons
Between wildernesses of dwarf pine and mountain torrent
To the forlorn caustic rubble fields sparsely strewn with the gen-
        tian's bluestars
Aloft to the redeeming womb-funnel of Etna—
Empedocles in a fever before the fatal lava-drop—
Sweat-seared and with the thick wrath-mush of impotent revolt
        around my gnawed mouth—
Rearing desperatestly helplessly brutal and as for a last time against
        the sun's impudent kick—
Again and again the hardness of my animality
Changed by enchantment into asphodel mildness—
Again and again the swords of my madness
Enleafed themselves with seraphic childhood smiles.
Again and again I was bowed down
Defenseless and tamed
In the light's last vestiges
On the scant sleep of the flocks
By the spice of your flute-fruit, O boys.

Meiner Hufe Mord und Höllen-Taifun stillte Wunder-Öl himm-
　　lischer Tauben.
Und Geschmack des bitteren Mittags löste sich im Leichen-Rachen.
Schlimmen Schlund kühlten süss Zitronen und Kristall-Gewässer.
... Würze euerer Flöten-Frucht, o Knaben ...
Eingespannt im sengenden Schicksal-Joch der Welt. Gepeinigt.
Meiner Wildheit Falte löschte. Meine Sphäre zeitlos und gereinigt.

Und aus Pforten verschütteter Augen bricht
Lange gedämmt
Magischer Glanz zurück in die Schluchten der Räume.
Und vom Bug meiner Lippen aus, verfluchten einst, spricht
Der Gott den Segen aus über das verworrene Netz meiner uferlosen
　　ursündlichen Träume.
Worte unaufhaltsam
Nichtmehr zu tilgen aus den Reihen der Nächsten.
Unerschütterlich Zentrum. Der heiligen Engel
Gerechtes Erbteil und einzig sicherer Besitz.

AN EINER PERLENSCHNUR

An einer Perlenschnur hängt erdrosselt die Tänzerin. Berge
Rollen ins Meer und stolze Donner wehen aus den Grüften. In das
Gläserne Netz eines
Tödlichen Auges gebannt: o dass ich
Nicht wüsste ... O du: süsser
Stern-Atem der Welt!

My hooves' murder and hell-hurricane was stilled by the miracle
    oil of heavenly doves.
And the bitter noonday taste vanished in the corpse-throat.
Sweetly lemons and crystal waters cooled the corrupt gorge.
. . . Spice of your flute-fruit, O boys . . .
Harnessed in the burning doom-yoke of the world. In pain.
My savagery's wrinkle smoothed. My sphere timeless and made
    pure again.

And from the gateways of buried eyes breaks
Long dammed
A magic radiance back into the gulfs of space.
And from my lips' edge, once accursed, the god
Pronounces blessing on the tangled net of my shoreless original sinful
    dreams.
Words impetuous
No longer to be uprooted from my neighbors' numbers.
Unshakeable center. Just inheritance
Of the holy angels and their one sure property.

1921

THROTTLED ON A STRING OF PEARLS
(from the cycle 'Transfiguration')

Throttled on a string of pearls, she hangs, the dancer. Mountains
Roll into the sea and proud thunders blow from the tombs. Charmed
Into the glassy net of a
Death-stricken eye: O if it was not
Known to me . . . O you: sweet
Star-breath of the world!

Umgestürzt treibt tief in den bleiernen Lüften das
Siegreiche Schiff, bewachsen von
Rauchender Wolke . . . Ein
Verkohlter Balken: das ist die Nacht—eingekerbt
Herzmal an Herzmal. Unverwelkbar aber in aller
Völker Gedächtnis haftet die Schrift. Es
Leuchtet die heilige Rune.

—ein schwebender Tisch—ein hohler
Kürbis gefüllt mit Blut . . . Es
Trinken und selig singend aufsprangen von den glühenden Bänken
    die Beter. Eine
Saphirene Säule: das ist die Nacht—und bekleidet mit der
Fliessenden Hülle des Mondes . . .
Rings um die blau klaffende Wunde, um die Quelle hatten spät sich
    gelagert, schlaftrunken,
Christi Gefährten im Öl-Garten. Aber hinab
Unter die Erde wurde gezogen
Abgehauen
Das Haupt des Unsterblichen.

Als du noch ein Kind warst, da spieltest oft du dich hinaus aus der
    Zeit mit
Bunten Steinen und Faltern. Blind nun
Tastest du dich fort
Gebunden
Ein Tier
Unentwirrbar
Ruhmlos
Unter den zermalmenden Böden . . .

Eine Tat ist nicht getan. *Ein*
Name ungenannt—Trommeln.
Dunkelheiten. Düfte.—

Capsized deep in the leaden winds the conquering
Ship plies, overgrown
With smoking cloud . . . A
Charred beam : this is the night, notched
Heartmark to heartmark. But imperishable
In all the peoples' memory the scripture remains. The
Holy rune shines.

—a swaying table—a hollow
Gourd filled with blood . . . At prayer
People drink and blissfully singing leapt up from the glowing
     benches. A
Sapphire column : this is the night—and clothed with the
Moon's flowing robe . . .
Round the blue-gaping wound, round the source, drunk with sleep,
Christ's companions had camped late in the olive garden. But down
Under the earth was dragged
Hacked off
The Immortal's head.

When you were still a child, often you played yourself out of time
With bright stones and butterflies. Blind now
You grope your way
In bonds
A beast
Unravellable
With no fame
Under the pulverizing floors . . .

One deed is not done. *One*
Name not named—Drums.
Darknesses. Fragrances.—

1922

YVAN GOLL

MOND

I

Wie unerbittlich aber schwelltest du
Kleiner Modistinnen einsames Herz
Und polternder Klaviere Himmelssehnsucht.

Wie unerbittlich streutest du dein Leuchten
In dunkelnde und fröstelnde Alkoven
Und hinters Gitter der Gefangenen.

Aus der entbrannten Hölle ihres Herzens
Schrieen die Menschen und verzweifelten
Und rissen sich die Brust im Irrsinn auf
Und starben dran, dass du so schön gewesen.

II

Und als du plötzlich, wie ein wunder Vogel,
Vom Himmel flattertest und deine Flammen
In roten Federn niederfallen liessest:

Wie grässlich fuhr dein Strahl über die Erde!
Die Tiere hatten Phosphor in den Augen,
Die Häuser brannten ab wie Scheiterhaufen.

Die Menschen, die um dunkle Plätze irrten,
Apachen und Kokotten und Gendarmen,
Sie glaubten wie Indianer an dein Sterben
Und feierten den Tod in dieser Nacht.

MOON

I

But yet how unrelentingly you swelled
The solitary hearts of little dressmakers
And blustering pianos' sky-desires.

How unrelentingly you shed your brightness
Into the darkening and shivering alcoves
And behind iron bars of prisoners.

Out of the blazing hell of their hearts
Men cried aloud and came into despair
And tore their breasts wide open in their madness
And died of it, you had been so beautiful.

II

And when abruptly, like a wounded bird,
You fluttered down from heaven and your flames
Were falling in red feathers everywhere:

How cruelly your ray drove over the earth!
The animals had eyes of phosphorus,
The houses burned to ash like funeral pyres.

The people wandering among dark squares,
Apaches and policemen and cocottes,
They all, like Indians, thought you were dying
And in that night they celebrated death.

III

Wie sollten wir dich anders denn verstehn,
O roter Mund, der sündig sich verzerrte:
Wir Schmachtenden, auf stummer Erde hockend!

Kalt in Mansarden warfst du dein Gemecker,
Und über die verstummten Krankensäle
Liessest du goldne Lerchen zwitschern.

Wir alle standen an die Welt gekreuzigt
Und mussten dich mit unsern Augen schaun,
Und mussten an den Schmerz und an das Sterben glauben
Und mussten doch noch immer weiter hoffen!

IV

Und eines Nachts troff Blut auf unser Antlitz:
Dein Blut, zu unsres Krieges Blut gemischt,
Rann um die Erde wie ein runder Ring.

Verwundete, tiefkniend bei Kartätschen,
Aufschäumten ihre Lippen von dem Roten,
Und Sterbende ersoffen an dem Trank.

Es war kein Heil im Himmel noch auf Erden:
Wir mussten unsre Häupter tief vergraben,
Wir mussten unsre Lieben tief verschütten,
Und klagten, dass wir eher nicht gestorben.

V

Doch da, als Tänzer und geschminkte Maske,
Befreitest du die Gräber. Säulen barsten,
Der Marmor klirrte, Kränze lösten sich.

Aus deinem Schwelen gläsern stieg ein Christ,
Und blau bemalte, blecherne Marien
Erstrahlten mitten in Geranientöpfen.

III

How else then can we ever understand you,
O red mouth, curled so sinfully awry:
We languishers, who squat on the dumb earth!

Your nagging you flung coldly into attics,
Made golden larks to twitter high above
The silenced dormitories in hospitals.

Nailed crucified against the world we stood
And had to look at you with our own eyes,
And had to believe in agony and dying,
Yet still we had to hope and go on hoping.

IV

And one night drops of blood fell on our faces:
Your blood with blood of our war interfused
Ran round the earth, an all-encircling ring.

The wounded kneeling hunched among the shrapnel
With bubbles on their lips, a froth of crimson,
In that same drink the dying too were drowned.

There was no help in heaven or on earth:
We had to hide our heads deep under ground,
Our loves we had to bury in deep graves,
And we lamented not to have rather died.

V

But even then as painted mask and dancer
You set the graves all free. The columns crumbled,
Marble came rattling down, wreaths fell apart.

Out of your smoke a Christ of glass rose up,
Blue-painted metal Virgin Marys shining
Stood in the midst of pot geraniums.

O Tänzer, der die Toten all erlöste,
Indessen wir in Schutt und Schmerz und Schlaf
Hinschnarchten und ein Glück verschmähten:
Die Toten lebten und wir waren tot.

REISE INS ELEND

Wie aber schmerzt die Menscheneinsamkeit,
Wenn Landschaften mit gleichem Leid wie du sich von dir wenden
Und in sich selbst versinken, dir so fremd!
Wenn klein ein Bahnhof dich in kalten Regen stösst,
Ein Güterwagen leer und ohne Zukunft dich anbettelt.
Da kriecht ein fahler Gaul auf dunklem Acker,
O, wenn der wüsste, dass du existierst
Und du ihn liebst, ihm würden Flügel blau zum Himmel wachsen.
Manchmal schaut Wasser auf zu dir mit grossen Augen,
Und weil es nicht dein Lächeln sah,
Fällt's freudelos und schal in sich zurück.
So lässt du jedes dort allein. Es reisst dein Schicksal dich dahin.
Die alte Bucklige am Damm wird ewig nach dir blicken,
Untröstlich steht das schreiende Plakat am schiefen Giebel.
So lässt du alles dort allein in unerfüllter Liebesdemut
Selbst doch ein Einsamer, den eine Stadt erwartet,
In der du weinen wirst die lange Nacht im billigen Hotel.

DER SALZSEE

Der Mond leckt wie ein Wintertier das Salz deiner Hände,
Doch schäumt dein Haar violett wie ein Fliederbusch,
In dem das erfahrene Käuzchen ruft.

You who have ransomed all that died, o dancer,
While deep in filth and torment, fast asleep,
We went on snoring, blind to a little gladness:
Ourselves it was had died; the dead, they lived.

[1916]

JOURNEY INTO MISERY

Yet how the solitude of man torments
When landscapes with a sorrow like your own turn from you
And shrink into themselves, are so estranged!
A station, small, may push you out into cold rain,
A goods truck, empty and futureless, may ask for alms.
There on the dark ploughland crawls a sallow nag,
O if he only knew that you exist
And love him, he would sprout blue wings to heaven.
Sometimes with large eyes water may look up at you,
And since it did not see your smile,
Into itself it falls back flat and joyless.
So you leave each thing there alone. Fate hurries you on.
The old hunchback on the road, forever she'll watch you go,
On the slant gable the loud placard stands inconsolable.
So you leave all things there alone in loving and unanswered
          humbleness,
Solitary yourself, for whom a town is waiting
Where in your cheap hotel you'll sob the long night through.

[1917]

THE SALT LAKE

The moon like a winter animal licks the salt of your hands,
Yet your hair foams violet like a lilac bush,
In which experienced the little owl calls.

Da steht für uns erbaut die gesuchte Traumstadt,
In der die Strassen alle schwarz und weiss sind.
Du gehst im Glitzerschnee der Verheissung,
Mir sind gelegt die Schienen der dunklen Vernunft.

Die Häuser sind mit Kreide gegen den Himmel gezeichnet
Und ihre Türen bleigegossen;
Nur oben unter Giebeln wachsen gelbe Kerzen
Wie Nägel zu zahllosen Särgen.

Doch bald gelangen wir hinaus zum Salzsee.
Da lauern uns die langgeschnäbelten Eisvögel auf,
Die ich die ganze Nacht mit nackten Händen bekämpfe,
Bevor uns ihre warmen Daunen zum Lager dienen

DER REGENPALAST

Ich hab dir einen Regenpalast erbaut
Aus Alabastersäulen und Bergkristall
   Dass du in tausend Spiegeln
   Immer schöner dich für mich wandelst

Die Wasserpalme nährt uns mit grauem Most
Aus hohen Krügen trinken wir silbernen Wein
   Welch ein perlmutternes Konzert!
   Trunkne Libelle im Regenurwald!

Im Käfig der Lianen ersehnst du mich
Die Zauberbienen saugen das Regenblut
   Aus deinen blauen Augenkelchen
   Singende Reiher sind deine Wächter

Aus Regenfenstern blicken wir wie die Zeit
Mit Regenfahnen über das Meer hinweht
   Und mit dem Schlachtheer fremder Stürme
   Elend in alten Morästen endet

There raised for us two stands the long-sought dream town,
All of whose streets are black and white.
You walk in the glittering snow of promise,
For me the rails of dark reason have been laid.

The houses are marked with chalk against the sky
And their doors are of cast lead;
Only under the gables above there grow yellow candles
Like nails for countless coffins.

But soon we come out and reach the salt lake.
There the long-beaked halcyons lie in wait for us,
Which all night long I fight with my bare hands
Before their warm down will serve for our couch

1951: *Traumkraut*

THE RAIN PALACE

I have built for you a rain palace
Of alabaster columns and rock crystal
　　So that a thousand mirrors
　　Tell me how you change in beauty

The water-palm feeds us with gray fruit juice
From tall jugs we drink a silver wine
　　What a concerto of mother-of-pearl!
　　Tipsy dragonfly in the rain jungle!

In the liana cage you crave for me
The magic bees gorge the rain blood
　　Out of your azure eye-cups
　　Singing herons are your guardsmen

Through rain windows we see how time
Wafts with rain banners across the sea
　　And with the army of alien storms
　　Piteously ends in ancient swamps

Mit Regendiamanten bekleid ich dich
Heimlicher Maharadscha des Regenreichs
　Des Wert und Recht gewogen wird
　Nach den gesegneten Regenjahren

Du aber strickst mir verstohlen im Perlensaal
Durchwirkt von Hanf und Träne ein Regentuch
　Ein Leichentuch breit für uns beide
　Bis in die Ewigkeit warm und haltbar

With rain diamonds I mantle you
Secret maharajah of the rain realm
  Whose worth and right are weighed
  By the goodness of the rain years

But stealthily in the room of pearl you knit
Threaded of tear and hemp my rain cloth
  A cerecloth broad for the two of us
  Warm and durable into eternity

1951 : *Traumkraut*

ANTON SCHNACK

NÄCHTLICHE LANDSCHAFT

Ein Gestirn wie ein Tag; und dahinter ein Rand, berührt und
    bezogen von Licht und Geleucht,
Das ging oder kam, das fiel oder stand, unruhig, gespenstisch; und
    ging es, so war es hohe Nacht;
Und kam es, so lag ein Dorf irgendwo, weiss und verhuscht, und ein
    Wald war gemacht
Und ein Tal voller Schlaf, mit Gewässern, verworrenem Zeug, mit
    Gräbern und Türmen von Kirchen, zerstört, mit steigenden
    Nebeln, grosswolkig und feucht,
Mit Hütten, wo Schlafende lagen, wo ein Traum ging umher, voll
    Fieber, voll Fremdheit, voll tierischem Glanz, wo urplötzlich
    zerriss
Irgendein Vorhang von Wolken; dahinter wuchs Meer der Gestirne
    oder ein Reich von Raketen, sprang aus dem Abgrund ein
    Licht,
Fürchterlich, brausend, rauschte Gerassel auf Wegen, trat einer
    dunkel ins Dunkle mit einem schrecklichen Traumgesicht,
Sah wandern den Flug von Feuern, hörte Gemetzel im Grunde, sah
    brennen die Stadt ewig hinter der Finsternis.
Hörte ein Rollen im Erdbauch, schwerfällig, gewaltig, uralt, hörte
    Fahren auf Strassen, ins Leere, in die geweitete Nacht, in ein
    Gewitter, schaurig im Westen.—Ruhlos das Ohr
Von den tausend Hämmern der Front, von den Reitern, die kamen,
    stampfend, eilfertig, von den Reitern, die trabten hinweg,
    um ein Schatten zu werden, verwachsen der Nacht, um zu
    verwesen,
Schlachtet sie Tod, um unter Kräutern zu liegen, gewichtig,
    versteint, Hände voll Spinnen, Mund rot von Schorf,
Augen voll urtiefem Schlaf, um die Stirne den Reif der Verdunklung,
    blau, wächsern, faul werdend im Rauche der Nacht,

NOCTURNAL LANDSCAPE

A constellation like day; the horizon behind it by lights and flares
fingered and shrouded,

That went and came, fell or stood, restless, phantom-like; and if it
went, deep night fell,

And if it came, then somewhere a town lay, white, shifting furtive,
a forest was made and a vale

Full of sleep, with torrents and indeterminate things, with graves
and churchtowers, smashed, with climbing mists, moist, big-
clouded,

With huts, where sleepers lay, where a dream walked, full of fever,
full of strangeness, full of animal splendor, where abruptly a
screen

Of cloud split open; and behind it swelled an ocean of stars, a
dominion of rockets, a light sprang from the ravine,

Terrible, roaring, rumble of wheels on roads, and a man stepped
darkly into the dark, by a dreadful nightmare amazed,

Saw the flight of fires migrating, heard butchery below, saw behind
the darkness the city that ceaselessly blazed,

Heard in earth's belly a rolling, ponderous, gigantic, primeval,
heard traffic travelling the roads, into the void, into the
widening night, into a storm, grim in the west. Frantic, the
ear

With the front's countless hammers, with the riders who came,
stamping, hurrying, with the riders who rode away, to turn
into shadows, melt into the night, there to rot,

Death slaughters them, and they lie under weeds, heavy, fossil, with
hands full of spiders, mouths scabbed red and brown,

Eyes full of uttermost sleep, the circlet of shadow around their
brows, blue, waxen, decaying in the smoke of the night

Die niedersank, die weit überschattete, die gewölbt sich spannte
    von Hügel zu Hügel, über Wald und Verwesung, über
    Gehirne voll Traum, über hundert Tote, unaufgelesen,
Über die Unzahl der Feuer, über Gelächter und Irrsinn, über
    Kreuze auf Wiesen, über Qual und Verzweiflung, über
    Trümmer und Asche, über Fluss und verdorbenes Dorf . . .

Which sank down, threw shadows far, which spread its vault from hill
　　to hill, over forest and rottenness, over brains full of dreams,
　　over the hundred dead none carried away,
Over the mass of fire, over laughter and madness, over crosses in
　　fields, over pain and despair, over rubble and ash, over the
　　river and the ruined town . . .

1920

GERTRUD KOLMAR

DAS EINHORN

Der Pfauen Pracht,
Blau, grün und gülden, blühte in Dämmerung
Tropischer Wipfelwirrnis, und graue Affen
Fletschten und zankten, hangelten, tummelten, balgten sich im
    Geschlinge.
Der grosse Tiger, geduckt, zuckte die Kralle, starrte, verhielt,
Als das stumme seltsame Wild durch seine indischen Wälder floh,
Westwärts zum Meere.

Das Einhorn.

Seine Hufe schlugen die Flut
Leicht, nur spielend. Wogen bäumten sich
Übermütig,
Und es lief mit der wiehernd springenden, jagenden silbermähnigen
    Herde.
Über ihnen
Schrieb Flug schwarzer Störche eilige Rätselzeichen an den Himmel
    Arabiens,
Der mit sinkender Sonne eine Fruchtschale bot:
Gelbe Birnen, gerötete Äpfel,
Pfirsich, Orange und prangende Trauben,
Scheiben reifer Melone.
Schwarze Felsen glommen im Untergange,
Amethystene Burgen,
Weisse glühten, verzauberte Schlösser aus Karneol und Topas.

Spät hingen Rosennebel über den tausendfarb dunkelnden Wassern
    der Bucht.

THE UNICORN

The peacocks' pride,
Blue, green and golden, flowered in the twilight
Of tropical overgrowth, of tree-top, and gray monkeys
Grinned, quarrelled, dangled and romped, scuffled among tendrils.
The great tiger crouched, flashed claws, stared, lay low
As the dumb bewildering beast flew through his Indian forests,
Westward to the sea.

The unicorn.

His hoofs beat the water,
Playful, lightly. Waves reared,
Exuberant,
And the unicorn ran with the whinnying, cavorting, chivying
    silvermaned herd.
Over them
Black storks flying wrote rapid enigmas on the sky of Arabia;
Sunset there, proffering a dish of fruit:
Pears yellow, and red apples,
Peach and orange and plump grape,
Slices of ripe melon.
Black cliffs smouldered in sundown,
Fortresses of amethyst,
Whitenesses glowed, enchanted castles of cornelian and topaz.

The rose mists hung late over the dovecolored darkening waters of
    the bay.

Das Einhorn.

Seine Hufe wirbelten Sand,
Der lautlos stäubte. Es sah
Einsame Städte, bleich, mit Kuppel und Minarett und den Steinen
    der Leichenfelder
Schweigend unter dem klingenden Monde.
Es sah
Trümmer, verlassene Stätten, nur von Geistern behaust, in funkeln-
    der Finsternis
Unter kalten Gestirnen.
Einmal lockte der Wüstenkauz,
Und im Fernen heulten Schakale klagend;
Hyänen lachten.
Am Eingang des Zeltes unter der Dattelpalme
Hob das weisse syrische Dromedar träumend den kleinen Kopf,
    und seine Glocke tönte.

Vorüber das Einhorn, vorüber.

Denn seine leichten, flüchtigen Füsse kamen weither aus dem
    Goldlande Ophir,
Und aus seinen Augen glitzerten Blicke der Schlangen, die des
    Beschwörers Flöte aus Körben tauchen, gaukeln und tanzen
    heisst,
Doch das steile Horn seiner Stirnmitte goss sanfteres Licht, milchig
    schimmerndes,
Über die nackten Hände und weich umschleierten Brüste der Frau,
Die da stand
Zwischen Mannassträuchern.

Ihr Gruss:
Demut
Und der stille Glanz tiefer, wartender Augen
Und ein Hauchen, leise quellendes Murmeln des Mundes.—
Brunnen in Nacht.

The unicorn.

His hoofbeats whirled the sand up,
Raising dust without sound. He saw
Lonely cities, pallid, with cupola and minaret,
Tombstones in graveyards, tranquil under a ringing moon,
He saw
Ruins, homes desolate, tenanted by ghosts, in glistening darkness,
Under cold constellations.
The desert owl enticed him once,
And distant jackals howled lamenting;
Hyenas laughed.
Under the date palm, at the tent door,
The white Syrian dromedary raised from dream his small head, and
        his bell tinkled.

Onward the unicorn, onward.

For his light flying feet came from afar in Golden Ophir,
And from his eyes glittered the gaze of snakes which the charmer's
        flute commands to rise from baskets, to sway and dance,
But the steep horn central upon his brow shed a light more tender,
        milky, shimmering
Over the bare hands and soft-veiled breasts of the woman
Who stood there,
Among the clumps of manna grass.

Her greeting:
Humbleness,
And the quiet radiance of deep awaiting eyes,
And a breathing, the mouth's faint murmur flowing.—
Fountain in night.

[Before 1943.] 1955

DIE ALTE FRAU

Heut bin ich krank, nur heute, und morgen bin ich gesund.
Heut bin ich arm, nur heute, und morgen bin ich reich.
Einst aber werde ich immer so sitzen,
In dunkles Schultertuch frierend verkrochen, mit hüstelnder
  rasselnder Kehle,
Mühsam hinschlurfen und an den Kachelofen knöchrige Hände tun.
Dann werde ich alt sein.

Meiner Haare finstere Amselschwingen sind grau,
Meine Lippen bestaubte, verdorrte Blüten,
Und nichts weiss mein Leib mehr vom Fallen und Steigen der roten
  springenden Brunnen des Blutes.
Ich starb vielleicht
Lange schon vor meinem Tode.

Und doch war ich jung.
War lieb und recht einem Manne wie das braune nährende Brot
  seiner hungrigen Hand,
War süss wie ein Labetrunk seinem dürstenden Munde.
Ich lächelte,
Und meiner Arme weiche, schwellende Nattern lockten umschlin-
  gend in Zauberwald.
Aus meiner Schulter sprosste rauchblauer Flügel,
Und ich lag an der breiteren buschigen Brust,
Abwärts rauschend, ein weisses Wasser, vom Herzen des Tannen-
  felsens.

Aber es kam der Tag und die Stunde kam,
Da das bittere Korn in Reife stand, da ich ernten musste.
Und die Sichel schnitt meine Seele.
„Geh", sprach ich, „Lieber, geh!
Siehe, mein Haar weht Altweiberfäden,
Abendnebel nässt schon die Wange,
Und meine Blume schauert welkend in Frösten.

THE OLD WOMAN

Today I'm ill, only today, tomorrow I'll be well.
Today I'm poor, only today, tomorrow I'll be rich.
But some day I shall always sit like this,
Shrinking icy into a somber shawl, with a dry hacking cough,
Shuffle slow when I walk, and put bony hands to the fire.
Then I shall be old.

My hair's dark blackbird wings are gray,
My lips fusty withered blossoms,
And my body knows no longer the rise and fall of the red springing
  fountain of the blood.
I died perhaps
Long before my death.

And yet I was young.
Was loved by, went with a man, like nourishing brown bread in his
  hungry hand,
Was sweet as solacing drink to his thirsty mouth.
I smiled,
And the soft fleshy snakes of my arms allured, clinging in magical
  woodlands.
Smokeblue wings grew from my shoulders,
And I lay on his broader breast,
A white stream spilled murmuring down from the heart of the
  fir-crag.

But the day came and the moment came
When the bitter corn stood ripe that I had to harvest.
And the sickle cut my soul.
'Go', I said, 'Go, my dear!
Look, my hair's threaded with old woman's silver,
Evening mist moistens my cheek,
My flower wilts under frost, and shivers.

Furchen durchziehn mein Gesicht,
Schwarze Gräben die herbstliche Weide.
Geh; denn ich liebe dich sehr."

Still nahm ich die goldene Krone vom Haupt und verhüllte mein
Antlitz.

Er ging,
Und seine heimatlosen Schritte trugen wohl anderem Rastort ihn
zu unter helleren Augensternen.

Meine Augen sind trüb geworden und bringen Garn und Nadelöhr
kaum noch zusammen.
Meine Augen tränen müde unter den faltig schweren, rotumrän-
derten Lidern.

Selten
Dämmert wieder aus mattem Blick der schwache, fernvergangene
Schein
Eines Sommertages,
Da mein leichtes, rieselndes Kleid durch Schaumkrautwiesen floss
Und meine Sehnsucht Lerchenjubel in den offenen Himmel warf.

Furrows cross my face,
Black dykes through autumn pasture.
Go: for I love you, my love.'

Silent I took the gold crown from my head and I hid my face then.
He went,
And his homeless footsteps brought him for sure to another haven,
    under brighter eye-stars.

My eyes have gone dim and can hardly bring needle and cotton
    together.
My eyes water wearily under their heavy wrinkled red-rimmed lids.

Seldom
From my dull glance dawns now the faint far-ago shine
Of a summer day,
When my light frock flowed rustling through fields of cuckoo-flower,
And my desire hurled raptures of larksong into the open sky.

[Before 1943.] 1955

ALBIN ZOLLINGER

KLOSTER FAHR

Fortblühender Garten Vergangenheit, stiller Vorort des Himmels
In Wolkenstreifen und Pappeln, Kornhügeln und spiegelndem
    Wasser,
Die Nonnen ergehen sich durch Gemüsebeete, der Sommerwind
Spielt in lässigen Fahnen
Ihrer Gewände, und Wohlgeruch
Weisser Nelken
Mit einer Wärme von Hühnerhof brandet herüber.

Spröde verschliessen
Sie sich der süssen Welt und lesen
Sich in die Tiefe Gottes, himmlische Vatikane
Blenden die Seele, die sehnlich
Und müde der langen Geduld
Sich verzehrt
In der Stille der Prüfung—
O unabsehlich
Unnennbar flimmern die Fensterfronten!

Nichts lieben sie so wie
Ihr Grab
Im Hofe, im schattigen Schotter, dort werden sie modern,
Und einer Kirche
Abgeregnetes Innere, Jüngstes Gericht
Am Gemäuer, moosig im Eppich
Mit Engelsgewölk, erkaltete Brandstätte hält
Ihrer Ewigkeit strengen Schlaf.

THE CONVENT AT FAHR

Still flowering garden of the past, calm suburb of heaven
In wisps of cloud, and poplars, wheat hills, and shining water,
Through vegetable plots the nuns meander, summer wind
Plays in their robes'
Indolent flags, and the fragrance
Of white carnations
Surges across with a warm breath of chicken yard.

Coyly they close
Their doors on the sweet world, gather themselves
Into God's depth, heavenly vaticans
Dazzle the soul which eagerly,
And by long patience fatigued,
Consumes itself
In the calm of scrutiny—
O infinitely
Beyond words the windows glitter!

More than all else they love
Their grave
In the burial ground, in shadowy shale, there they will crumble
Where the rain-gutted
Sanctum of a church, with an Apocalypse
Upon the walls and moss-cold angel
Clouds amid ivy, every flame extinct, contains
Their eternity's severe repose.

Still dunkeln indessen die Fische
Durch Erlengebüsch, quellen die Ernten und sprosst
In den Wiegen der Pächter Geschlecht um Geschlecht
Rauher Bauern, die Pferde stampfen, die Ställe
Duften mit Strömen der heiligen Milch,
Wenn morgens Laternen
Mit blauem Schein
In Heuhöhen zünden.
Goldnes Stroh
In den Strassen versät
Blitzt sommerlich wallende Funken.

Aber die falbe Salbei
Und Gebüsche Phloxes
Entblättern in Kerzen
Den Heiligen
Müd um die Füsse.
Gefangene Gottes
Flackern in Zellen, da ferne
Mit Silos und schwarzem Gestänge,
Gasometern und Domen die Abendstadt
Höllenrot angeglüht
Unter den Bergen dunkelt.

Quietly yet the fish now darken
Through bushy alder, harvests gush, in farmers' cradles
Thrives generation on generation
Of rugged countrymen, the horses stamp, the byres
Are redolent with streams of holy milk
When lanterns at daybreak
With a blue radiance
Gleam in the haylofts.
Golden straws
That litter the road
Sparkle and shift like summer lightning.

But wearily from dun sage
And phlox in clusters
The petals flake into candles
Encircling the feet
Of the saints.
God's prisoners
Waver in cells, while far off
With black spikes and silos,
Gasometers and cathedrals, the sunset town
Bathed in its hellish crimson
Is darkening under the hills.

1936: *Sternfrühe*

BERTOLT BRECHT

VOM ARMEN B. B.

Ich, Bertolt Brecht, bin aus den schwarzen Wäldern.
Meine Mutter trug mich in die Städte hinein,
Als ich in ihrem Leibe lag. Und die Kälte der Wälder
Wird in mir bis zur meinem Absterben sein.

In der Asphaltstadt bin ich daheim. Von allem Anfang
Versehen mit jedem Sterbsakrament:
Mit Zeitungen. Und Tabak. Und Branntwein.
Misstrauisch und faul und zufrieden am End.

Ich bin zu den Leuten freundlich. Ich setze
Einen steifen Hut auf nach ihrem Brauch.
Ich sage: es sind ganz besonders riechende Tiere,
Und ich sage: es macht nichts, ich bin es auch.

In meine leeren Schaukelstühle vormittags
Setze ich mir mitunter ein paar Frauen,
Und ich betrachte sie sorglos und sage ihnen:
In mir habt ihr einen, auf den könnt ihr nicht bauen.

Gegen Abend versammle ich um mich Männer,
Wir reden uns da mit „Gentleman" an.
Sie haben ihre Füsse auf meinen Tischen
Und sagen: Es wird besser mit uns. Und ich frage nicht: Wann?

Gegen Morgen in der grauen Frühe pissen die Tannen,
Und ihr Ungeziefer, die Vögel, fängt an zu schrein.
Um die Stunde trink ich mein Glas in der Stadt aus und schmeisse
Den Tabakstummel weg und schlafe beunruhigt ein.

OF POOR B. B.

I, Bertolt Brecht, came out of the black forests.
My mother moved me into the cities while I lay
Inside her body. And the chill of the forests
Will be inside me till my dying day.

In the asphalt city I'm at home. From the very start
Provided with every unction and sacrament:
With newspapers. And tobacco. And brandy.
To the end mistrustful, lazy and content.

I'm polite and friendly to people. I put on
A stiff hat because that's what they do.
I say: they're animals with a quite peculiar smell
And I say: Does it matter? I am too.

Sometimes in the morning on my empty rocking chairs
I'll sit a woman or two, and with an untroubled eye
Look at them steadily and say to them:
Here you have someone on whom you can't rely.

Towards evening it's men that I gather around me
And then we address one another as 'gentlemen'.
They're resting their feet on my table tops
And say: Things will get better for us. And I don't ask: When?

In the gray light before morning the pine-trees piss
And their vermin, the birds, raise their twitter and cheep.
At that hour I drain my glass in town, then throw
The cigar butt away and worriedly go to sleep.

Wir sind gesessen ein leichtes Geschlechte
In Häusern, die für unzerstörbare galten
(So haben wir gebaut die langen Gehäuse des Eilands Manhattan
Und die dünnen Antennen, die das Atlantische Meer unterhalten).

Von diesen Städten wird bleiben: der durch sie hindurchging, der
    Wind!
Fröhlich machet das Haus den Esser: er leert es.
Wir wissen, dass wir Vorläufige sind,
Und nach uns wird kommen: nichts Nennenswertes.

Bei den Erdbeben, die kommen werden, werde ich hoffentlich
Meine Virginia nicht ausgehen lassen durch Bitterkeit,
Ich, Bertolt Brecht, in die Asphaltstädte verschlagen
Aus den schwarzen Wäldern, in meiner Mutter, in früher Zeit.

GESANG DER REISKAHNSCHLEPPER

In der Stadt oben am Fluss
Gibt es für uns einen Mundvoll Reis,
Aber der Kahn ist schwer, der hinauf soll,
Und das Wasser fliesst nach unten.
Wir werden nie hinaufkommen.

> *Zieht rascher, die Mäuler*
> *Warten auf das Essen.*
> *Zieht gleichmässig. Stosst nicht*
> *Den Nebenmann.*

We have sat, an easy generation
In houses thought to be indestructible
(Thus we built those tall boxes on the island of Manhattan
And those thin antennae that amuse the Atlantic swell.)

Of those cities will remain: what passed through them, the wind!
The house makes glad the consumer: he clears it out.
We know that we're only tenants, provisional ones,
And after us there will come: nothing worth talking about.

In the earthquakes to come, I very much hope,
I shall keep my Virginia alight, embittered or no,
I, Bertolt Brecht, carried off to the asphalt cities
From the black forests inside my mother long ago.

1921

SONG OF THE RICE BARGEES

In the town up river
We'll get a mouthful of rice,
But the barge we're hauling is heavy,
And the water flows downward.
We'll never arrive up there.

> *Pull faster, mouths*
> *Are waiting for food.*
> *Pull together, don't jostle*
> *The man beside.*

Die Nacht kommt schon bald. Das Lager,
Zu klein für eines Hundes Schatten,
Kostet einen Mundvoll Reis.
Weil das Ufer zu glatt ist,
Kommen wir nicht vom Fleck.

Zieht rascher, die Mäuler
Warten auf das Essen.
Zieht gleichmässig. Stosst nicht
Den Nebenmann.

Länger als wir
Hält das Tau, das in die Schultern schneidet.
Die Peitsche des Aufsehers
Hat vier Geschlechter gesehen.
Wann sieht sie das letzte?

Zieht rascher, die Mäuler
Warten auf das Essen.
Zieht gleichmässig. Stosst nicht
Den Nebenmann.

Unsere Väter zogen den Kahn von der Flussmündung
Ein Stück weit höher. Unsere Kinder
Werden die Quelle erreichen, wir
Sind dazwischen.

Zieht rascher, die Mäuler
Warten auf das Essen.
Zieht gleichmässig. Stosst nicht
Den Nebenmann.

Im Kahn ist Reis. Der Bauer, der
Ihn geerntet hat, bekam
Eine Handvoll Münzen, wir
Kriegen noch weniger. Ein Ochse
Wäre teurer. Wir sind zu viele.

Soon night will come. The camp,
Too small for a dog's shadow,
Costs a mouthful of rice.
The shore is so slippery
We can't move an inch.

> *Pull faster, mouths*
> *Are waiting for food.*
> *Pull together, don't jostle*
> *The man beside.*

The rope that cuts
Our shoulders lasts longer than us.
The overseer's whip
Has seen four generations.
When will it see the last?

> *Pull faster, mouths*
> *Are waiting for food.*
> *Pull together, don't jostle*
> *The man beside.*

Our fathers pulled the barge from the rivermouth
Up stream a little further. Our children
Will reach the source. We
Come between.

> *Pull faster, mouths*
> *Are waiting for food.*
> *Pull together, don't jostle*
> *The man beside.*

There's rice in the barge. The farmer who
Picked it was given
A handful of coin, we
Get still less. An ox would cost
More. There's too many of us.

Zieht rascher, die Mäuler
Warten auf das Essen.
Zieht gleichmässig. Stosst nicht
Den Nebenmann.

Wenn der Reis in der Stadt ankommt,
Und die Kinder fragen, wer
Den schweren Kahn geschleppt hat, heisst es :
Er ist geschleppt worden.

Zieht rascher, die Mäuler
Warten auf das Essen.
Zieht gleichmässig. Stosst nicht
Den Nebenmann.

Das Essen von unten kommt
Zu den Essern oben. Die
Es schleppen, haben
Nicht gegessen.

ÜBER DAS LEHREN OHNE SCHÜLER

Lehren ohne Schüler
Schreiben ohne Ruhm
Ist schwierig.

Es ist schön, am Morgen wegzugehen
Mit den frisch beschriebenen Blättern
Zu dem wartenden Drucker, über den summenden Markt
Wo Fleisch verkauft wird und Handwerkszeug :
Du verkaufst Sätze.

Pull faster, mouths
Are waiting for food.
Pull together, don't jostle
The man beside.

When the rice reaches the town
And the children ask who
Dragged the heavy barge they're told:
It was just dragged.

Pull faster, mouths
Are waiting for food.
Pull together, don't jostle
The man beside.

The food from below comes
To the feeders above. Those
Who haul it up, they
Have not eaten.

1927

ON TEACHING WITHOUT PUPILS

Teaching without pupils
Writing without fame
Are difficult.

It is good to go out in the morning
With your newly written pages
To the waiting printer, across the buzzing market
Where they sell meat and sets of workmen's tools:
What *you* are selling is sentences.

Der Fahrer ist schnell gefahren
Er hat nicht gefrühstückt
Jede Kurve war ein Risiko
Er tritt eilig in die Tür:
Der, den er abholen sollte
Ist schon aufgebrochen.

Dort spricht der, dem niemand zuhört:
Er spricht zu laut
Er wiederholt sich
Er spricht Falsches:
Er wird nicht verbessert.

VIER PSALMEN

Der erste Psalm

1. Wie erschreckend in der Nacht ist das konvexe Gesicht des schwarzen Landes!
2. Über der Welt sind die Wolken, sie gehören zur Welt. Über den Wolken ist nichts.
3. Der einsame Baum im Steinfeld muss das Gefühl haben, das alles umsonst ist.
   Er hat noch nie einen Baum gesehen. Es gibt keine Bäume.
4. Immer denke ich: wir werden nicht beobachtet.
   Der Aussatz des einzigen Sternes in der Nacht, vor er untergeht!
5. Der warme Wind bemüht sich noch um Zusammenhänge, der Katholik.
6. Ich komme sehr vereinzelt vor. Ich habe keine Geduld. Unser armer Bruder That's-all sagte von der Welt: sie macht nichts.
7. Wir fahren mit grosser Geschwindigkeit auf ein Gestirn in der Milchstrasse zu. Es ist eine grosse Ruhe in dem Gesicht der Erde. Mein Herz geht zu schnell. Sonst ist alles in Ordnung.

The driver has driven fast
He has eaten no breakfast
Every bend was a risk
In haste he steps through the doorway:
He whom he came to fetch
Has already gone.

There speaks he to whom no-one is listening:
He speaks too loud
And repeats himself.
He says things that are wrong:
No one corrects him.

[1935]

FOUR PSALMS

The First Psalm

1. How terrifying it is in the night, the convex face of the black land!
2. Above the world are the clouds, they belong to the world. Above the clouds there is nothing.
3. The solitary tree on the rocky ground must be feeling it is all in vain. It has never seen a tree. There are no trees.
4. I keep on thinking: we are not observed.
   The leprosy of the sole star in the night before it perishes!
5. The warm wind is still trying to make connections, the Catholic.
6. I am very much an isolated case. I have no patience. Our poor brother Thatsall said of the world: it's not doing anything.
7. We are traveling at high speed toward a constellation in the Milky Way. There is a great calm in the earth's face. My heart beats too fast. Otherwise all is well.

Der zweite Psalm

1. Unter einer fleischfarbenen Sonne, die vier Atemzüge nach Mitternacht den östlichen Himmel hellmacht, unter einem Haufen Wind, der sie in Stössen wie mit Leilich bedeckt, entfalten die Wiesen von Füssen bis Passau ihre Propaganda für Lebenslust.

2. Von Zeit zu Zeit teilen die Eisenbahnzüge voll von Milch und Passagieren die Weizenfeldmeere; aber die Luft steht still um die Donnernden, das Licht zwischen den grossen Versteinerungen, der Mittag über den unbewegten Feldern.

3. Die Gestalten in den Feldern lasterhafte Visagen, arbeiten in langsamen Bewegungen für die Bleichgesichter in den Versteinerungen, wie es auf dem Papier vorgesehen ist.

4. Denn Gott hat die Erde geschaffen, dass sie Brot bringe, und uns die Braunbrüstigen gegeben, dass es in die Mägen komme, vermischt mit der Milch der Kühe, die er geschaffen hat. Aber für was ist der Wind da, herrlich in den Baumwipfeln?

5. Der Wind macht die Wolken, dass da Regen ist auf die Äcker, dass das Brot entstehe. Lasst uns jetzt Kinder machen aus Lüsten für das Brot, dass es gefressen werde.

6. Das ist der Sommer. Scharlachene Winde erregen die Ebenen, die Gerüche werden Ende Juni masslos. Ungeheure Gesichte zähnefletschender nackter Männer wandern in grossen Höhen südwärts.

7. In den Hütten ist das Licht der Nächte wie Lachs. Man feiert die Auferstehung des Fleisches.

Der dritte Psalm

1. Im Juli fischt ihr aus den Weihern meine Stimme. In meinen Adern ist Kognak. Meine Hand ist aus Fleisch.

2. Das Weiherwasser gerbt meine Haut, ich bin hart wie eine Haselrute, ich wäre gut fürs Bett, meine Freundinnen!

3. In der roten Sonne auf den Steinen liebe ich die Gitarren: es sind Därme von Vieh, die Klampfe singt viehisch, sie frisst kleine Lieder.

The Second Psalm

1. Under a fleshcolored sun that brightens the eastern sky four breaths after midnight, under a heap of wind that covers them in gusts as with shrouds, the meadows from Füssen to Passau spread their lust-for-life propaganda.

2. From time to time the trains full of milk and passengers cleave the wheat fields; but around the thunderers the air stands still, the light between the great petrefacts, the noon over the motionless fields.

3. The figures on the fields, how wicked they look, work with slow movements for the palefaces in the petrefacts, the documents provide for this.

4. For God created the earth that it might bring bread, and gave us the brownbreasts that it might enter our stomachs, mixed with the milk from the cows which he created. But what is the wind for, glorious in the tops of the trees?

5. The wind makes the clouds, that rain should be on the ploughland, that bread should come. Let us now make children out of our lusts, for the bread, that it may be devoured.

6. This is Summer. Scarlet winds excite the plains, the smells at the end of June are beyond bound. Vast visions of teeth-gnashing naked men travel in great hills southward.

7. In the cottages the night's light is like salmon. The resurrection of the flesh is celebrated.

The Third Psalm

1. In July you fish my voice from the ponds. There is cognac in my veins. My hand is flesh.

2. The pond water tans my skin, I am hard as a hazel switch, I would be good in bed, ladies.

3. In the red sun on the stones I love the guitars: they are cow's guts, the banjo sings like a beast, it eats little songs.

4. Im Juli habe ich ein Verhältnis mit dem Himmel, ich nenne ihn
Azurl, herrlich, violett, er liebt mich. Es ist Männerliebe.

5. Er wird bleich, wenn ich mein Darmvieh quäle und die rote
Unzucht der Äcker imitiere sowie das Seufzen der Kühe beim
Beischlaf.

Der vierte Psalm

1. Was erwartet man noch von mir?
Ich habe alle Patiencen gelegt, alles Kirschwasser gespien
Alle Bücher in den Ofen gestopft
Alle Weiber geliebt, bis sie wie der Leviathan gestunken haben.
Ich bin schon ein grosser Heiliger, mein Ohr ist so faul, dass es
nächstens einmal abbricht.
Warum also ist nicht Ruhe? Warum stehen immer noch die
Leute im Hof wie Kehrichttonnen—wartend, das man etwas
hineingibt? Ich habe zu verstehen gegeben, das man das Hohe
Lied von mir nicht mehr erwarten darf.
Auf die Käufer habe ich die Polizei gehetzt.
Wer immer es ist, den ihr sucht : ich bin es nicht.

2. Ich bin der praktischste von allen meinen Brüdern—
Und mit *meinem* Kopf fängt es an!
Meine Brüder waren grausam, ich bin der grausamste—
Und *ich* weine nachts!

3. Mit den Gesetzestafeln sind die Laster entzweigegangen.
Man schläft schon bei seiner Schwester ohne rechte Freude.
Der Mord ist vielen zu mühsam
Das Dichten ist zu allgemein.
Bei der Unsicherheit aller Verhältnisse
Ziehen es viele vor, die Wahrheit zu sagen
Aus Unkenntnis der Gefahr.
Die Kurtisanen pökeln Fleisch ein für den Winter
Und der Teufel holt seine besten Leute nicht mehr ab.

4. In July I have an affair with the sky, I call him Little Azure, glorious, violet, he loves me. It's homosexual.

5. He goes pale when I torture my gut beast and imitate the red incest of the fields as well as the sighing of cows when we sleep with one another.

The Fourth Psalm

1. What do people still expect of me?
   I have played all the patiences, spat out all the kirsch
   Stuffed all the books into the stove
   Loved all the women till they stank like Leviathan.
   Now I am a great saint, my ear is so rotten it will soon drop off.
   So why still no calm? Why do the people stand in the yard like rubbish bins—waiting for something to be put into them? I have made it plain it is no use any more to expect of me the Song of Solomon.
   I have set the police on the buyers.
   Whoever it is you are looking for: it is not me.

2. I am the most practical of all my brothers—
   And it all starts in *my* head!
   My brothers were cruel, I am the cruellest—
   And it is *I* who weep at night!

3. Wickedness broke with the tables of the law.
   Now one can sleep with one's sister and not like it much.
   Murder is too much trouble for many
   Writing poems is too common a thing.
   Since everything is uncertain
   Many prefer to tell the truth
   Being ignorant of the danger.
   The courtesans pickle meat for the winter
   And the devil no longer carries away his best people.

[Mid-1930's]

GENERAL, DEIN TANK IST EIN STARKER WAGEN

Er bricht einen Wald nieder und zermalmt hundert Menschen.
Aber er hat einen Fehler:
Er braucht einen Fahrer.

General, dein Bombenflugzeug ist stark.
Es fliegt schneller als ein Sturm und trägt mehr als ein Elefant.
Aber es hat einen Fehler:
Es braucht einen Monteur.

General, der Mensch ist sehr brauchbar.
Er kann fliegen, und er kann töten.
Aber er hat einen Fehler:
Er kann denken.

AN DIE NACHGEBORENEN

I

Wirklich, ich lebe in finsteren Zeiten!
Das arglose Wort ist töricht. Eine glatte Stirn
Deutet auf Unempfindlichkeit hin. Der Lachende
Hat die furchtbare Nachricht
Nur noch nicht empfangen.

Was sind das für Zeiten, wo
Ein Gespräch über Bäume fast ein Verbrechen ist,
Weil es ein Schweigen über so viele Untaten einschliesst!
Der dort ruhig über die Strasse geht,
Ist wohl nicht mehr erreichbar für seine Freunde,
Die in Not sind?

GENERAL, THAT TANK

General, that tank of yours is some car.
It can wreck a forest, crush a hundred men.
But it has one failing:
It needs a driver.

General, you've got a good bomber there.
It can fly faster than the wind, carry more than an elephant can.
But it has one failing:
It needs a mechanic.

General, a man is a useful creature.
He can fly, and he can kill.
But he has one failing:
He can think.

1938: *Deutsche Marginalien*

TO POSTERITY

I

Truly, the age I live in is bleak.
The guileless word is foolish. A smooth brow
Denotes insensitiveness. The laughing man
Has only not yet received
The dreadful news.

What times are these when a conversation
About trees is almost a crime.
Because it includes a silence about so many misdeeds!
That one there calmly crossing the street,
Hasn't he ceased to be at home to
His friends in need?

Es ist wahr: ich verdiene noch meinen Unterhalt.
Aber glaubt mir: das ist nur ein Zufall. Nichts
Von dem, was ich tue, berechtigt mich dazu, mich sattzuessen.
Zufällig bin ich verschont. (Wenn mein Glück aussetzt,
Bin ich verloren.)

Man sagt mir: Iss und trink du! Sei froh, dass du hast!
Aber wie kann ich essen und trinken, wenn
Ich es dem Hungernden entreisse, was ich esse, und
Mein Glas Wasser einem Verdurstenden fehlt?
Und doch esse und trinke ich.

Ich wäre gerne auch weise.
In den alten Büchern steht, was weise ist:
Sich aus dem Streit der Welt halten und die kurze Zeit
Ohne Furcht verbringen
Auch ohne Gewalt auskommen,
Böses mit Gutem vergelten,
Seine Wünsche nicht erfüllen, sondern vergessen,
Gilt für weise.
Alles das kann ich nicht:
Wirklich, ich lebe in finsteren Zeiten!

II

In die Städte kam ich zur Zeit der Unordnung,
Als da Hunger herrschte.
Unter die Menschen kam ich zur Zeit des Aufruhrs,
Und ich empörte mich mit ihnen.
So verging meine Zeit
Die auf Erden mir gegeben war.

Mein Essen ass ich zwischen den Schlachten.
Schlafen legte ich mich unter die Mörder.
Der Liebe pflegte ich achtlos
Und die Natur sah ich ohne Geduld.
So verging meine Zeit
Die auf Erden mir gegeben war.

True enough: I still earn my living.
But, believe me, it's only luck.
Nothing I do gives me the right to eat my fill.
It happens that I've been spared. (When my luck gives out
I shall be lost.)

They tell me: Eat and drink. Be glad that you can!
But how can I eat and drink, when
From the hungry man I snatch what I eat, and
My glass of water deprives the man dying of thirst?
And yet I eat and drink.

And I'd also like to be wise.
In the old books you read what is wise:
To keep out of the strife of the world and spend
Your brief span without fear.
And to refrain from violence
Render good for evil
Not fulfil one's desires, but forget
Is accounted wise.
All these are beyond me:
Truly, the age I live in is bleak.

II

I came into the cities at the time of disorder
When hunger was rife.
I mixed with men at the time of rebellion
And revolted as they did.
So passed the time
Granted to me on earth.

I ate my meals between battles.
I lay down to sleep between the murderers.
Love I pursued unheeding
And on nature looked without patience.
So passed the time
Granted to me on earth.

Die Strassen führten in den Sumpf zu meiner Zeit.
Die Sprache verriet mich dem Schlächter.
Ich vemochte nur wenig. Aber die Herrschenden
Sassen ohne mich sicherer, das hoffte ich.
So verging meine Zeit
Die auf Erden mir gegeben war.

Die Kräfte waren gering. Das Ziel
Lag in grosser Ferne.
Es war deutlich sichtbar, wenn auch für mich
Kaum zu erreichen.
So verging meine Zeit
Die auf Erden mir gegeben war.

III

Ihr, die ihr auftauchen werdet aus der Flut
In der wir untergegangen sind,
Gedenkt
Wenn ihr von unseren Schwächen sprecht
Auch der finsteren Zeit
Der ihr entronnen seid.

Gingen wir doch, öfter als die Schuhe die Länder wechselnd
Durch die Kriege der Klassen, verzweifelt
Wenn da nur Unrecht war und keine Empörung.

Dabei wissen wir doch:
Auch der Hass gegen die Niedrigkeit
Verzerrt die Züge.
Auch der Zorn über das Unrecht
Macht die Stimme heiser. Ach, wir
Die wir den Boden bereiten wollten für Freundlichkeit,
Konnten selber nicht freundlich sein.

Ihr aber, wenn es soweit sein wird
Dass der Mensch dem Menschen ein Helfer ist
Gedenkt unsrer
Mit Nachsicht

The streets led into morasses in my time.
Speech betrayed me to the butcher.
There was little I could do. Yet the rulers
Sat more secure but for me, that was my hope.
So passed the time
Granted to me on earth.

My resources were not great. The goal
Lay far ahead.
It was clearly visible, if for me
Scarcely attainable.
So passed the time
Granted to me on earth.

III

You that will emerge from the deluge
In which we drowned,
When you speak of our shortcomings
Remember too
The bleak age
Which you have escaped.

For, changing countries more often than shoes, we walked
Through the wars of the classes, despairing
When there was injustice only and no rebellion.

And yet we know well:
Even hatred of vileness
Distorts a man's features.
Even anger at injustice
Makes hoarse his voice. Ah, we
Who desired to prepare the soil for kindness
Could not ourselves be kind.

But you, when the times permit
Men to be the helpers of men
Remember us
With indulgence.

1938

VOM SPRENGEN DES GARTENS

O Sprengen des Gartens, das Grün zu ermutigen!
Wässern der durstigen Bäume! Gib mehr als genug und
Vergiss nicht das Strauchwerk, auch
Das beerenlose nicht, das ermattete
Geizige. Und übersieh mir nicht
Zwischen den Blumen das Unkraut, das auch
Durst hat. Noch giesse nur
Den frischen Rasen oder den versengten nur:
Auch den nackten Boden erfrische du.

GEDANKEN ÜBER DIE DAUER DES EXILS

I

Schlage keinen Nagel in die Wand,
Wirf den Rock auf den Stuhl.
Warum versorgen für vier Tage?
Du kehrst morgen zurück.

Lass den kleinen Baum ohne Wasser.
Wozu noch einen Baum pflanzen?
Bevor er so hoch wie eine Stufe ist,
Gehst du froh weg von hier.

Zieh die Mütze ins Gesicht, wenn Leute vorbeigehen!
Wozu in einer fremden Grammatik blättern?
Die Nachricht, die dich heimruft,
Ist in bekannter Sprache geschrieben.

So wie der Kalk vom Gebälk blättert,
(Tue nichts dagegen!)
Wird der Zaun der Gewalt zermorschen,
Der an der Grenze aufgerichtet ist
Gegen die Gerechtigkeit.

ON WATERING THE GARDEN

O the spraying of gardens, to encourage green!
Watering of thirsty trees! Give them more than enough and
Do not forget the shrubs,
Even those without berries or those
Exhausted, grown mean. And don't overlook
The weeds between the flowers—these too
Are thirsty. Nor water only
The fresh parts of the lawn, or only the scorched:
Even the naked soil take care to refresh.

[c. 1940–45]

THOUGHTS ON THE LENGTH OF EXILE

I

Don't knock any nails in the wall,
Just throw your coat on the chair.
Why plan for four days?
Tomorrow you'll go back home.

Leave the little tree without water.
Why ever plant a tree?
You'll pack your bags and be away
Before it's as high as a doorstep.

Pull your cap over your eyes when people pass!
What use thumbing through a foreign grammar?
The message that calls you home
Is written in a language you know.

As plaster peels from the ceiling
(Don't bother about repairs!)
It will crumble, the block of force
That has been set up at the frontier
To keep out justice.

II

Sieh den Nagel in der Wand, den du eingeschlagen hast:
Wann, glaubst du, wirst du zurückkehren?
Willst du wissen, was du im Innersten glaubst?

Tag um Tag
Arbeitest du an der Befreiung,
Sitzend in der Kammer schreibst du.
Willst du wissen, was du von deiner Arbeit hältst?
Sieh den kleinen Kastanienbaum im Eck des Hofes,
Zu dem du die Kanne voll Wasser schlepptest!

RÜCKKEHR

Die Vaterstadt, wie find ich sie doch?
Folgend den Bomberschwärmen
Komm ich nach Haus.
Wo denn liegt sie? Wo die ungeheuren
Gebirge von Rauch stehen.
Das in den Feuern dort
Ist sie.

Die Vaterstadt, wie empfängt sie mich wohl?
Vor mir kommen die Bomber. Tödliche Schwärm
Melden Euch meine Rückkehr. Feuersbrünste
Gehen dem Sohn voraus.

II

Look at the nail you knocked into the wall:
When, do you think, will you return?
Do you want to know what your heart of hearts is saying?

Day after day
You work for liberation.
You sit in your room, writing.
Do you want to know how your work really strikes you?
That little chestnut tree in the corner of the yard,
Look, that was a canful of water you carried to it.

1945 (first version).

RETURN

Hometown, how will it look then?
Behind the swarms of bombers
I have come home.
But where's the town? Where the towering
Mountains of smoke stand.
There in the flames,
It's there.

Hometown, how will it receive me then?
Before me the bombers come. Death-bearing swarms
Announce my return. Raging fires
Precede the homecoming son.

[*c.* 1948.] 1957

EISEN

Im Traum heute nacht
Sah ich einen grossen Sturm.
Ins Baugerüst griff er
Den Bauschragen riss er
Den eisernen, abwärts.
Doch was da aus Holz war
Bog sich und blieb.

DER RADWECHSEL

Ich sitze am Strassenhang.
Der Fahrer wechselt das Rad.
Ich bin nicht gern, wo ich herkomme.
Ich bin nicht gern, wo ich hinfahre.
Warum sehe ich den Radwechsel
Mit Ungeduld?

IRON

In a dream last night
I saw a great gale rage.
It gripped the scaffolding
Tore down the supports
Of solid iron.
But whatever was made of wood
Bent and remained.

[1953]

CHANGING THE WHEEL

I sit on the roadside bank.
The driver changes a wheel.
I do not like the place I have come from.
I do not like the place I am going to.
Why do I watch him changing the wheel
With impatience?

[1953]

BÖSER MORGEN

Die Silberpappel, eine ortsbekannte Schönheit
Heut eine alte Vettel. Der See
Eine Lache Abwaschwasser, nicht rühren!
Die Fuchsien unter dem Löwenmaul billig und eitel.
Warum?
Heut nacht im Traum sah ich Finger, auf mich deutend
Wie auf einen Aussätzigen. Sie waren zerarbeitet und
Sie waren gebrochen.

Unwissende! schrie ich
Schuldbewusst.

DER BAUER KÜMMERT SICH UM SEINEN ACKER

I

Der Bauer kümmert sich um seinen Acker
Hält sein Vieh instand, zahlt Steuern
Macht Kinder, damit er die Knechte einspart und
Hängt vom Milchpreis ab.
Die Städter reden von der Liebe zur Scholle
Vom gesunden Bauernstamm und
Dass der Bauer das Fundament der Nation ist.

II

Die Städter reden von der Liebe zur Scholle
Vom gesunden Bauernstamm und
Dass der Bauer das Fundament der Nation ist.
Der Bauer kümmert sich um seinen Acker
Hält sein Vieh instand, zahlt Steuern
Macht Kinder, damit er die Knechte einspart und
Hängt vom Milchpreis ab.

A BAD MORNING

The silver poplar, a beauty of local fame
An old hag today. The lake
A puddle of dirty suds—do not touch:
The fuchsias among the snapdragon cheap and vain.
But why?
Last night in a dream I saw fingers pointing at me
As at a leper. They were callous, stained with work and
They were broken.

Ignorant lot! I cried,
Conscious of guilt.

[1953]

THE FARMER'S CONCERN

I

The farmer's concern is with his field,
He looks after his cattle, pays taxes,
Produces children, to save himself laborers and
Depends on the price of milk.
The townspeople speak of love for the soil
Of healthy peasant stock
And call farmers the pillars of the nation.

II

The townspeople speak of love for the soil
Of healthy peasant stock
And call farmers the pillars of the nation.
The farmer's concern is with his field,
He looks after his cattle, pays taxes,
Produces children, to save himself laborers and
Depends on the price of milk.

ERICH KÄSTNER

GEFÄHRLICHES LOKAL

Mir träumte neulich, dass mein Stammcafé
auf einer Insel unter Palmen stünde.
Persönlich kenne ich bloss Warnemünde.
Doch Träume reisen gern nach Übersee.

Ich sass am Fenster und versank in Schweigen.
Wo sonst die Linie 56 hält
war eine Art von Urwald aufgestellt.
Und Orang Utans hingen in den Zweigen.

Sie waren sicher noch nicht lange da.
So leicht verändern sich die Metermasse!
Bevor ich kam, war's noch die Prager Strasse.
Man setzt sich hin, schon ist es Sumatra.

Erst wollte ich den Oberkellner fragen.
Dann dachte ich, es hätte keinen Zweck.
Was soll ein Kellner namens Urbanek,
selbst wenn er wollte, weiter dazu sagen?

Dann ging die Tür. Das war der Doktor Uhl.
Und hinter ihm erschien ein schwarzer Panther,
der setzte sich, als sei er ein Bekannter,
an meinem Tisch auf einen leeren Stuhl.

Ich fragte ihn betreten, ob er rauche.
Er sah mich an. Und sagte keinen Ton.
Dann kam der Wirt in eigener Person
und kitzelte den seltnen Gast am Bauche.

DANGEROUS ESTABLISHMENT

My favorite café—so I dreamed recently—
stood amidst palm trees in an island port.
Now, Margate is *my* holiday resort;
but dreams are rather apt to cross the sea.

I settled near the window, ill at ease:
where once the number 2 bus used to stop
they'd set a sort of pristine jungle up
and apes—orang-outangs—hung on the trees.

I'm sure they'd not been there so very long:
you can't just change dimensions, yards and feet.
Before I came it was still Bishop's Street;
you pick a place, and now it's Belitong.

At first I felt like asking the headwaiter.
But then I thought this wasn't any good.
What sort of comment should a man called Slater
make on this business, even if he could?

Now the door opened. It was Dr Clare.
And, close behind him, a black panther who
sat down as any Tom or Dick might do—
and at my table, on a vacant chair.

I asked him softly if he'd care to smoke.
He did not stir, but stared at me defiant.
Now the proprietor approached this client,
solemnly tickled him, but never spoke.

Der Ober brachte Erbspüree mit Speck.
Er hatte grosse Angst und ging auf Zehen.
Der Panther liess das gute Essen stehen
und frass den Kellner. Armer Urbanek!

Von oben drang der Klang der Billardbälle.
Der schwarze Panther war noch beim Diner.
Ich sass bestürzt in meinem Stammcafé.
Und sah nur Wald. Und keine Haltestelle.

Weil man mich dann zum Telephone rief
(ein Kunde wollte mich geschäftlich sprechen),
war ich genötigt, plötzlich aufzubrechen.
Als ich zurückkam, sah ich, dass ich schlief . . .

The waiter brought us scrambled egg on toast.
He walked on tip-toe and seemed liverish.
The panther did not touch this wholesome dish
but ate poor Slater. Peace be with his ghost!

From up above came sounds of ball and cue.
The panther dined. He saw no need to hurry.
What could I do but sit there, watch and worry,
with jungle all around, no number 2?

Because they called me to the phone (old Deeping,
my senior clerk, to tell me he was sick),
I was obliged to make my exit quick.
When I came back I saw that I was sleeping. . .

1930: *Ein Mann gibt Auskunft*

PETER HUCHEL

DER POLNISCHE SCHNITTER

Klag nicht, goldäugige Unke,
im algigen Wasser des Teichs.
Wie eine grosse Muschel
rauscht der Himmel nachts.
Sein Rauschen ruft mich heim.

Geschultert die Sense
geh ich hinab die helle Chaussee,
umheult von Hunden,
vorbei an russiger Schmiede,
wo dunkel der Amboss schläft.

Draussen am Vorwerk
schwimmen die Pappeln
im milchigen Licht des Mondes.
Noch atmen die Felder heiss
im Schrei der Grillen.

O Feuer der Erde,
mein Herz hält andere Glut.
Acker um Acker mähte ich,
kein Halm war mein eigen.

Herbststürme, weht!
Auf leeren Böden
werden die hungrigen Schläfer wach.
Ich geh nicht allein
die helle Chaussee.

THE POLISH REAPER

Don't be sad, goldeyed toad
in the pond among waterweed.
Like a great shell
the sky murmurs at night.
Its murmur calls me home.

Shouldered my scythe,
down the bright road I go,
howled round by dogs,
past the sootblack smithy
where the anvil sleeps in the dark.

Outside the farmyard,
poplars are swimming
in milky moonlight.
Fields breathe hot still
in the grasshoppers' cry.

O fire of earth,
my heart has another warmth.
Field upon field I've mown,
not a cornblade was mine.

Autumn winds, blow!
The hungry sleepers
wake on vacant ground.
It's not alone I walk
down the bright road.

Am Rand der Nacht
schimmern die Sterne
wie Korn auf der Tenne,
kehr ich heim ins östliche Land,
in die Röte des Morgens.

On the edge of the night
the stars glitter
like corn on the threshing floor,
and I'm going home to the eastern land,
to the crimson of morning.

1933: *Herkunft*

MÜNZE AUS BIR EL ABBAS

Reibe die schartige Münze nicht blank.
Lass es schlafen, das fremde Gesicht,
Unter der grünen Schicht des Metalls
Wie unter dem grünen Wasser
Verschlammter Löcher der letzten Oase.

Die Münze klirrt.
Du hörst Getöse der Öde,
Die lange Klage der Karawanen,
Zerfallen zu Staub.
Vom Wind gewetzt,
Zerschneidet die Sichel des Sandes
Das Lagerfeuer,
Das schwarze Zelt aus Ziegenhaar,
Der Eselstute Nüster und Huf.

Ruhlose Münze,
Von Brunnen zu Brunnen getragen,
Auf schrundigem Rücken dürrer Kamele
Von Markt zu Markt,
Aus schmutzigem Kopftuch der Greisin fallend
Ins schmutzige Leder des Fladenhändlers,
Verborgen unter der Achsel des Diebes
Und wieder geworfen aus Räuberhand
Dem Leprakranken in den Napf,
Geschoben auf den dünnen Teppich,
Dass vor der Liebe die Ulad noch tanze,
Drehend den Leib wie eine Töpferscheibe
Und über dem starren, gekalkten Gesicht
Den kleinen Mond aus Tierhaut schwingend,
Der dröhnend umkreist den Flötenton—

COIN FROM BIR EL ABBAS

Do not rub the notched coin clean.
Let it sleep, the alien face,
Under the metal's green film
As under the green water
Silted holes of the last oasis.

The coin clinks.
You hear the roaring of emptiness,
The long lamentation of the caravans,
Crumbled into dust.
Sharpened by the wind,
The sickle of sand slices up
The camp fire,
The black tent of goat hair,
Nostril and hoof of the she-ass.

Restless coin,
Carried from fountain to fountain,
On the cracked rumps of thin camels,
From market to market.
Falling from an old woman's dirty headscarf
Into the dirty leather of the dung-merchant,
Hidden in the armpit of the thief
And thrown again from robber hands
Into the leper's begging-bowl,
Pushed across the thin carpet
That before love the Ulad may repeat her dance
Whirling her body like a potter's wheel,
And over her rigid whitened face
Waving the small moon of animal skin
That circles with a hum the sound of flutes—

Ruhlose Münze,
Verschenkt und verloren,
Von Fersen getreten, von Zähnen geprüft,
Geschrieben ins Schuldbuch, ins Salz der Tränen,
Wenn unter der Fron der Mahlstein knirschte,
Du Zeuge des Schachers um Amber und Perlen,
Dem Richter den Spruch vom Munde nehmend:
Du nur kennst die Wege der Welt.
Du rolltest durch den Hunger des Volks,
Durch Prunk und Aufruhr alter Provinzen,
Durch Stammesfehden und Lachen von Blut,
Bis dich die Tatze der Wüste begrub.

Wo Öde wuchert an Wall und Mauer,
Mit stumpfer Hacke die Hitze schlägt,
Lagst du im Schutt purpurner Scherben,
Dem Schweigen nun auf Zins geliehen—
Vom Spaten gehoben,
Das einzige Grün im grellen Sand,
Der Mammon der Toten,
Der nicht zu stillen vermochte
Den nie verlöschenden Durst der Welt.

Restless coin,
Given away and lost,
Trodden underfoot, tested by teeth,
Inscribed in the creditor's list, in the salt of tears
When in sweat-work the millstone crunched,
Witness of the haggler for amber and pearls,
Taking from his mouth the judge's words:
You alone know the ways of the world.
You rolled through the people's hunger,
Through the splendor and tumult of old provinces,
Through tribal feuds and pools of blood
Till the paw of the desert buried you.

Where emptiness thrives by mound and wall,
And heat strikes with its blunt pick,
You lay in the rubbish of purple shards,
Put out at interest in silence now,
Raised by the shovel,
The only green in the dazzling sand,
Mammon of the dead,
That had no power to slake
The never sated thirst of the world.

1959

WALTER BAUER

SINGEN IN ALTEN MASSEN

Singen in alten Massen
und tun, als gäbe es immer noch Harfen—
woher nehmen die Leute den Mut?
Und wieso sprechen sie immer noch von Göttern?
Ist hier nicht alles einsam geworden?
Ja, vielleicht flüstern—
das kann man,
als spräche man mit sich selber,
oder mit Worten von der Schärfe des Pflugs
den Acker aufzureissen dieser verrotteten Zeit—
das mag es sein, das ist uns erlaubt.
Zu viele Gräber liegen auf unsern Stimmen,
zu viele Tote machen sich über uns bitter lustig
in ihrem Verfall,
wenn wir sagen: wir singen.
Und so, kaum hörbar, flüstere ich zu mir selber
oder zu dir . . . ich weiss nicht . . .
dieses Wort vom Lächeln im Gesicht eines Fremden,
das plötzlich ungerufen erschien
wie der Gruss eines in sich selber Verschütteten.
Oder von der Linie unbeschreiblich zart und kühn,
die ein Vogelflug an die Tafel des Himmels schreibt.

TO SING IN ANCIENT MEASURES

To sing in ancient measures,
to act as if harps still existed,
where do people get the courage?
And how do they still manage to speak of gods?
Hasn't everything here become lonely?
Yes, perhaps a whisper,
one can do that,
as if one spoke to oneself,
or used words which are sharp as ploughshares
to rip open the ground of this rotten age—
that may be, that is permitted us.
Too many graves lie upon our voices,
too many dead men mock us with bitter joy
in their decay,
if we say that we are singing.
And so, scarcely audible, I whisper to myself
or to you . . . I do not know . . .
a word concerning the smile on the face of a stranger,
which suddenly appeared, without provocation,
like the greeting of one who is buried inside himself;
or about the indescribably delicate brave line
which a bird's flight inscribes on the tablet of the sky.

1954

HIER ZU SEIN

Wo sind die schmetternden Hörner von Ninive,
wo sind die Heere, die durch die Tore von Babylon zogen—
gegen welchen Feind?
Wo liegen die Gräber der Sieger und der Besiegten?
Wie Schiffe fahren die Völker über das Meer der Zeiten—
zu welchem Ziel?
Unterzugehen und als Strandgut ein paar zerbrochene Tore
zu hinterlassen, Tafeln und Statuen.
Und alle wollten ewig sein.
O, lass uns so leben,
dass wir mit einem Lachen fortgehn:
das wir hier waren, dass wir einander liebten
und dass uns nichts fehlte, wenn wir beieinander lagen.
Lass uns mit Freude erwachen auf dieser Erde,
die voll toter Völker ist und verwehter Stämme,
und streu die grossen Namen mit leichter Hand in die Luft
wie Asche.

BEING HERE

Where are the shattering horns of Nineveh,
where the armies which marched through Babylon's gates,
against what enemy?
Where are the graves of the conquerors and the conquered?
Like ships the nations pass over the seas of time—
to what destination?
To perish and leave behind as jetsam
a few broken doors, tablets, statues.
And they all wanted to go on forever.
O let us so live
that we go out laughing
to have been here, to have loved each other,
to have wanted nothing as long as we lay together.
Let us wake up with joy on this earth
which is full of dead nations and perished races.
Let's scatter the big names with a light hand into the air
like ashes.

1954

JESSE THOOR

AUS: 'REDEN UND RUFE' (1944–49)

Meine Freunde, hört:—unser Nachbar ist krank!—Ach, unser
    Nachbar!
Der ein Träumer war zur Nacht . . und wachsam bis in den Schlaf
    hinein.
Und der erzählt hat die Geschichten von der Torheit der Gerechten.
Und dass einer umgeht in uns, der auch meine Stimme vernommen
    hat.

Denn noch immer brennen die hellen Wundermale der Verwirrung
    in mir.
Und fallen die Tränen fort . . wachsen Rosen . . und lauter Anmut
    hervor.
Und die Lieder der Heimkehr, und die hohen Gesänge der Vernunft.
Und die Gespräche der Verwandlung und der fröhlichen Gemein-
    schaft.

Ach, ihr Leute . . entschuldigt meine Worte, achtet nicht meiner
    Reden.
Ihr Gebete von Madrid . . und ihr Kathedralen an den raschen
    Flüssen.
Das polnische Kreuz . . das wie die Sonne zwischen meinen Augen
    kreist.

Ach, Unbegreiflicher . . der du bist—und wie aus der Mitte der Zeit.
Und wie die Zuversicht . . und wie die Mitteilung der Ermunterung.
Und dass wieder der Grund wie Gold sei, rufen die Diener des
    Trostes.

From SPEECHES AND INVOCATIONS

Listen, my friends:—our neighbor is ill!—Oh, our neighbor!
Who was a dreamer by night and watchful even in sleep.
And who told us the stories about the follies of the just.
And that one walks about within us, who has heard my voice also.

For still the bright stigmata of confusion smart in me.
And the tears fall away . . . roses grow . . . and all manner of grace
And the songs of homecoming, and the solemn hymns of wisdom.
And the discourse of transformation and of glad community.

Ah, you people, excuse my words, do not heed my speeches.
You prayers of Madrid . . . and you cathedrals by the fast-flowing
      rivers.
The Polish Cross . . . that revolves like a sun between my eyes.

Ah, incomprehensible one . . . that you are—and as though from the
      middle of time.
And like confidence . . . and like the communication of cheer.
And that the ground is like gold once more, exclaim the servants of
      comfort.

1956

AUS: 'REDEN UND RUFE' (1944-49)

Herr Herr . . sie haben meinen Verstand zerstochen, dass ich
    schreibe:
Sie haben meinen Verstand zerstochen, die Elenden!
Herr . . die der Mord freigelassen hat!—Lausige Knechte, die
der neuen Obrigkeit ihre Dienstbarkeit beweisen, dass ich schreibe:

Rattenzüngiger Dreck, der über den Ruinen tanzt.
Der du den Verdacht des Wahnsinns in mein Gemüt niedergelegt
    hast.
Verwischt die Spuren der Einfalt und der Frömmigkeit, zerbrochen
den Hammer, der das Gold hämmert in meiner Hand, dass ich
    schreibe:

Meinen Tod habe ich erwartet mit Ungeduld . . und tagelang.
Das ich weine ohne Ursache, dass ich rede ohne Schmerz.
Der ich einhergehe . . verlegen—oder läppisch—dass ich schreibe:

Gestossen wurde ich über den Rand des Ertragens . . gehenkt
    dreimal.
Verbrannt wie Reisig . . zerrieben wie trockene Erde . .
Was soll bestehn—wenn nichts als Speichel allein uns verbindet?

From SPEECHES AND INVOCATIONS

Lord Lord . . . they have stabbed my reason, so that I write:
They have stabbed my reason, the wretched ones!
Lord . . . those whom murder let loose! Lousy lackeys who
show their servility to the new masters, so that I write:

Filth with the tongues of rats that dances over the ruins.
That have put the suspicion of madness into my mind.
Erased the traces of innocence and devotion, broken
the hammer that beats the gold in my hand, so that I write:

I have awaited my death with impatience . . . day after day.
That I weep without cause, that I speak without anguish.
I who wander about . . . embarrassed—or silly—so that I write:

I was pushed over the rim of endurance . . . three times hanged.
Burnt like dry sticks . . . ground into powder like sun-parched clay . . .
What shall remain—when nothing but spittle holds us all together?

1956

WERNER ZEMP

VORÖSTERLICHE LANDSCHAFT

So hub es an: dass wir mit jedem Schritt,
Der uns der Stadt entführte, jedem Schritt
Durchs Schattennetz der unbelaubten Bäume,
Dass zwischen emsigen Wässern, trillernden Vögeln
Wir uns verjüngten.
Beginnen, o noch einmal neu beginnen,
Wie ringsum, vor des Himmels Blumenbläue,
Mit Wäldern, leuchtenden wie rosa Marmor,
Mulden, im Dunst des silbernen Flusstals schwebend—
Die Landschaft neu beginnt: da ist kein Stein,
Darunter nicht ein Engelsfittich schliefe!

Das zweite war, dass wir in einem Kreuzgang
Auf Gräberplatten tote Namen lasen,
Wie man ein Buch liest, doch mit eins verstummten.
Denn dies war wirklich:
Dass hier, unter den nassen Kränzen,
Seit Stunden eine Tote lag,
Bei ihren Schwestern lag, wie Stein bei Stein.

Als endlich wir aus Dunkelheit und Grab
Wie Lazarus verstört ins Offene traten,
Siehe, da hatte sich der Tag verfinstert.
Wind lief vom Hügel, der smaragden grünte
Vorm Wolkenturm, und mit ihm lief ein Duft
Von jungen Knospen, und in einem Pferch
Stampfend und wiehernd toste ein schwarzes Ross.
Dies aber war das Letzte, das wir sahen,
Dieweil der irre Schrei des schönen Lebens
Stieg wie Fanfaren:

LANDSCAPE BEFORE EASTER

With this it all began: that with each step
Which led us from the city, with each step
Through nets of shadow under leafless trees,
That between busy waters, trilling birds,
Youth was restored to us.
Beginning, o beginning once again,
As round us facing heaven's blue of flower,
With woodland, shining roseate like marble,
Coombs hovering in the silver valley's haze,
The countryside begins: no stone is there
Without a wing of angel sleeping under it.

The second thing was that we read dead names
On gravestones in a cloister, as one reads
A book, but suddenly we both fell silent.
For this was real:
That here under the wet wreaths
A woman not long buried lay,
Among her sisters lay, as stone by stone.

When finally we walked from dark and grave
Disturbed like Lazarus into the open air,
Look, for by now the day had darkened.
Wind ran from the hill that mounted emerald
Fronting the towered cloud, and fragrance ran
Of fresh and tender shoots, and in a pen
A black horse stamped and whinnied in a rage.
But this, this was the last thing that we saw,
Though still the reckless cry of living's beauty
Rose like a fanfare:

Ein weisses Antlitz, durch ein Fenster spähend—
Das Letzte, ehe langsam, Stück um Stück,
Das Kloster hinterm Hügel uns versank:
Ein weisses Antlitz unter weissem Stirnband,
Ins ferne fremde Licht des Tagmonds spähend.

Out of a window peering, a white face—
The last thing seen before the convent vanished,
Little by little gone behind the hill:
A white face underneath as white a headband,
Peering at strange and distant early moonlight.

1956

WOLFGANG WEYRAUCH

EVEREST AUS TRÄNEN

Ich sehne mich nach Dir,
araberhäutige.
Aber unsere Ebene schrumpfte
unter den Heuschrecken.
Unsere Lerchen versteinerten im Flug.
Unser Lied wurde eine Lautlosigkeit.
Ein Everest aus Tränen
schwärzte unsere Himmel.
Ich sehne mich nach Dir,
dotterhaarige.
Du aber sprangst in das Delta,
wo die Rochen warten.

EVEREST OF TEARS

I long for you,
Arabian-skinned.
But our lowland shriveled
under the locust's attack.
Our larks turned to stone as they flew.
Our songs became a silence.
An Everest of tears
blackened our sky.
I long for you,
yolk-yellow-haired.
But you leapt into the delta
where the rayfish wait.

1956

ROTER STAUB

Ich ging in meinen Wald, ich war allein,
ging bis zur Mitte, bis zu meinem Stein,
den ich dorthin gewälzt hatte,
wo der Wald so stumm wie die Stummheit ist.

Dann baute ich aus Ast und Blatt ein Nest,
auch verwandte ich vertrocknete Boviste,
zusammengeschrumpfte Salamanderhüllen,
und kroch hinein, war fort, fort war die Pest
der Sekunden, Millimeter,
die Lepra der Summe der Zahlen, Buchstaben.

Ich atmete nicht mehr, war blind und taub,
merkte, wie ich sofort einunddasselbe
mit Mistkäfer und Sumpfanfang wurde;
ich lächelte. Dann war ich roter Staub.

RED DUST

I went into the woods, I was alone,
went to the center, as far as my stone
which I had rolled to that place
where the wood is mute as muteness.

Then out of branch and leaf I built a nest,
also using desiccated puffballs,
shrivelled skins of salamanders,
and crawled inside, was gone, gone was the pest
of seconds and of millimeters,
the leprosy of the sum of numbers, letters.

I ceased to breathe, grew deaf and blind,
noticed how immediately I became
one with dung-beetles, bogland, one and the same;
I smiled. And then I was red dust.

1956

GÜNTER EICH

DENKE DARAN . . .

Denke daran, dass der Mensch des Menschen Feind ist
Und dass er sinnt auf Vernichtung.
Denke daran immer, denke daran jetzt,
Während eines Augenblicks im April,
Unter diesem verhangenen Himmel,
Während du das Wachstum als ein feines Knistern zu hören glaubst,
Die Mägde Disteln stechen
Unter dem Lerchenlied,
Auch in diesem Augenblick denke daran!

Während du den Wein schmeckst in den Kellern von Randersacker
Oder Orangen pflückst in den Gärten von Alicante,
Während du einschläfst im Hotel Miramar nahe dem Strand von
    Taormina,
Oder am Allerseelentage eine Kerze entzündest auf den Friedhof
    in Feuchtwangen,
Während du als Fischer das Netz aufholst über der Doggerbank,
Oder in Detroit eine Schraube vom Fliessband nimmst,
Während du Pflanzen setzst in den Reis-Terrassen von Szetschuan,
Auf dem Maultier über die Anden reitest,—
Denke daran!

Denke daran, wenn eine Hand dich zärtlich berührt,
Denke daran in der Umarmung deiner Frau,
Denke daran beim Lachen deines Kindes!

Denke daran, dass nach den grossen Zerstörungen
Jedermann beweisen wird, dass er unschuldig war.

THINK OF THIS

Think of this, that man is the enemy of man
And that he meditates on destruction.
Think of this always, think of this now
During this moment in April,
Beneath a foreboding sky;
While you believe you are listening to growth like a gentle rustling,
And girls are cutting thistles
Under the skylark's song;
Even in this moment, think of this!

While you taste wine in the cellars of Randersacker
Or pick oranges in the gardens of Alicante,
While you fall alseep in the Miramar Hotel near the beach of
      Taormina,
Or light a candle on All Souls' Day in the churchyard in Feucht-
      wangen,
While you, a fisherman, haul up the net over the Dogger Bank,
Or in Detroit take a screw from the conveyor belt,
While you lay plants in the rice groves of Setzuan,
Or ride a mule across the Andes—
Think of this!

Think of this, when a hand touches you tenderly,
Think of this in the embrace of your wife,
Think of this when you hear the laughter of your own child.

Think of this, that after the great destructions
Everyone will prove that he was innocent.

Denke daran:
Nirgendwo auf der Landkarte liegt Korea und Bikini,
Aber in deinem Herzen.
Denke daran, dass du schuld bist an allem Entsetzlichen
Das sich fern von dir abspielt—

BOTSCHAFTEN DES REGENS

Nachrichten, die für mich bestimmt sind,
weitergetrommelt von Regen zu Regen,
von Schiefer- zu Ziegeldach,
eingeschleppt wie eine Krankheit,
Schmuggelgut, dem überbracht,
der es nicht haben will—

Jenseits der Wand schallt das Fensterblech,
rasselnde Buchstaben, die sich zusammenfügen,
und der Regen redet
in der Sprache, von welcher ich glaubte,
niemand kenne sie ausser mir—

Bestürzt vernehme ich
die Botschaften der Verzweiflung,
die Botschaften der Armut
und die Botschaften des Vorwurfs.
Es kränkt mich, dass sie an mich gerichtet sind,
denn ich fühle mich ohne Schuld.

Ich spreche es laut aus,
dass ich den Regen nicht fürchte und seine Anklagen
und den nicht, der sie mir zuschickte,
dass ich zu guter Stunde
hinausgehen und ihm antworten will.

Think of this:
Nowhere on the map lies Korea and Bikini,
But in your own heart.
Think of this, that you are responsible for every atrocity
Enacted far from you.

1955

MESSAGES OF THE RAIN

News intended for me,
drummed out from rain to rain,
from slate roof to tiled roof,
introduced like an illness,
contraband, delivered to him
who has no wish to receive it.

Beyond the wall my metal window-sill clamors,
pattering letters link up
and the rain speaks
in that language which once I believed
none but I could decipher—

Disconcerted now I hear
the messages of despair,
the messages of poverty
and the messages of reproach.
It hurts me to think they're addressed to me,
feeling guiltless of any offense.

And I say out loud
that I do not fear the rain or its accusations,
nor him who sent them to me;
and that all in good time
I will go out and give him my answer.

1955

TAUBEN

Taubenflug über die Äcker hin,—
ein Flügelschlag, der schneller ist als die Schönheit.
Sie holt ihn nicht ein, sondern bleibt mir
als Unbehagen zurück im Herzen.

Als wäre auch Taubengelächter vernehmbar
vor den Schlägen, den grün gestrichenen Zwerghäusern,
und ich beginne nachzudenken,
ob der Flug ihnen wichtig ist,
welchen Rang die Blicke zum Erdboden haben
und wie sie das Aufpicken des Korns einordnen
und das Erkennen des Habichts.

Ich rate mir selbst, mich vor den Tauben zu fürchten.
Du bist nicht ihr Herr, sage ich, wenn du Futter streust,
wenn du Nachrichten an ihre Federn heftest,
wenn du Zierformen züchtest, neue Farben,
neue Schöpfe, Gefieder am Fuss.
Vertrau deiner Macht nicht,
so wirst du auch nicht verwundert sein,
wenn du erfährst, dass du unwichtig bist,

dass neben deinesgleichen heimliche Königreiche bestehen,
Sprachen ohne Laut, die nicht erforscht werden,
Herrschaften ohne Macht und unangreifbar,
dass die Entscheidungen geschehen im Taubenflug.

PIGEONS

Flight of pigeons over the ploughed fields—
a wingbeat more swift than beauty
that cannot catch up with such speed
but remains in my heart as discomfort.

As if the laughter of pigeons too could be heard
in front of the dovecotes, dwarf dwellings painted green,
and I begin to consider
whether flight is important to them,
what rank they accord to the earthward glance
and how they value the pecking of grain,
how the recognition of hawks.

I advise myself to be afraid of pigeons.
You are not the master, I say, when you throw them food,
when you fasten messages to their legs,
when you breed curious variants, new colors,
new crests, or tufts of feathers above the feet.
Put no trust in your power,
then you'll not be astonished
when you discover how little you count,

that beside your kind there are hidden kingdoms,
languages without sounds that cannot be studied,
dominions without power and unassailable;
that decisions are made by the pigeons' flight.

1955

FRANZ BAERMANN STEINER

8. MAI 1945

Hastig ist der vogelflug. weh, was jemals sich heben wollte,
Hat der steine gewicht,
Die unter der erde dauern, verkittet mit leibern und jahren der
liebe.

Bürger begruben ihren ruchlos verzärtelten krieg.
Mohnblumen blühen aus bier.
Girlanden schnüren die leiber fiebernder häuser.

Die nassen fahnen tropfen in schwüle festluft.
Hinter dem trommelwirbel
Zickzackt ein eisläufer über gefrorenen blutsee.

ELEFANTENFANG

Die zahmen tiere drohten schweigend,
Köpfe gesenkt vor schwarzem meer,
Das rastlos mahlte in der friedung,
Gellte, schnob.

Doch als die wildlinge, bemeistert
Von hungertagen und verschnürter welt,
Nicht kraft mehr fanden, alte angst verstanden,
Liess man die zahmen zu.

Die schlugen ein mit rüsseln und mit zähnen.
Erbarmungslos der wohlgenährten hass
Dem waldruch galt, dem fernherkommen:
Strafte mit lust.

8th MAY 1945

Hasty is the flight of birds. Woe, all that was ever ready to soar
Has the weight of stones
That endure under the earth, cemented with the bodies and years
   of love.

People have buried their wickedly pampered war.
Poppies bloom out of beer.
Paper-chains lace up the bodies of feverish houses.

The wet flags drip into sultry, festive air.
Behind the roll of drums
A skater zigzags over a frozen lake of blood.

[1945, 2nd version 1947]

CAPTURING ELEPHANTS

The tame beasts menaced silently,
Their heads they bowed to the black sea
That churned and churned in the pen,
Trumpeting, shrill.

But when these wild ones, mastered now
By days of hunger in a world strung up
Had no more strength, knew ancient fear,
The tame ones went to them.

With trunk and tusk these stove the wild ones in.
Fat bodies' hatred, without pity aimed
Against the jungle smell and foreign kind,
Wreaked glad revenge.

So schlachten sie die eigne, kleine wildheit
Im bruderleibe mal um mal,
Aber die blutenden, fast zahm geschreckten
Klagten nicht an.

KAFKA IN ENGLAND

Weder via Belsen, noch als dienstmädchen
Kam der fremde, keineswegs ein flüchtling.
Dennoch wars ein trauriger fall:
Die nationalität war strittig,
Die religion umlispelte peinlichkeit.

,,Haben sie Kafka gelesen?'' fragt Mrs Brittle beim frühstück,
,,er ist recht unausweichlich und ziemlich fundamental!''
,,haben sie Kafka gelesen?'' fragt Mr Tooslick beim tee.
,,man versteht dann die welt viel besser—
Doch freilich ist nichts real.''
Miss Diggs sagt: ,,aber wirklich?
Ist das nicht reaktionär?''
Nur der kleine Geoffrey Piltzman
Träumt: ,,wer?

Ich meine, wer daran verdient,
Sie müssen doch tot sein,
Ich mein die leute in Prag—nun, wer auch immer . . .''
Doch aus dem tor bricht trotzdem der schimmer . . .

They slaughter so their own small savageness
In brother-bodies, one by one.
But these, all bleeding and near-tamed by terror,
Did not complain.

[1942]

KAFKA IN ENGLAND

Neither via Belsen, nor as a maid of all work
The stranger came, by no means a refugee.
And yet the case was a sad one:
His nationality was in doubt,
His religion occasioned lisping embarrassment.

"Have you read Kafka?" asks Mrs Brittle at breakfast.
"He's rather inescapable and quite fundamental, I feel".
"Have you read Kafka?" asks Mr Tooslick at tea,
"Then you'll understand the world much better—
Though nothing in him is real".
Miss Diggs says: "Is that so?
I thought that was reactionary. Don't you?"
Only little Geoffrey Piltzman
Dreams: "Who?

"I mean, who does well out of this,
They must be dead, after all,
I mean those people in Prague—well, no matter what name..."
Yet the glory of him shines through the gateway all the same.

[1946, 2nd version 1952]

RUDOLF HAGELSTANGE

ARAN

Aus dem Chaos gebrochen,
der erste Wurf von der Hand
des schaffenden Gottes:
ARAN.

Wurzellos stehst du
auf geschichtetem Fels.
Wirf deinen Namen über den Absturz
vierhundert Fuss in die Tiefe!
Meer—ist ein Name für Namenloses,
ein bitterer Schluck aus der Flut
unseres Ungenügens. Du möchtest
den kleinen Vogel Hoffnung
auf die Schwinge des Adlers setzen,
die, hoch oben, reglos sich spannt?—
Du bist nicht mehr
als der flüchtige Schatten der Möwe
über die salzgefurchte
westwärts gewendete Stirne der Insel ...

Hassen und Lieben, Schuld und Ruhm—
eine Handvoll Staub,
für eine Stunde im Lichte geduldet.

Denke an Aufbruch ...

ARAN

Quarried from chaos,
the first rough image carved
by the Creator's hand:
Aran.

Rootless you stand
on the many-layered rock.
Cast your name over the sheer drop,
four hundred feet to fall!
Sea—is the name for the nameless,
a bitter draught from the flood
of our insufficiency. So you'd like
to set the small bird hope
upon the eagle's pinions
stretching motionless high above?—
You are no more
than the passing seagull's shadow
above the salt-furrowed
western brow of the island . . .

Hatred and love, guilt and fame—
a handful of dust
held for an hour in the tolerant light.

Think of departure . . .

1953

MEMENTO

An den Wassern Babylons
Haben wir nicht gesessen.
Aber keines Klagetons
Schwingung sei uns vergessen.

Vor den Mauern Jerichos
Haben wir nicht geblasen.
Aber der stürzenden Mauern Stoss
Schreckt uns noch unterm Rasen.

In den Tempeln Jerusalems
Haben wir nicht gebetet.
Doch mit dem Blute Seths und Sems
Ist unser tägliches Brot geknetet.

MEMENTO

By the waters of Babylon
We did not sit and weep.
But the pulse of the plaint lifted there
Let us keep—let us keep.

We did not blow the blast before Jericho
Made walls sunder and spill.
But even under the turf those walls tumbling
Appal us still.

Not by us in Jerusalem's temple
Was one prayer said.
Yet the blood of Seth and of Shem is kneaded
Into our daily bread.

1953

HANS EGON HOLTHUSEN

MEIN LEBEN, MEIN TOD

Geboren hat mich ein zwanzigjähriges Mädchen,
Die trug eine Bluse mit Fischbeinkragen und Brüsseler Spitzen.
Weisst du das bräunliche Foto, das schwankende Lächeln,
Frühreifes Glück und kleine, unsichere Trauer:
Ein Leib und eine Zeit, umnachtet von Ewigkeit,
In der wir nicht sind und niemand auf Erden uns sieht.
Hier bin ich: zwischen Ungeboren und Nimmermehr
Liegt eine Spanne Schmerz, Fleisch, Lust und Schuld,
Der unbegreifliche Zwischenfall meines Lebens.

Ich bin über knisternde Treppen geschlichen,
Ich habe mit Frauen zusammengelegen,
Als es Fasching war und Mitternacht war schon vorüber,
Matrose und Colombine.
Meine Hand war unter dem Nacken der Freundin,
Das war in der Heide, und hoch stand die Sonne und schwarz der
    Wacholder.
Warum muss man sie alle verlassen, von Abschied zu Abschied
Durch labyrinthische Jahre? Da bleibt eine feine
Blutspur hinter dem Fuss. Aber man sieht sich nicht um . . .
O du schwarzer Wacholder, dunkler Schatten des Glücks!
Ewiger Doppelgänger der Liebe: Tod.

Ein Schoss ist tiefer als das Meer,
Matrose und Colombine.
Die Lust ist Ewigkeiten schwer,
Matrose und Colombine.

MY LIFE, MY DEATH

Born I was of a girl of twenty
Who wore a blouse with a whalebone collar and Brussels lace.
Remember that brownish photo, the wavering smile,
Precocious bliss and slight, uncertain sadness:
A time, a body, shrouded in night of eternity
In which we are not and are seen by no-one on earth.
Here I am: between unborn and nevermore
Lies a span of pain, flesh, lust and guilt,
The incomprehensible incident of my life.

I have sneaked over creaking stairs,
I have lain together with women
At carnival time, and midnight was already past,
Sailor and Columbine.
My hand beneath the nape of the girl's neck,
That was on the heath, and the sun stood high, and black the juniper
        tree.
Why must one leave them all, move from parting to parting
Through labyrinthine years? There remains a fine
Trail of blood behind the foot. But one does not turn . . .
O black juniper tree, dark shadow of happiness!
Ever the echo of love: death.

The womb is deeper than the sea,
Sailor and Columbine.
Lust heavy with eternity,
Sailor and Columbine.

Zum Grunde hin, vom Grunde her,
Das ist der Toten Wiederkehr,
Matrose und Colombine.
Ach Erde, wir vergessen dich nicht
Mit Mann und Weib und Wind und Licht,
Matrose und Colombine.

Das Sterben wird sein voller Angst und Gewalt:
Ein Schuss ins Genick, ein Autounfall, ein böses Geschwür,
Ein übermenschliches Knie auf der Brust. Man wird uns mit
     Strenge
Würgen und abtun, ungeduldig und unter der Hand,
Wie man in Terrorkellern Gefangne erschiesst.
Die Seele will nicht, will nicht! Irdischer Eigensinn
Klammert sich noch an die Welt. All das Verworrene,
Aufgehäufte, Verknotete, alles in Hoffnung und Ohnmacht
Ratlos Verstrickte, es will sich noch immer nicht lösen.
Niemals hat sie verstanden, was alles bedeuten soll,
Alles ist immer zu schnell gegangen, und niemals,
Niemals hat sie geliebt, und wann hat sie jemals erkannt?
Immer drängte die Zeit, drängten die Umstände, immer
Fehlte der Atem, die Freiheit, das alles zu sagen,
Was zu sagen nicht war. Am Ende schwieg man mit Toten.
So werden wir töricht, das Gesicht nach unten,
Zu all den andern in die offene Erde geworfen
Und sanfter auf den Grund des Seins gelegt.
Ist es denn wahr, was uns die andern sagen,
Dass wir hier wirklicher sind als oben im Licht?

Towards the depths and free from the depths,
That is the return of the dead,
Sailor and Columbine.
O earth, remembered always
With men and women, wind and light,
Sailor and Columbine.

Death will be violent and full of fear:
A shot in the neck, a car accident, a malignant growth,
A knee, superhuman, upon the chest. Implacably
They will strangle us, kill us, impatiently, secretly,
As one shoots prisoners in underground cellars of terror.
The soul is unwilling, unwilling! Earthly stubbornness
Clings yet to the world. All that is confused,
Amassed, entangled, caught up perplexedly
In hope and impotence, still it will not unravel.
The soul at no time understood all the meaning of it,
Everything always went too quickly, and never
Did the soul love, or really know.
Time, circumstances, were always pressing, breath,
Freedom was always lacking to say all
That could not be said. In the end
Silence was kept with the dead.
Thus foolishly we are thrown, face downward,
Where the others are, into the gaping earth,
And laid more gently on the ground of being.
Can it be true, what the others tell us,
That we are more real here than there above in the light?

1952

ABSCHIEDSBRIEF

(Entwurf aus den nachgelassenen Papieren eines Selbstmörders)

Ich will dieses ganze ekelhafte Gebräu
Aus salzigen Suppen und einigen süssen Likören,
Dieses aus Missverständnissen, Vorläufigkeiten
Und unbestimmten Auskünften peinlich Gemischte,
Dieses verwirrte Herumstehn, sinnlos, dieses
Törichte Buchstabieren am falschen Fahrplan,
Als wäre der Bahnhof verhext und ringsum wäre
Ein ganzer Maskenverleih von schiefen Visagen
An Pfosten aufgehängt, und diese gemeine
Verstrickung in klobige Hindernisse und zwanzig
Abgedroschne Motive, man meinte, das sei
Ein Schicksal—nein, ich halt das nicht mehr aus.
Ich will mich bescheiden. Ich will den Abstand, ich lehne
Mich ab. Ich will nach so viel Zweifel und Zwielicht
Den reinen Schmerz, das glatte Resultat.
Ich will ein Nein, so klar und wasserhell
Wie neunzigprozentiger Wodka. Ich will wissen,
Was man noch tun kann. Ich will endlich wissen,
Was man noch tun kann, nur für sich.

Gewiss, das gab es, ein paar verzehrende Nächte:
Schwellung und Andrang, ein Schluchzen, Saugen und Schmelzen,
Oh paradiesisch . . . Es gab diese föhnigen Himmel,
Weiss, blau, resedengrün, und silbrige Seen,
Föhn und Musik, es gab die mäandernde Lust,
Die wie mit Bienenrüsseln am schwärmenden Herzen
Schlürft, und wir konnten nicht enden, wir liebten
Gifte: Kola und Mohn, Nikotin, Belladonna,
Oder wir tranken.

LAST LETTER
(Rough Draft Found Among a Suicide's Papers)

I want—this whole revolting brew
Of salty soups and a few sweet liqueurs,
This embarrassing mixture of misunderstandings,
Uncertain information, temporary solutions,
This senseless, confused hanging around, these foolish
Attempts at spelling out the wrong time-table, as if
The station were bewitched, and all around a mass
Of hired out masks of crooked faces
Strung up on posts, and this vulgar
Entanglement in clumsy obstacles and twenty
Hackneyed motives, one imagined that was
Destiny—no, I can't stand it any more.
I will be modest. I want distance. I
Reject myself. After so much doubt and obscurity
I want the pure pain, the blunt result,
I want a No, as clear and translucent
As vodka, ninety percent proof. I want to know
What one can still do. I want to know at last
What one can still do for oneself, only for oneself.

True, they existed, those few consuming nights,
A rush of blood welling up, a sobbing, sucking and melting,
O paradisal. They existed, those windy warm skies,
White, blue, reseda-green, and silvery lakes,
Warm southerly winds and music, meandering lust,
Sucking as with bees' tongues at the doting
Heart, and we could not stop, we loved
Poisons: cola and poppy, nicotine, belladonna,
Or we drank.

Das ist vorbei. Und nun kein Lieben mehr,
Nicht mehr dies bittre Hingehalten werden
Ein Leben lang, von zweien oder dreien,
Die qual- und liebevoll zusammenhängen
An einem Ort, der weder Trennung noch
Vereinigung erlaubt, nur immer Worte,
Die blind das hoffnunglose Bett umkreisen
Und Pfeffer in entzündete Wunden streun,
Denn einer war immer das Schwert in der Brust des andern.

Ich muss etwas zerstören. Ist es vielleicht
Die dunkle Witterung zwischen mir und Gott?
Oh dieser schreckliche Provokateur und Erpresser,
Der immer Neues herauslockt, immer noch feinere,
Immer gewagtere Flötentöne der Hoffnung
Aus der gedrosselten Kehle. Ich will ihn nicht festlegen
Auf Gleichmut, Zorn oder Gnade. Ich erwarte
Nur Kälte, Kälte, unerforschte Arktis,
Nur strenge, weisse Unzugänglichkeit.
Er wird zu seinen Füssen ein wenig Blutschaum
Finden: meine Seele. Ich bin nicht sicher,
Ob er den kleinen, ganz verzweifelten Farbfleck
Beachten wird.

Ein Körper bleibt zurück. Aber die leidende
Unruhe hat ihn verlassen, und dieses Herz
Ist nur noch toter Muskel: welch ein Fortschritt!
Es bleibt ein Rest von Zeit, der mir den Weg
Ins Freie noch drei Tage lang blockiert,
Und Freunde, denen man ein Bündel bleiches
Entsetzen in einem abgetragenen Anzug
Nachts in die Küche warf: ein kleiner Halbkreis
Betretener Männer, vielleicht auch einige Frauen,
Schluchzend, flüsternd, verworren. Nun hab ich endlich den
     Abstand,

That is over. No more loving now,
No longer this bitter being put off, kept on,
A whole life through, by two and three
Who hang together, in love and torment,
In a place which does not permit separation
Or union, only words, words,
Which blindly encircle the hopeless bed
And dash pepper into inflamed wounds
For one was ever the sword in the breast of the other.

I must destroy something. Is it perhaps this somber
Atmosphere between me and God?
O this terrible provocateur and extortioner,
Always drawing out something new, ever finer,
Ever more daring flute-like tones of hope
From the strangled throat. I won't tie him down
To wrath, indifference or mercy. I only expect
Coldness, coldness, unexplored arctic,
Inaccessibleness, severe and white.
At his feet he will find a little froth of blood:
My soul. I am uncertain
If he will notice that small and quite despairing
Speck of color.

A body remains. But the painful
Disquiet has left it, and this heart
Is nothing but dead muscle now: what progress!
There is a remainder of time, which for three days
Still blocks my way into the open,
And friends, into whose kitchen in the night
They threw a bundle of pale horror
In a worn suit: a small semicircle
Of disconcerted men, perhaps some women too,
Sobbing, whispering, confused. Now at last I have that distance,

Und meine Hand, die trocken vom Bettrand herabhängt,
Weiss, pulslos, trocken, wenn der Todesschweiss
Verdunstet ist, sie gibt das erste und letzte
Wahrhaft gebieterische Zeichen: ich habe nun
Die Welt gelöscht und Sein und Nichts vertauscht,
Ich habe die Zeit in Ewigkeit ertränkt.

And my hand, which hangs open from the bed's side
White, dry and pulseless, after the sweat of death
Has evaporated, gives the first and last
Truly commanding sign: I have extinguished
The world, exchanged being for nothingness,
I have drowned time in eternity.

1952

KARL KROLOW

LIEBESGEDICHT

Auf der linken oder rechten Seite liegen gilt gleich,
Eine Melone zerschneiden oder das Wasser im Glas
Leuchten lassen. Die Anmut der Kerze
Dahinter: belanglos wie schwebende Luft
In der Nacht ohne dich.

Als Nachmittag war, liess vor dem Fenster der Pfau sich
Wie ein schattiger Blumenstrauss nieder.
Du hieltest in der 6-Uhr-Sonne deinen Löffel
Über einen Teller durchscheinender Himbeeren.
Nun dulde das Dunkel ich,
Diese Nacht, die du nicht gemacht hast,
Mit zäher, schwarzer Tusche ausgezogen,
Mit dem Geschmack von Tränen im Mund
Und scharfem Wind in den Blumen.

Hinter dem von Schwärze rissigen Ziegel
Wird die Zikade still, und ich habe
Das Aroma der Einsamkeit zu schmecken bekommen am Tisch
Zwischen Schweigen und Schweigen
In der Nacht ohne dich.

Auf der linken oder rechten Seite liegen gilt gleich
In der Umarmung der Stille, wenn die Armbanduhr leicht
Die Zeit zählt, das Mundstück der Zigarette verascht . . .
Mit dem Finger durchstreich' ich das Jenseits,
In dem ich noch eben gelebt,
Ohne rotes Halstuch und braune Schuhe,
In der Nacht ohne dich:

Ich hör' unter Sternen dich atmen!

LOVE POEM

It is the same if I lie on the left or the right side,
Cut a melon, or let the water
Shine in the glass, the candle's grace
Behind it: meaningless this as floating air
In the night without you.

Outside my window, a peacock alighted
In the afternoon, like a shadowy bouquet of flowers.
You held your spoon in the six o'clock sun
Over your plate of translucent raspberries.
Now I endure the dark,
This night not made by you,
With black and viscous color coated over,
With the taste of tears in the mouth
And sharp wind in the flowers.

Behind the tile cracked with blackness
The cicada stops, and I have had
The flavor of loneliness to taste at table,
Between silence and silence
In the night without you.

It is the same if I lie on the left or the right side
In the embrace of silence, when the wristwatch
Lightly counts time, and the end of the cigarette turns to ash ...
My finger gently moves through the beyond
Where I lived even now,
Without red kerchief and brown shoes,
In the night without you:

I hear you breathing under stars!

1952

DU GINGST FORT . . .

> „Und ich liebe des Zimmers Wände,
> Die ich bemale mit deinem Knabenantlitz."
> (Else Lasker-Schüler)

Du gingst fort. Du wirst fortgehen immer,
Wenn der Tag graue Tauben ans Herz nimmt
Und die Dämmerung ihr Tuch über uns wirft.

Die Nacht kommt mit gefärbten Haaren und dem Geruch von
    Mandelkern.
Mond steht in den von Minze parfümierten Stoppeln
Und früher Tau fällt auf Flüsse, in denen die Aale wachsen.

Du gingst fort. Schwarz wurde das Blau in den Flöten des Enzian.
Zurück blieben das Zimmer und das Grün einer Cordjacke überm
    wollenen Rock,
Abwesende Blicke, die wie neugierige Mücken waren.

Die Wände: tapeziert mit Unruhe und der Bronze eines Nackens!
Du gingst fort. Und ich liebe des Zimmers Wände,
Die ich bemale mit deinem Knabenantlitz . . .

SCHATTEN IN DER LUFT

Schatten in der Luft: Gespenster
Aus blauer Uniform wie grosse Schmetterlinge.

Die Träume sind gekleidet mit Verdacht:
Prähistorische Faune,
Die nüchtern wurden an der Gegenwart
Der luftigen Ereignisse.

Schatten von oben: wenig sicher wie
Montagsgedanken; und der Sonntag war
Voll Vogelfedern, heller Mädchenhandschuh.

YOU WENT AWAY

You went away. You will always go
When day takes gray doves to his heart
And dusk covers us with her great shawl.

Night comes with tinted hair and a scent of almonds.
Moon shines on mint-perfumed stubble
And early dew falls on streams where eels grow.

You went away. Blue turned to black in the gentian's trumpet.
The room remained, the green of a cord jacket over a woolen skirt,
Glances, absent-minded, like curious mosquitos.

The walls, papered with unrest and a bronzed neck!
You went away: and I love the walls of this room
Which I paint with your boylike face.

1952

SHADOWS IN THE AIR

Shadows in the air: such phantoms,
Uniform blue like giant butterflies.

All dreams come clothed in doubt:
Prehistoric fauns
Grown suddenly sober in the presence
Of such airy happenings.

Shadows from above: not very confident,
Like Monday thoughts; and Sunday
Was full of bird-plumage, a girl's bright glove.

Das sanfte Wasser Himmel: einmal badeten
In ihm geschloss'ne Augen, viele Blätter.
Nun aber
Ist Kälte da, Geruch
Von Einsamkeit. Kein Goldfisch schwimmt
Im Glas des Mittags mehr.

Luft voller Schatten! Und der Marmor
Vergangenen Fleisches fröstelt.
Eine schwarze Fahne
—Schlaf ohne Traum—
Entrollt sich und fliesst langsam über Schultern.

The sky's calm water: once
Closed eyes bathed in it, and many leaves.
But now
The cold is come, the odor
Of solitude. No goldfish swim
In noon's glass any longer.

Air full of shadows! And the marble
Of gone flesh shivers.
A black banner
—a dreamless sleep—
unfolds and slowly flows over shoulders.

1954

CHRISTINE LAVANT

DASS DU NICHT GRÖSSER ALS EIN SPERLINGSHAUPT

Dass du nicht grösser als ein Sperlingshaupt
am Himmel aufkommst, Sonne, Sonne, Sonne!
Und eh der Kuckuck dreimal hat geschrien
soll sich der Regen wieder um dich schliessen.
Wir mögen nicht mehr nach dem Blauen sehn,—
mein Bruder da, die wilde Hundezwiebel,
er blühte blau und niemand trug ihn heim
um sich zu trösten hinterm Rand des Sommers.
Und was ist Sterngold wenn Johanniskraut
des öden Bahndamms Bitternis nie einholt
und keins der neuen Mädchen darin hinkniet
um nach des Liebsten Liebe bang zu fragen?
Was nützt es noch, wie Mohn gekrönt zu sein
wenn man des Schlafes Wunder anders fristet
und Träume anstarrt wie ein Nachtgesicht
bis sie sich flüchten ins Gefühl der Irren?
Dort ruht schon viel. Auch mein Gefühl ist voll
und schreit aus mir im Ton des Regenrufers:
„Dass du nicht grösser als ein Sperlingshaupt
am Himmel aufkommst, Sonne, Sonne, Sonne!"

DON'T DARE BE LARGER THAN A
SPARROW'S HEAD

Don't dare be larger than a sparrow's head
as you rise in the sky, o sun, sun, sun!
And ere the cuckoo has called out three times
the rain must close around you once again.
We now no longer want to see the blue—
my little brother, the wild dog's-tongue, bore
so blue a flower, yet no girl took it home
to comfort her, behind the rim of summer.
What use is star-gold, when the golden gorse
can never overtake the arid rail track,
and none of the new maidens kneels in it,
to ask whether her lover truly loves her?
What use still to be crowned as poppies are,
when one must spend the wonder-spell of sleep
staring the dreams away, like nightmare visions,
till they escape into the minds of madmen,
where so much rests. My mind is crowded too,
I feel it crying, on the rain-bird's note:
"Don't dare be larger than a sparrow's head
As you rise in the sky, o sun, sun, sun!"

1956

JESUS CHRISTUS, ICH BETE UND BETE

Jesus Christus, ich bete und bete,
aber ich weiss, dass du abwarten musst
die Zeit meiner eigenen Heilung.
Jetzt liegt mir ja Gift im Blut herum
und mein Herz ist eine offene Falle,
auch meine Gedanken, wenn sie nicht beten,
sind schlaue grausame Schlingen.
So wie ich bin, kann ich nicht verlangen,
dass du jetzt eingehst unter mein Dach,
denn selbst meine eigene Mutter würde
kaum noch bei mir übernachten.
Ich glaub nicht, dass ich mich reinigen kann,
ich finde in mir kein Bröselchen Würde,
und die Demut, wenn sie mich überkommt,
wird süchtig von allen Giften.
Auch ist mein Herz so nach Liebe aus,
nach der einfachen, wärmenden Menschenliebe,
von der es meint, dass sie heilig macht
und den Zustand des Himmels bereitet.
Deshalb, Herr Christus, ist mein Gebet
vielleicht ein Köder, der gar nicht dich meint,
obwohl ich an deine Herrlichkeit glaube,
obwohl ich täglich schöner dich schaue
mit meinen unwürdigen Augen.

JESUS CHRIST, I PRAY WITH ALL MY MIGHT

Jesus Christ, I pray with all my might,
but I know that you have to wait
for the time when I myself am healed,
now poison lies round in my blood
my heart has become a trap, set and open,
and my very thoughts, when they cease to be prayers,
have turned into snares, crafty and cruel.
Such as I am, I cannot expect
to receive you under my roof,
for even my own mother might now refuse
to spend the night in my house.
I don't think I can purify myself,
I have not a crumb of dignity left,
and humility, when it comes over me,
is addicted to all poisons.
Besides, my heart is greedy for love,
for that uncomplicated, warming human love,
which, so it believes, sanctifies us
and prepares the conditions of Heaven.
Therefore, Lord Christ, my prayer might be
only a bait, not meant for you at all,
though I believe in your might and glory
and each day your splendor increases
in the sight of my unworthy eyes.

1956

CHRISTINE BUSTA

SCHNEE IM ADVENT

Leiser wird nichts verkündigt:
      so reden Liebende nachts,
die fern voneinander schlafen,
         und finden am Morgen die fremde
Erde wieder als Nest
        voll von himmlischem Flaum.

SNOW AT ADVENT

Nothing's announced more softly;
        so lovers converse in the night,
then sleep remote from each other
        and waking at daybreak discover
the strange earth changed to a nest
        full of heavenly down.

1955

HANS WERNER COHN

DER SKLAVE

Keuchend und krumm
kriecht er durchs Rohrwerk der Blutgefässe
beklopft mit krampfigen Fingern die weichen Wände
sucht nach schadhaften Stellen.
Dann wieder entziffert sein heisses Ohr
Nachrichten von entlegenen Zentren
Die ihn auf bebenden Nervenbahnen erreichen.
Angst schnürt ihm die Kehle
bedenkt er das riesige Netz, die vielen Verzweigungen
und Knotenpunkte, die Hierarchie der Organe
vom unnahbaren Gehirn zum aufdringlichen Geschlecht,
bedenkt er die möglichen Fehlerquellen
und Störungsherde Versäumnisse Widerstände
die katzenpfötige Zerrüttung, das tückische Chaos.

So hockt er in seinem Körper und lauscht
und spürt nicht der Sonne Hand auf der Haut
und sieht nicht des Himmels deutende Zeichen
und hört nicht des Nachbarn Ruf übern Zaun.

Im Bauche des Schiffs das ihm nicht mehr gehört
dessen Kurs er nicht kennt
hockt er und lauscht und berechnet und prüft:
die Fahrt ist gefährdet
Bewegung ist Wagnis
denn das Meer ist furchtbar.

Er kann es freilich nicht sehen hier unten
in seines Daseins Eingeweiden.

THE SLAVE

Gasping and bent
he crawls through the conduits of blood vessels
knocks with crooked fingers on soft walls
looks for defects.
Then again his hot ear decodes
messages from distant centers
that reach him on quivering nerve routes.
Fear stifles him
if he thinks of the giant skein, the many branchings
and nodal points, the hierarchy of organs
from the unapproachable brain to the importunate sex,
if he thinks of the possible sources of error
the roots of trouble failures blockages
cat-pawed dislocation, insidious chaos.

So he squats in his body and listens
and does not feel the sun's hand on his skin
and does not see the sky's interpreting signs
and does not hear his neighbor shout over the fence.

In the belly of the ship that has ceased to be his
whose course he does not know
he squats and listens and calculates and tests:
the journey is jeopardized
to move is much risk
for the sea is terrible.

Of course he cannot see it down here
in the intestines of his existence.

[1959]

VOM MANNE DER IM KELLER SITZT

Der Mann sitzt im Keller
und bleicht dahin:
ein Kartoffelsprössling im Winkel.
Seine Hände hängen schlaff über die Knie'
seinen Kopf verschlingen die Schultern.

Manchmal kommt
die Frau in den Keller
und kämmt sein Haar
und wäscht seine Ohren
und zieht ihn am Arm
wie an einer Leine
in die gute Stube:
da sitzen die Freundinnen um den Tisch.
Sie sagen: wie hübsch! und auch: wie gescheit!
Denn bei Licht sieht er garnicht so übel aus,
der Mann,
und Gedanken wuchern
in der Kellerluft
und nun kramt er sie aus vor den Freundinnen,
der Mann.
Am Ende der Vorstellung zieht die Frau den Mann
in den Keller zurück.

Das ist ihre Stunde.
Zwar: er freut sich darauf
denn ein wenig Licht
dringt durch den Samt
der Vorhänge
in der guten Stube.
Doch: es ist ihre Stunde.

OF THE MAN WHO SITS IN THE CELLAR

The man sits in the cellar
and he wilts:
a potato sprout in the corner.
His hands hang limp over his knees
his shoulders swallow his head.

Sometimes the woman
comes into the cellar
and combs his hair
and cleans his ears
and pulls him by the arm
as on a lead
into the best room:
there her lady friends sit round the table.
They say: how nice! they say: how clever!
For in the light he does not look at all bad,
the man,
and thoughts thrive
in the cellar air
and now he trundles them out for the lady friends,
the man.
The performance over, the woman pulls the man
back into the cellar.

It is her moment.
True: he looks forward to it
for a little light
pierces the velvet
of the curtains
in the best room.
Yet: it is her moment.

Seine Stunde kommt
seine Stunde kommt
in der Nacht.
Die Frau liegt im Bett
doch der Mann ist wach.
Seine Stunde kommt.
Sein Kopf schiesst zwischen
den Schultern hervor
und stösst an die Decke
rot und wild
im Herztakt.
Die Hände straffen sich
rot und wild
und schlagen im Herztakt
an die Kellertür.

Die Frau liegt im Bett
gebadet in Angst
in Angst.

His moment comes
his moment comes
at night.
The woman lies in bed
but the man is awake.
His moment comes.
His head thrusts up
between the shoulders
and thumps on the ceiling
savage and red
in heart beat.
The hands clench
savage and red
and pound in heart beat
on the cellar door.

The woman lies in bed
bathed in fear
in fear.

[1959]

RAINER BRAMBACH

GRANIT

Über Granit gebeugt—aus südlichen Brüchen.
Während dein Hammer fällt
steigt dir ein Himmel aus Milchglass ins Auge
während dein Meissel die Rinne gräbt
schmeckst du den Staub versteinerter Wälder.

Über Granit gebeugt—
O Ginster und Aloe schiefergrau verschwommen
während dein Knie sich
an die ausgetrockneten Ebenen presst
—aus südlichen Brüchen
während dein schweissnasser Rücken gestreift wird
vom kühlen Hauch nördlichen Sommers.

DER BAUM

Seit ich weit draussen
das Haus in der Siedlung bewohne
wächst aus dem Keller ein Baum
durch Diele und Mansarden.
Laub hängt fahnengleich
zu allen Fenstern hinaus,

der Wipfel wiegt sich
über dem moosgrauen Dach.

GRANITE

Stooped over granite—from southern quarries.
When your hammer falls
a sky of frosted glass appears,
when your chisel cuts the groove
you taste the dust of petrified forests.

Stooped over granite—
O gorse and aloe slategray interfused
when your kneecap
presses hard on dried-out planes
—from southern quarries
when drenched in sweat your back is stroked
by the cool breath of northern summer.

1956

THE TREE

Ever since I've been living far out
in the house on the new estate,
a tree has been growing from the cellar
up through hall and attic.
Foliage hangs like flags
out of all the windows,

the treetop sways
over the mossgray roof.

Ich hause unbesorgt nah dem Gezweig,
im Hof fault der Spaltklotz,
auf dem Speicher rostet die Säge.
Nachbarn freilich rufen sich zu:
Sein Haus ist wie unsere Häuser,
was ist der Narr fröhlich—
Hört, er singt in der Frühe, redet
und lacht wenn es dämmert!

Der Baum wächst.

I live beside the branches unperturbed,
the chopping-block is rotting in the yard,
the saw is rusting in the storehouse.
Neighbors, it's true, call to each other:
His house is the same as our houses,
what's the fool got to be so happy about—
Listen, he sings at daybreak, talks
and laughs when the night falls!

The tree is growing.

1956

WOLFDIETRICH SCHNURRE

STROPHE

Als der Falke
der Taube
die Fänge ins Fleisch schlug,
sank eine Feder
der Welt auf den Mund.
Reglos hing sie
an den dörrenden Lippen
und harrte des Atems.
Er kam nicht; es
war der Abendwind,
der sie fortnahm.

DENUNZIATION

Mond,
Milchspinne der Frauen,
Lästerer;
Mond:
Wir klagen dich an.
Du hast Spionage getrieben,
das Weiss deiner Hände, es lügt.
So weiss ist Chlor, so weiss ist Schnee;
Chlor, das auf Erschossene rieselt,
Schnee, der die Erfrorenen wärmt.
So weiss ist Nebel, so weiss ist Linnen;
Nebel, der ins Pesttal sich senkt,
Linnen, das die Ermordeten kühlt.

STROPHE

When the hawk
struck his talons
into the dove's flesh,
a feather drifted
on to the mouth of the world.
Unmoving it clung
to those wilting lips
and waited for them to breathe.
No breath came; it
was the evening breeze
that bore the feather away.

1956

DENUNCIATION

Moon,
milk spider of the women,
blasphemer;
moon,
we accuse you.
You have practised espionage,
the whiteness of your hands deceives:
the whiteness of chlorine, whiteness of snow;
chlorine that drizzles on those shot dead ,
snow that warms those frozen to death;
the whiteness of mist, the whiteness of linen;
mist that settles on the plague-filled valley,
linen that cools the murdered.

Mond,
Heuschreckenmünze der Männer,
Verhöhner;
Mond:
Du hast Spionage getrieben.
Dein Auftraggeber ist uns bekannt;
er wohnt jenseits der Liebe.

HAUCH AUF DER SCHERBE

Nicht mit dem Donner,
nicht unterm Faustschlag
des Winds weht es heran:
sanft,
auf Kolibrischwingen,
mild wie das Gift
im Dolchzahn der Viper
wird es sich zeigen,
als goldener Ausschlag
erscheint es
auf Papierdrachenfetzen ,
auf brüchigen Fellen,
auf Schläfen, verdorrt
zu Fledermauspergament:
das zarte Entsetzen.

Moon,
locust coin of the men,
scoffer;
moon,
you have practised espionage.
Your employer is known to us;
he lives on the far side of love.

1956

BREATH ON A PIECE OF BROKEN GLASS

Not with the thunder,
not under the clenched blow
of the wind does it approach:
gently,
on hummingbird wings,
mild as the venom
in the viper's dagger tooth
it will reveal itself,
as a golden rash
it appears
on scraps of paper kites,
on mangy pelts,
on temples withered
to batskin parchment:
the delicate horror.

1956

PAUL CELAN

TODESFUGE

Schwarze Milch der Frühe wir trinken sie abends
wir trinken sie mittags und morgens wir trinken sie nachts
wir trinken und trinken
wir schaufeln ein Grab in den Lüften da liegt man nicht eng
Ein Mann wohnt im Haus der spielt mit den Schlangen der schreibt
der schreibt wenn es dunkelt nach Deutschland dein goldenes Haar
    Margarete
er schreibt es und tritt vor das Haus und es blitzen die Sterne er
    pfeift seine Rüden herbei
er pfeift seine Juden hervor lässt schaufeln ein Grab in der Erde
er befiehlt uns spielt auf nun zum Tanz

Schwarze Milch der Frühe wir trinken dich nachts
wir trinken dich morgens und mittags wir trinken dich abends
wir trinken und trinken
Ein Mann wohnt im Haus der spielt mit den Schlangen der schreibt
der schreibt wenn es dunkelt nach Deutschland dein goldenes Haar
    Margarete
Dein aschenes Haar Sulamith wir schaufeln ein Grab in den Lüften
    da liegt man nicht eng

Er ruft stecht tiefer ins Erdreich ihr einen ihr andern singet und
    spielt
er greift nach dem Eisen im Gurt er schwingts seine Augen sind blau
stecht tiefer die Spaten ihr einen ihr andern spielt weiter zum Tanz
    auf

FUGUE OF DEATH

Black milk of daybreak we drink it at nightfall
we drink it at noon in the morning we drink it at night
drink it and drink it
we are digging a grave in the sky it is ample to lie there
A man in the house he plays with the serpents he writes
he writes when the night falls to Germany your golden hair
      Margarete
he writes it and walks from the house the stars glitter he whistles his
      dogs up
he whistles his Jews out and orders a grave to be dug in the earth
he commands us now on with the dance

Black milk of daybreak we drink you at night
we drink in the mornings at noon we drink you at nightfall
drink you and drink you
A man in the house he plays with the serpents he writes
he writes when the night falls to Germany your golden hair Margarete
Your ashen hair Shulamith we are digging a grave in the sky it is
      ample to lie there

He shouts stab deeper in earth you there you others you sing and
      you play
he grabs at the iron in his belt and swings it and blue are his eyes
stab deeper your spades you there and you others play on for the
      dancing

Schwarze Milch der Frühe wir trinken dich nachts
wir trinken dich mittags und morgens wir trinken dich abends
wir trinken und trinken
ein Mann wohnt im Haus dein goldenes Haar Margarete
dein aschenes Haar Sulamith er spielt mit den Schlangen

Er ruft spielt süsser den Tod der Tod ist ein Meister aus Deutschland
er ruft streicht dunkler die Geigen dann steigt ihr als Rauch in die
     Luft
dann habt ihr ein Grab in den Wolken da liegt man nicht eng

Schwarze Milch der Frühe wir trinken dich nachts
wir trinken dich mittags der Tod ist ein Meister aus Deutschland
wir trinken dich abends und morgens wir trinken und trinken
der Tod ist ein Meister aus Deutschland sein Auge ist blau
er trifft dich mit bleierner Kugel er trifft dich genau
ein Mann wohnt im Haus dein goldenes Haar Margarete
er hetzt seine Rüden auf uns er schenkt uns ein Grab in der Luft
er spielt mit den Schlangen und träumet der Tod ist ein Meister aus
     Deutschland

dein goldenes Haar Margarete
dein aschenes Haar Sulamith

Black milk of daybreak we drink you at night
we drink you at noon in the mornings we drink you at nightfall
drink you and drink you
a man in the house your golden hair Margarete
your ashen hair Shulamith he plays with the serpents

He shouts play sweeter death's music death comes as a master from
      Germany
he shouts stroke darker the strings and as smoke you shall climb to
      the sky
then you'll have a grave in the clouds it is ample to lie there

Black milk of daybreak we drink you at night
we drink you at noon death comes as a master from Germany
we drink you at nightfall and morning we drink you and drink you
a master from Germany death comes with eyes that are blue
with a bullet of lead he will hit in the mark he will hit you
a man in the house your golden hair Margarete
he hunts us down with his dogs in the sky he gives us a grave
he plays with the serpents and dreams death comes as a master from
      Germany

your golden hair Margarete
your ashen hair Shulamith

1952

DIE KRÜGE

An den langen Tischen der Zeit
zechen die Krüge Gottes.
Sie trinken die Augen der Sehenden leer und die Augen der
    Blinden,
die Herzen der waltenden Schatten,
die hohle Wange des Abends.
Sie sind die gewaltigsten Zecher:
sie führen das Leere zum Mund wie das Volle
und schäumen nicht über wie du oder ich.

SCHIBBOLETH

Mitsamt meinen Steinen,
den grossgeweinten
hinter den Gittern,

schleiften sie mich
in die Mitte des Marktes,
dorthin,
wo die Fahne sich aufrollt, der ich
keinerlei Eid schwor.

Flöte,
Doppelflöte der Nacht:
denke der dunklen
Zwillingsröte
in Wien und Madrid.

Setz deine Fahne auf Halbmast,
Erinnrung.
Auf Halbmast
für heute und immer.

THE JUGS

At the long tables of time
the jugs of God carouse.
They drink empty the eyes that see and the eyes of the blind,
the hearts of the mastering shadows,
the hollow cheek of the evening.
They are the most mighty carousers:
they carry empty and full alike to their mouths
and do not flow over like you or like me.

1952

SHIBBOLETH

Together with all my stones
that had grown big with weeping
behind the bars,

they dragged me out into
the middle of the market,
there,
where the flag unfurls to which
I swore no kind of allegiance.

Flute
double flute of the night:
remember the dark
twin redness
of Vienna and of Madrid.

Set your flag at half mast,
memory.
At half mast
today and forever

Herz:
gib dich auch hier zu erkennen,
hier, in der Mitte des Marktes.
Ruf's, das Schibboleth, hinaus
in die Fremde der Heimat:
Februar. No pasaran.

Einhorn:
du weisst um die Steine,
du weisst um das Wasser,
komm,
ich führ dich hinweg
zu den Stimmen
von Estremadura.

Heart:
here too reveal what you are,
here, in the midst of the market.
Call the shibboleth, call it out
into your alien homeland:
February. *No pasaran.*

Unicorn:
you know of the stones,
you know of the waters;
come,
I shall lead you away
to the voices
of Estremadura.

1955

IN MEMORIAM PAUL ELUARD

Lege dem Toten die Worte ins Grab,
die er sprach. um zu leben.
Bette sein Haupt zwischen sie,
lass ihn fühlen
die Zungen der Sehnsucht,
die Zangen.

Leg auf die Lider des Toten das Wort,
das er jenem verweigert,
der du zu ihm sagte,
das Wort,
an dem das Blut seines Herzens vorbeisprang,
als eine Hand, so nackt wie die seine,
jenen, der du zu ihm sagte,
in die Bäume der Zukunft knüpfte.

Leg ihm dies Wort auf die Lider:
vielleicht
tritt in sein Aug, das noch blau ist,
eine zweite, fremdere Bläue,
und jener, der du zu ihm sagte,
träumt mit ihm: Wir.

IN MEMORIAM PAUL ELUARD

Lay these words into the dead man's grave
which he spoke in order to live.
Pillow his head amid them,
let him feel
the tongues of longing,
the tongs.

Lay that word on the dead man's eyelids
which he refused to him
who addressed him as thou,
the word
his leaping heart-blood passed by
when a hand as bare as his own
knotted him who addressed him as thou
into the trees of the future.

Lay this word on his eyelids:
perhaps
his eye, still blue, will assume
a second, more alien blueness,
and he who addressed him as thou
will dream with him: We.

1955

HELMUT HEISSENBÜTTEL

KOMBINATION XI

1

Die Nacht ist ein Muster aus Bogenlampen und Autorücklichtern.
Auf der reglosen Fläche der Alster stehen die weissen Fahnen der
Nacht.
Unter den Bäumen gehen die Schatten.
Ich bins.

2

Dunkelkammergespräche.
Dunkelkammergedächtnis.
Schattengitter über dem schmelzenden Eis.
Auf Spiegelstelzen stehen die Lichter am Ufer.
Die unbelichteten Stellen verblühn.

3

All diese Sätze.
Das Inventar der Gelegenheiten.
Vergiss nicht.
Gerede von Schallplatten.
Das Gedächtnis von Tonfilmstreifen die abgespielt sind.

4

Und die Fragen sind die Sätze die ich nicht aussprechen kann.
Und die Gedanken sind die Vögel die wegfliegen und nicht wieder-
kommen.

COMBINATION XI

1

Night is a pattern of arc-lamps and the rearlights of cars.
The white flags of night stand on the Alster's immobile surface.
The shadows walk beneath the trees.
It's me.

2

Darkroom colloquies.
Darkroom memory.
Bars of shadow over the melting ice.
The lights stand ashore on mirror stilts.
The unexposed areas fade.

3

All these sentences.
The inventory of occasions.
Don't forget.
Talk from gramophone records.
The memory of soundtracks that have been played to a stop.

4

And the questions are the sentences I cannot articulate.
And the thoughts are the birds that fly away and do not return.

1954

BRUCHSTÜCK III

Alle Horizonte sind rund.
Auf der platten Scheibe der Ebene bin ich
Der Mittelpunkt ferner Kirchturmspitzen.

Die Stimme des Radios sagt
FREIHEIT IST EIN DING DER UNMÖGLICHKEIT.
Es folgt
Das vierte Streichquartett von Arnold Schönberg.

Fern in meine Zelle scheint die Sonne.
Im Wind
Das Klappern der Hochbahn auf den Viadukten
Ist eine Melodie.

Unausfüllbarer Hunger nach Unausdenkbarem.
Kombination von Abfahrtzeiten
Ohne Ankunft.

FRAGMENT III

All horizons are round.
On the flat disc of the plain I am
The center of distant steeple-points.

The radio's voice says:
FREEDOM IS AN IMPOSSIBLE THING.
There follows
The fourth string quartet of Arnold Schönberg.

The sun shines into my cell far off.
In the wind
The clatter of the railway on the viaducts
Is a melody.

Insatiable hunger for the inexcogitable.
Combination of times of departure
Without arrival.

1954

HANS CARL ARTMANN

DOD EN WOSSA

waun s me aussezan
waun s me aussezan
aus de donau
untan wintahofm
bei oewan
wiad ma des monogram
wos ma mei muta r amoe
en s hemt zeichnt`hod
lenx fawoschn sei:
a monogramdintn
is aa nua r a mendsch
und hoet ned ewech . .

waun s me aussezan
waun s me aussezan
untan wintahofm
bei oewan
en heabst
how e a neix monogram
a leichz und a schweas
wäu s me amoe auffedrad hod
und amoe owe aum grund
und hii und hea
wia s en wossa scho is . .
und da suma woa laung
und de schdrömung ned schdoak
und de wassreche gengd
hod es iwreche gmacht . .

DEATH BY WATER

when they pull me out
when they pull me out
out of the danube
near albern
where the ships tie up for winter
the monogram
my mother once
stitched in my shirt
will long have been washed out:
a monogram
is also only human
and doesn't last for ever . . .

when they pull me out
when they pull me out
near albern
where the ships tie up for winter
in the fall
I'll have a new monogram
a light wound and a deep one
because a whirlpool drew me
down to the river bed
and back and forth
and the sort of thing a river does . . .
and the summer was long
and the current mild
and the water around me
did the rest . . .

a fisch fia de wön
und a r aunka fia n grund
oes monogram unta d aung
is bessa r oes kans—
owa drozzdem ka easoz
fia des schene blaue
wos ma mei muta seinazeid
en s hemad einezeichnt hod . .

waun s me aussezan
waun s me aussezan
en heabst
bei oewan
untan wintahofm : . .

a fish for the waves
and an anchor for the bottom
are a better monogram than none
yet cannot compare
with the handsome blue one
my mother once
stitched in my shirt . . .

when they pull me out
when they pull me out
in the fall
near albern
where the ships tie up for winter . . .

1958

ERICH FRIED

NACHHER

Dann kommen die Mädchen
aus den verbrannten Städten
in ihre Kleider
teilt sich der Wind mit den Hecken

Und manche nimmt einen Baum zum Liebsten
und manche ein Tier
sonderbare
Geburten werden geschlachtet

Da und dort noch
ein Fähnlein lachender Männer
mitleidig nehmen die Wölfe
sie in ihr Rudel

Denn die allein bleiben
werden zu Tode gejagt
oder im Winterschlaf
von Weibern erschlagen

Und grün wird alles
rund um die Knochen und Steine
die Wälder reichen
wieder hinab zum Meer

AFTERWARD

Then girls will be coming
out of the cindered cities
their dresses are parted
between the wind and the hedges

And one takes a tree for her lover
another a beast
curious beings
no sooner born but are slaughtered

Here and there still
a troop of men laughing
pitying wolves take them
into their pack

For who remain alone are
hunted down till they die
or in their winter sleep
murdered by women

And all is green
around the bones and boulders
once more the woodland
stretches down to the sea

1958

ALTES ZIMMER

Im Zimmer der Staub
zart auf den Fensterscheiben,
im Zimmer der leise Staub
auf dem Tisch
auf dem alten Kissen:
Pfirsichflaum
der streichelt die streichelnde Hand,
der zeigt der Sonne
den Weg durch geschlossene Fenster

Müde sein
und nicht weinen wollen
und nicht
sterben wollen:
geweint haben und schon tot sein.
Im leichten Staub
der dem Sonnenlicht seinen Weg zeigt
auf dem Kissen liegen
nicht Wieder, nein, Immer, noch immer
und schon für immer
Staub auf Staub unter Staub

Staub auf dem Tisch
auf dem Bett
auf den Fensterscheiben:
Ich liebe dich!
Ich liebe dich Staub!
Ich liebe
den Staub im Staub
die Sonne im Staub
den Staub in der Sonne!
Ich Staub im Zimmer der Sonne
ich Staub auf dem Kissen
ich Wieder, ich Noch, ich Immer
im Zimmer aus Staub

OLD ROOM

The dust in this room
delicate on the windowpanes
the quiet dust in this room
on the table
on the old cushion:
peach skin down
that fondles the fondling hand,
that shows the sun
the way through fastened windows

To be tired
and unwilling to weep
and unwilling
to die:
to have wept and to be already dead.
In the light dust
that shows the sunlight the way,
to lie on the cushion
not Again, no, Ever, and still
and already for ever
dust on dust among dust

Dust on the table
on the bed
on the windowpanes:
I love you!
I love you dust!
I love
the dust in the dust
the sun in the dust
the dust in the sun!
I, dust in the room of the sun
I, dust on the cushion
I Again, I Still, I Ever
in the room of dust

[1959]

DIE BLINDEN

Ich sagte „Ich sehe"
du sagtest „Ich sehe dich sehen"
So tappten wir uns vorbei
an den Höhlen der Augen

Die Augen kamen gerollt
aus den hellen Höhlen
sie wollten uns ins Gesicht
sie hüpften uns bis ans Kinn

„Sie äugen uns weil wir lügen"
Wir packten die weichen Steine
wir warfen sie weit von uns weg
wir tasteten uns nach Hause

Man fühlte uns ins Gesicht
man fragte „Was habt ihr begriffen?"
„Wir haben gesehen
wir waren im Lande der Augen

„Wir waren voll Augen
die wollten ihr Licht in uns bohren
sie rollten aus alten Höhlen
Wir haben uns freigemacht"

THE BLIND

I said "I see"
you said "I see you see"
So we tapped our way
past the hollows of eyes

The eyes came rolling
from the bright hollows
they tried to get into our faces
they hopped right up to our chins

"Because we are lying they're eyeing us"
We grabbed the soft stones
we flung them away from us
we groped our way home

They fingered our faces
they asked "Did you grasp anything?"
"We have seen
we were in the country of eyes

"We were full of eyes
their light tried to pierce us
they rolled out of old hollows
We shook ourselves free"

[1959]

WALTER HÖLLERER

DER LAG BESONDERS MÜHELOS AM RAND

Der lag besonders mühelos am Rand
Des Weges. Seine Wimpern hingen
Schwer und zufrieden in die Augenschatten.
Man hätte meinen können, dass er schliefe.

Aber sein Rücken war (wir trugen ihn,
Den Schweren, etwas abseits, denn er störte sehr
Kolonnen, die sich drängten) dieser Rücken
War nur ein roter Lappen, weiter nichts.

Und seine Hand (wir konnten dann den Witz
Nich oft erzählen, beide haben wir
Ihn schnell vergessen) hatte, wie ein Schwert,
Den hartgefrornen Pferdemist gefasst,

Den Apfel, gelb und starr,
Als wär es Erde oder auch ein Arm
Oder ein Kreuz, ein Gott: ich weiss nicht was.
Wir trugen ihn da weg und in den Schnee.

PARTICULARLY EFFORTLESS HE LAY

Particularly effortless he lay
Beside the road. His lashes hung
Into the shadows of his eyes, content and heavy.
One might quite well have thought he was asleep.

But his back was (we carried him,
And he was heavy, a bit aside, for he disturbed
The columns that were crowding on) this back
Was just a swab of red and nothing more.

And his hand (those days we couldn't tell the joke
Often, and afterward we both
Forgot it fast) had seized like a sword
A piece of horse dung that was frozen hard,

The apple, yellow, stiff,
As if it might be earth or even an arm,
Perhaps a cross, a god: I don't know what.
We carried him away and into the snow.

1952

GESICHT DES FISCHERS

Europaspur im Antlitz, Geleitzug von
Triëren, Koggen, Masken des Dionys,
Verwandelte, in dunklen Rillen
Um seine Brauen.

Mehr, als du ahnst, Gesang.
Fernblickend Inseln.
Prall wie am ersten Tag die Segel.

THE FACE OF THE FISHERMAN

In his face the trace of Europe. Escort of
Triremes, galleons, masks of Dionysus,
Transformed, in dark furrows
Around his eyebrows.

More than you guess of song.
Islands distantly gazing.
Taut as the sails on the first day.

1952

HEINZ PIONTEK

MIT 30 JAHREN

Keine sichtbaren Narben,
keine Medaillen,
keine Titel—
aber das Auge scharf, unbezähmbar
wie Zorn und Entzücken,
dicht die Erinnerung
und leicht der Schlaf.

Fahrten, Märsche vor zwanzig.
Nachher genügten vier Wände:
Wir werden nicht
überschaubarer unterwegs!
Oft reichen drei Schritte.
Und immer genügt
weniger als wir vermuten.

Zum Beispiel die Stadt.
Man kann sie umwandern
in einer einzigen Stunde.
Ihre Steige bröckeln,
in den Türmen haust
die blinde Geschichte.
Helle von Silberkörnern,
wenn die Flussnebel fallen . . .

Mühsal ist wirklich:
Last und Hitze
und das steinerne Glück.

AT THIRTY YEARS

No visible scars,
no medals,
no titles—
but the eye sharp, untameable
as rage or as a rapture,
memory crowded
and sleep light.

Journeys, marches before the twentieth year.
Later four walls were enough:
to move about
does not make us more palpable!
Often three steps are enough.
And enough is always
less than we think.

The town, for instance.
You can walk all round it
in a single hour.
Its pavements are crumbling,
in its towers lives
blind history.
Brightness of silver grain
when the mists fall . . .

Effort is real:
burdens and heat
and stony joy.

Wirklich der überwundene Tod—
und alles Vergebliche wird
fest unter den Sohlen.
Mehr wissen wir nicht.

Erwachet früh—
wenn der Morgen
mit halben Farben erscheint
und satt das Holz leuchtet,
das geteert ist—
denn der Wind steht gegen euch!
Doch sputet euch nicht.
Wir leben gezählte Tage.

DIE TOCHTER DES SCHMIEDS

Ich hatte einen Vater,
mächtig wie der Pfosten des Ziehbrunnens
in Kobniza,
mit Augen aus blauem Eisen und Funken im Bart,
der hinkte und konnte in den Legenden lesen.

Er hatte eine Tochter,
schön wie der Fluss in den Wiesen
bei Kobniza.
Winters trug sie die zierlichen Stiefel,
sommers eine Fahne Katun um die Hüften.

Ihm träumte, er lebe als Köhler
und verstünde die Vögel.
Aber Schmied war er auf einem verlotterten Vorwerk
und bückte sich vor dem Vogt.

Real too is death overcome—
and all that was vain
grows solid under your feet.
That is all we know.

Awaken early—
when the morning
with muted colors appears
and wood had a mellow gleam,
wood that has been tarred—
for the wind is against you!
But do not hurry.
The days of our lives are counted.

1957

THE BLACKSMITH'S DAUGHTER

I had a father
powerful as the post of the well
at Kobnitza,
with eyes of blue iron and sparks in his beard,
who limped and knew what the legends mean.

He had a daughter,
lovely as the river in the meadows
near Kobnitza.
In winter she wore her dainty boots,
in summer a sash of cotton around her hips.

He dreamed that he was a charcoal-burner
and understood the language of birds.
But a blacksmith he worked in a tumbledown manor-farm
and went in fear of the bailiff.

Und sie, seine Tochter, wäre am liebsten
mit einem zwanzigjährigen Fähnrich geritten,
aber ein Posthalter nahm sie,
kaufte ihr Zwieback und eine Brille.

Ein Apfelschimmel schlug meinen Vater lahm.
Mein Vater kam nie in die Wälder.
Er schüttete Kohlengrus auf:
sein Herz war eine ausgeblasene Esse.
Er trank neun Krüge Dünnbier
und starb daran.

Ich lernte, das man vor seinem Gedächtnis
nie sicher ist.
Ich sehe des Morgens unseren kleinen Horizont,
und unter der Funzel schreib ich Adressen
für die Leute.

DIE VERSTREUTEN

Wir haben Wind unter den Sohlen.
Wir haben Wind im Nacken.

Des Nachbarn Stimme fing sich in Netzen Schnees.
Da stopften wir Silber und Brot in die Säcke, entriegelten die Tür.
Als die Nacht anhub zu flackern, liefen wir waffenlos zu den Ställen
und hinaus auf Strassen von wandernden Ratten.

Zerstossenes Blech und Kälte: das Land der Geschlagenen.
Wir fuhren im Schritt. Ein Mädchen kam nieder
zwischen den Speichen. Ein Blinder stolperte hinter barmherzigen
        Leuten
an einem Strick, und er schrie zu den Lüften: Wo sind wir?

And she, his daughter, would have liked best
to go out riding with an ensign twenty years old,
but a postmaster made her his wife,
bought her rusks and a pair of spectacles.

My father was lamed by a dapple-gray's kick.
His leg kept him out of the forests.
He stoked the fire with small coal:
his heart was a forge gone out.
He drank nine tankards of thin beer
and died of it.

I learned that one is never safe
from his memory.
In the mornings I see our little horizon
and in feeble lamplight I write addresses
for the customers.

1957

THE DISPERSION

We have the wind under our feet.
We have the wind at our backs.

Our neighbor's voice caught in the nets of snow.
So we crammed silver and bread into bags, unbolted the door.
As the night began to flicker, unarmed we ran to the stables,
and out onto roads where rat-hordes wandered.

Dented metal and the cold: the land of the defeated.
We inched along. A girl had a baby
between the wheels. A blind man on a string ran stumbling
behind compassionate folk, and called to the winds: "Where are
     we?"

Wir müssen vor den Kreuzungen warten.
Wir besitzen keine Dokumente.

Mancher starb kauernd—im Hader über seine verendeten Pferde,
mancher streckte sich schweigsam und mild unter Planen.
Und als wir einzeln eine getroffene Brücke passierten,
waren viele im Eis zu sehen, grün und wie schwebend.

Der Himmel ein Sieb, und hinter den Karawanen
blieb eine Fährte aus untilgbarer Stille,
ein zügiger Horizont blieb zurück, auf dem wir biwakiert,
der Schläfer, der die Verfolgung nicht mehr fürchtete.

Wir dürfen kein Feuer machen.
Wir dürfen den Zug ohne Erlaubnis nicht verlassen.

Man rief mich: „Erzähle! Wir wissen zu wenig von jenen,
die im April eines frommen Jahrhunderts sich aufgemacht hatten,
um ihre Reiche—zwölfhundert Ruten Wildnis—zu gründen,
vom Mehl der Gebeine auf unseren Friedhöfen erzähle!"

Ich sagte zu ihnen: Es war ein Volk, das auszog
nach dem gelobten Land und es nicht fand und verdarb.—
„Narr, sie erreichten es—süss und barbarisch zwischen Wasser-
        bächen!
Wir aber müssen nun unsre frühere Heimat erkunden."

Wir beugen die Rücken unter leichte Lasten.
Wir nähren uns von Schnee und Vögeln.

Unsere Scharen lichteten sich und strömten mit dünnen Schatten.
Einer verlor den andern. Der Osten—wie eine feurige Sage—
ging hinter Armeen zugrunde. Jammer war er
und Aschenflug über der Öde und dunkel wie einst.

We must wait before we come to the crossroads.
We do not possess any documents.

Some died cowering—squabbling over dead horses;
some lay flat, taciturn, calm under sheets of canvas.
And as we passed singly over a smashed bridge,
many could be seen in the ice, as if they hung there.

The sky a sieve, and behind the wagons
a trail remained, of indestructible stillness;
behind, where we had bivouacked, a chill horizon
slept, no longer in dread of the pursuers.

We may not light any fires.
We may not leave the convoy without permission.

They said to me: "Tell us! We know too little about the people
who set out in the April of a pious century to establish—
twelve hundred perch of wilderness—their kingdoms;
and about the powder of bones in our graveyards, tell us!"

I told them: "There was a people that left home
for the promised land, and did not arrive, and perished."
Fool! They found it, sweet and barbarous among streams of water!
But now it is we who must seek out our original country.

We bow our shoulders under easy burdens.
We feed upon birds and snowflakes.

Our swarms thinned and flowed in lean shadows onward.
We lost each other. The East—like a fiery legend—
collapsed behind armies. It was desolation
and a cloud of ash adrift over desert and dark as long ago.

Doch holte uns ein, der einen Knaben führte: ein rüstiger Mann,
den Waffenrock heftig von Sommern versengt
und einen Alten, den schlaffen Vater, auf den Schultern.
Da wurde es Tag vor unseren Augen mit rosenblättrigem Licht.

Wir werden zu einer festen Stadt kommen im Wind.
Wir werden Frieden finden auf Felsen.

But a man drew level, leading a boy, a man vigorous,
his tunic badly yellowed by many summers,
and an old man, his father, limp on his shoulders.
Then we saw dawn breaking about us, with light as of rose petals.

We shall come to a sure city in the wind.
We shall find peace rooted in rock.

1955 : 'Mein Gedicht ist mein Messer'

ALBERT ARNOLD SCHOLL

ETWAS KÜNDIGT SICH AN

Die grossen Veränderungen,
Von denen die Blätter berichten
Und die Gerüchte in unser aller Munde—
Sie meine ich nicht,

Auch nicht die kleinen Beunruhigungen,
Von denen wir ungern sprechen:
Das stetige Rieseln des Putzes
Selbst in den neuen Häusern,
Das häufige Bersten der Sicherung
Und die gefährlichen Spiele der Kinder.

Irgend etwas jedoch geschieht,
Von dem wir nicht wissen, was es bedeutet,
Die Dinge sind in Bewegung geraten,
Etwas kündigt sich an—

Und ist da:
Mitten in der Verwirrung,
Wenn sich der Nachrichtensprecher
Mehrmals verspricht—

Oder im Schweben der Hand
Vor dem letzten Stich,
Wenn die Blicke der Spieler sich kreuzen—

SOMETHING MAKES ITSELF KNOWN

The major alterations
Of which the papers inform us
And the rumors in the mouths of all of us—
I don't mean them.

Nor the small agitations
We speak of unwillingly:
The continuous sifting of plaster
Even in newly built houses,
The common blowing of fuses
And the dangerous games of children.

Yet something does happen
Of which we do not know the meaning,
Things have begun to move,
Something makes itself known—

And is there:
At the center of all the confusion
When the news announcer
Makes repeated mistakes—

Or in the hesitation of the hand
Before the last card is thrown
When the eyes of the players meet—

Auch Sonntags, am späten Mittag,
Während der Himmel die Dächer siedet
Und schwarz oder rot ein Fetzen auffliegt,
Schattenlos
In den Arkaden
Der ausgestorbenen Stadt.

Even Sundays, late in the noon,
While the sky simmers the roofs
And black or red a rag flies up
Shadowless,
In the arcades
Of the dead silent town.

1957

INGEBORG BACHMANN

ALLE TAGE

Der Krieg wird nicht mehr erklärt,
sondern fortgesetzt. Das Unerhörte
ist alltäglich geworden. Der Held
bleibt den Kämpfen fern. Der Schwache
ist in die Feuerzonen gerückt.
Die Uniform des Tages ist die Geduld,
die Auszeichnung der armselige Stern
der Hoffnung über dem Herzen.

Er wird verliehen,
wenn nichts mehr geschieht,
wenn das Trommelfeuer verstummt,
wenn der Feind unsichtbar geworden ist
und der Schatten ewiger Rüstung
den Himmel bedeckt.

Er wird verliehen
für die Flucht von den Fahnen,
für die Tapferkeit vor dem Freund,
für den Verrat unwürdiger Geheimnisse
und die Nichtachtung
jeglichen Befehls.

DAS ERSTGEBORENE LAND

In mein erstgeborenes Land, in den Süden
zog ich und fand, nackt und verarmt
und bis zum Gürtel im Meer,
Stadt und Kastell.

EVERY DAY

War is not declared any more,
but simply continued. The terrible
is an everyday thing. The hero
stays far from battles. The weakling
is moved into the firing lines.
The uniform of the day is patience,
its decoration the shabby star
of hope above the heart.

It is conferred
when nothing more happens,
when the drumfire stops,
when the enemy has become invisible,
and the shadow of eternal armament
darkens the sky.

It is conferred
for the deserting of flags,
for courage in the face of friends,
for the betrayal of despicable secrets
and disregard
of all commands.

1953

THE FIRSTBORN LAND

To my firstborn land, to the south
I went and found, naked, impoverished
and up to my waist in the sea,
city and citadel.

Vom Staub in den Schlaf getreten
lag ich im Licht,
und vom ionischen Salz belaubt
hing ein Baumskelett über mir.

Da fiel kein Traum herab.

Da blüht kein Rosmarin,
kein Vogel frischt
sein Lied in Quellen auf.

In meinem erstgeborenen Land, im Süden
sprang die Viper mich an
und das Grausen im Licht.

O schliess
die Augen schliess!
Press den Mund auf den Biss!

Und als ich mich selber trank
und mein erstgeborenes Land
die Erdbeben wiegten,
war ich zum Schauen erwacht.

Da fiel mir Leben zu.

Da ist der Stein nicht tot.
Der Docht schnellt auf,
wenn ihn ein Blick entzündet.

Trodden by dust into sleep,
I lay in the light,
and with leaves of Ionian salt there hung
a tree's skeleton over me.

No dream fell down from there.

No rosemary blooms there,
no bird refreshes
his song in springs.

In my firstborn land, in the south
the viper leapt at me,
and horror of light.

O close,
close the eyes!
Press your mouth to the wound!

As I drank myself
and the earthquake rocked
my firstborn land to sleep,
all eyes I awoke.

Then life fell to my share.

Stone there is no dead thing.
The wick flares up,
if a glance ignites it.

1956

NEBELLAND

Im Winter ist meine Geliebte
unter den Tieren des Waldes.
Dass ich vor Morgen zurückmuss,
weiss die Füchsin und lacht.
Wie die Wolken erzittern! Und mir
auf den Schneekragen fällt
eine Lage von brüchigem Eis.

Im Winter ist meine Geliebte
ein Baum unter Bäumen und lädt
die glückverlassenen Krähen
ein in ihr schönes Geäst. Sie weiss,
dass der Wind, wenn es dämmert,
ihr starres, mit Reif besetztes
Abendkleid hebt und mich heimjagt.

Im Winter ist meine Geliebte
unter den Fischen und stumm.
Hörig den Wassern, die der Strich
ihrer Flossen von innen bewegt,
steh ich am Ufer und seh,
bis mich Schollen vertreiben,
wie sie taucht und sich wendet.

Und wieder vom Jagdruf des Vogels
getroffen, der seine Schwingen
über mir streift, stürz ich
auf offenem Feld : sie entfiedert
die Hühner und wirft mir ein weisses
Schlüsselbein zu. Ich nehm's um den Hals
und geh fort durch den bitteren Flaum.

FOG LAND

In winter my loved one retires
to live with the beasts of the forest.
That I must be back before morning
the vixen knows well, and she laughs.
Now the low clouds quiver! And down
on my upturned collar there falls
a landslide of brittle ice.

In winter my loved one retires,
a tree among trees, and invites
the crows in their desolation
into her beautiful boughs. She knows
that as soon as night falls the wind
lifts her stiff, hoar-frost-embroidered
evening gown, sends me home.

In winter my loved one retires,
a fish among fishes, and dumb.
Slave to the waters she ripples
with her fins' gentle motion within,
I stand on the bank and look down
till ice floes drive me away,
her dipping and turning hidden.

And stricken again by the blood-cry
of the bird that tautens his pinions
over my head, I fall down
on the open field: she is plucking
the hens, and she throws me a whitened
collar bone. This round my neck,
off I go through the bitter down.

Treulos ist meine Geliebte,
ich weiss, sie schwebt manchmal
auf hohen Schuh'n nach der Stadt,
sie küsst in den Bars mit dem Strohhalm
die Gläser tief auf den Mund,
und es kommen ihr Worte für alle.
Doch diese Sprache verstehe ich nicht.

Nebelland hab ich gesehen,
Nebelherz hab ich gegessen.

My loved one, I know, is unfaithful,
and sometimes she stalks and she hovers
on high-heeled shoes to the city
and deeply in bars with her straw
will kiss the lips of the glasses,
and finds words for each and for all.
But this language is alien to me.

It is fog land I have seen,
It is fog heart I have eaten.

1956

GÜNTER GRASS

DIE SCHULE DER TENÖRE

Die Brust heraus, bis der Wind seinen Umweg macht.
Immer wieder Trompeten,
Spitzgedrehte Tüten voller silberner Zwiebeln.

Dann die Geduld.
Warten, bis der Dame die Augen davonlaufen,
Zwei unzufriedene Dienstmädchen.
Jetzt erst den Ton den die Gläser fürchten
Und der Staub
Der die Gesimse verfolgt bis sie hinken.

GEÖFFNETER SCHRANK

Unten stehen die Schuhe.
Sie fürchten sich vor einem Käfer
Auf dem Hinweg,
Vor einem Pfennig auf dem Rückweg,
Vor Käfer und Pfennig die sie treten könnten
Bis es sich einprägt.
Oben ist die Heimat der Hüte.
Behüte, hüte dich, behutsam.
Unglaubliche Federn,
Wie hiess der Vogel,
Wohin rollte sein Blick
Als er einsah, dass er zu bunt geraten?

THE SCHOOL FOR TENORS

Puff out your chests, till the wind takes its devious way.
Trumpet again and again,
Conical paper bags full of silver onions.

After that, patience.
Wait till the lady's eyes run away,
Two dissatisfied skivvies.
Only now that tone which the glasses fear,
And the dust
That pursues the ledges until they limp.

(Shortened Version) 1956 'Transit'

OPEN WARDROBE

The shoes are at the bottom.
They are afraid of a beetle
On the way out,
Of a penny on the way back,
Of a beetle and a penny on which they might tread
Till it impresses itself.
At the top is the home of the headgear.
Take heed, be wary, not headstrong.
Incredible feathers,
What was the bird called,
Where did its eyes roll
When it knew that its wings were too gaudy?

Die weissen Kugeln, die in den Taschen schlafen,
Träumen von Motten.
Hier fehlt ein Knopf,
Im Gürtel ermüdet die Schlange.
Schmerzliche Seide,
Astern und andere feuergefährliche Blumen,
Der Herbst, der zum Kleid wird,
Jeden Sonntag mit Fleisch und dem Salz
Gefälteter Wäsche gefüllt.
Bevor der Schrank schweigt, Holz wird,
Ein entfernter Verwandter der Kiefer,—
Wer wird den Mantel tragen
Wenn du einmal tot bist?
Seinen Arm im Ärmel bewegen,
Zuvorkommend jeder Bewegung?
Wer wird den Kragen hochschlagen,
Vor den Bildern stehen bleiben
Und alleine sein unter der windigen Glocke?

TIERSCHUTZ

Das Klavier in den Zoo.
Schnell, bringt das Zebra in die gute Stube.
Seid freundlich mit ihm.
Es kommt aus Bechstein.
Noten frisst es
Und unsere süssen Ohren.

The white balls asleep in the pockets
Dream of moths.
Here a button is missing,
In this belt the clasp grows weary.
Doleful silk,
Asters and other inflammable flowers,
Autumn becoming a dress.
Every Sunday filled with flesh
And the salt of folded linen.
Before the wardrobe falls silent, turns into wood,
A distant relation of pine trees,—
Who will wear the coat
One day when you're dead?
Who move an arm in the sleeve,
Anticipate every movement?
Who will turn up the collar,
Stop in front of the pictures
And be alone under the windy cloche?

1956

PREVENTION OF CRUELTY TO ANIMALS

The piano into the zoo.
Quick, get the zebra into the best room.
Be kind to it,
It comes from Bechstein.
Scores are its fodder,
And our sweet ears.

1956

WANDLUNG

Plötzlich waren die Kirschen da,
obgleich ich vergessen hatte,
dass es Kirschen gibt
und verkünden liess: Noch nie gab es Kirschen—
waren sie da, plötzlich und teuer.

Pflaumen fielen und trafen mich.
Doch wer da denkt,
ich wandelte mich,
weil etwas fiel und mich traf,
wurde noch nie von fallenden Pflaumen getroffen.

Erst als man Nüsse in meine Schuhe schüttete
und ich laufen musste,
weil die Kinder die Kerne wollten,
schrie ich nach Kirschen, wollt ich von Pflaumen
getroffen werden—und wandelte mich ein wenig.

TRANSFORMATION

Suddenly the cherries were there
although I had forgotten
that cherries exist
and caused to be proclaimed : There never have been cherries—
they were there, suddenly and dear.

Plums fell and hit me,
but whoever thinks
that I was transformed
because something fell and hit me
has never been hit by falling plums.

Only when they poured nuts into my shoes
and I had to walk
because the children wanted the kernels
I cried out for cherries, wanted plums
to hit me—and was transformed a little.

1959

HANS MAGNUS ENZENSBERGER

INS LESEBUCH FÜR DIE OBERSTUFE

lies keine oden, mein sohn, lies die fahrpläne:
sie sind genauer. roll die seekarten auf,
eh es zu spät ist. sei wachsam, sing nicht.
der tag kommt, wo sie wieder listen ans tor
schlagen und malen den neinsagern auf die brust
zinken, lern unerkannt gehn, lern mehr als ich:
das viertel wechseln, den pass, das gesicht.
versteh dich auf den kleinen verrat,
die tägliche schmutzige rettung, nützlich
sind die enzykliken zum feueranzünden,
die manifeste: butter einzuwickeln und salz
für die wehrlosen. wut und geduld sind nötig,
in die lungen der macht zu blasen
den feinen tödlichen staub, gemahlen
von denen, die viel gelernt haben,
die genau sind, von dir.

ODE AN NIEMAND

dein rauchiges herz ist zeuge,
einziger könig, im wind
dein auge aus trauer.
du bist der gesell des zaubers,
erleuchtet von vielen wüsten,
vom ungehorsam gekrönt.
du bist nicht gemodelt von zeit,
noch gesprenkelt von asche
ist deine getreue stirn.

FOR A SENIOR COLLEGE TEXTBOOK

don't read odes, boy, timetables
are more exact. unroll the sea-charts
before it is too late. be on your guard. don't sing.
the day will come when they paste upon the door
new blacklists and brand their mark on those who answer no.
learn to pass unrecognized, to change quarters,
identity and face : you'll need to more than i did.
become adept at minor treason,
the sordid daily escape. the encyclicals
will do to make a fire, manifestos
to wrap up butter and salt
for the defenceless. anger and endurance
are necessary to blow into the lungs of power
the deadly powder, ground fine
by such as you, who have learnt much
and are fastidious in their ways.

1956

ODE TO NOBODY

your smoky heart is witness,
singular king, in the wind
your eye of sorrow.
you are magic's journeyman,
enlightened by many deserts,
by disobedience crowned.
you are not modelled by time,
nor is your loyal brow
bespattered with ash.

du bist ein geist ohne narbe,
deine dünung ist feierlich,
du warst vordem, vollkommner
als der grosse schwebende rochen,
gesalbter, in deinem glanz,
todes quitt, könig.

aber du bist nicht fern und früh
oder spät. du bist hier.
dein gerechter blick fällt hin
wie ein schnee aus luft
und wohnt auf den werften,
geht über sternwarten weg
in staubige fundbüros, ruht
in nassen zementkellern,
wo die mörder jauchen, fällt
auf thrombosen und lunten,
schlachthöfe schmatzend
und wirre raffinerien,
wo das lachgas schwelt, ruht
auf den ränken der reedereien
und streift die kometen,
die karzinome der hohen finanz,
ruht auf den mauern der macht,
dahinter substanzen ticken
zum tod, und belagert sie,
bis deinem dröhnenden blick
anheim der himmel, verschimmelt
von fallschirmen, fällt.

unerkannt schreitest du,
schöne bö, nächtlich,
über den spanischen platz.
dein reich kehrt zu dir zurück,
verborgner, gläserner jäger.

you are a spirit without scar,
your sea swell is solemn,
you were before, more perfect,
than the great floating rayfish,
anointed, in your glory,
quit of death, king.

but you are not far and early
or late. you are here.
your just glance falls
like snow out of air
and dwells on the wharfs,
passes over observatories
into dusty lost property offices, rests
in wet cement cellars
where the murderers crap, falls
upon thromboses and cannon,
a smacking kiss on slaughterhouses
and tangled refineries
where laughing gas steams, rests
on the intrigues of shipping companies
and skims the comets,
the carcinoma of high finance,
rests on the ramparts of power
behind which substances tick
toward death, and besieges them
till to your throbbing glance
the sky, crusted with mould
of parachutes, falls.

you stride unrecognized,
beauteous squall, by night,
over the spanish square.
your kingdom is restored to you,
hidden one, glass huntsman.

in deiner grossmut wirst du,
so wie den unschuldigen spargel,
dein ebenbild, das gezeichnete,
erbeuten, vergessen.

dein ist der ruhm und die rache,
nie behelligter fels, gesell
des zaubers, zeuge geheim
und einzig! dein windhaar,
dein barer blick weht hin
über dein altes künftiges reich,
und bewahrt im rauch,
was wahr ist, im wind auf.

EHRE SEI DER SELLERIE

der steinbrech, der uhu, die milch,
unbezweifelbar wie das licht, der fels,
von tauben bewaldet, der föhn,
der dotter, das brom, warum nicht,
und meinetwegen der blitz, ja,
der wal und der blitz, sie stehen fest,
auf sie lasst uns bauen,
sie sind eine ode wert.

die zigarrenasche im spiegel,
das ebenbild, wer wär es nicht leid,
dieses scheckgesicht
aus behaartem bims,
diese blumenkohlohren
von schlagern verprügelt,
und später am blutigen himmel
diese suturen aus rauch!

both innocent asparagus and
your image, the brandmarked,
you in your bounty will
despoil and forget.

glory and vengeance are yours,
rock never molested, magic's
journeyman, occult and
singular witness! your windhair,
your bare glance blows across
your ancient kingdom to come,
and in the smoke treasures up,
in the wind, what is true.

1959

HONOR TO CELERY

saxifrage, owl, milk,
indubitable as light, rock
wooded by doves, south wind,
egg-yolk, bromine, why not,
lightning too, i don't mind, yes,
whale and lightning, they stand firm,
let's build on them,
they're worth an ode.

cigar ash in the glass,
the image, who would not grieve for it,
this check face
of hirsute dough,
these cauliflower ears
punched by popsongs,
and later in the bloody sky
these sutures of smoke!

gelobt sei die friedliche milch,
ruhm dem uhu, er weiss wie er heisst
und fürchtet sich nicht, ehre
dem salz und dem erlauchten wal,
und der barmherzigen sellerie,
gebenedeit unter den köchen,
die auf dem teller stirbt.

das zarte erdherz, die sellerie,
menschlicher als der mensch,
frisst nicht seinesgleichen,
noch der blitz, gelobt sei der blitz,
oder meinetwegen der dotter.

let us praise peaceful milk,
glorify the owl, he knows his name
and is not afraid, honor
salt and the illustrious whale,
and merciful celery,
blessed by cooks,
which expires on the plate.

the delicate earth-heart, celery,
more human than man,
does not eat its equals,
lightning too, let's praise lightning,
or egg-yolk, i don't mind.

1959

WIELAND SCHMIED

ALTE CHINESISCHE WELTKARTE

Überschattet von den Fächern
eines zerklüfteten Baumes, weiss und schwarz,
verästelt in hundert zarte Schriftzeichen,
die wir nicht mehr zu deuten wissen,
liegt vor uns die erste Karte der Welt.

Wir erschrecken
vor diesem ersten Versuch,
die Welt mit ihren Bergen,
Flüssen und Gewächsen
zu ordnen und zu übersehen.

Immer schon war es unsere Hoffnung,
das, was ist, und was unaufhörlich
an uns herandrängt,
zu erfassen
in ein paar einfachen Zeichen.

Aber wir erschrecken,
wenn uns diese eigenen Zeichen,
an die wir uns hielten,
fremd geworden sind
wie die ungedeutete Welt.

ANCIENT CHINESE MAP OF THE WORLD

Overshadowed by the sprays
of a cleft tree, white and black,
ramified into a hundred delicate characters,
which we no longer can interpret,
the first map of the world lies before us.

We are startled
by the first attempt
to order and to survey
the world with its mountains,
rivers and vegetation.

It has always been our hope
to comprehend
what is, and what ceaselessly
presses upon us,
in a few simple signs.

But we are startled
when these our own signs
on which we relied,
have become alien to us
as the uninterpreted world.

1957

MYTHEN

I

Auf einem Stier reitet die Sonne
hinab in das Jonische Meer.
Die Spur seiner blutigen Hufe
zieht über den Horizont.
Seine Hörner ragen als Klippen
vor der Brandung von Leukas bei Nacht.

II

Der Mondschein dringt wie ein Stachel
in das Fleisch der Nacht.
Zwei Tage lang blieb er
in den Zweigen der Fichten gefangen.
(Aber wer zählt die Zeit
die dem Zugriff des Mondes entfiel?)

III

Das Gewitter reitet den Damm entlang
hin zu den Quellen des Inn.
Der Donnervogel stürzt in das Flussbett
und raubt die Feuersteine.
In seinen Krallen blitzen Sterne:
Jetzt fliesst der Inn über den Himmel.

MYTHS

I

Athwart a bull, the sun
plunges into the Ionian Sea.
Hoof-prints glow blood-red
along the distant skyline.
Against the surf at Leukas after dark
his horns stand out as cliffs.

II

Moonlight, like a barb,
impales the flesh of night.
Two days long it was snarled
in the branches of the pines.
(Yet who should count the time
that slipped from the moon's jaws?)

III

Riding the dam, the storm
steers for the sources of the Inn.
Searching the river-bed,
the thunderbird filches firestones:
its talons sparkle with stars
as the Inn spreads over the sky.

1957

ANDREAS OKOPENKO

GRÜNE MELODIE

... grüne Melodie blaues Mädchen
weiss sind die Ferien.

Ich grüne in der Wiese des Jungdorfes
Mein Hof ist gelb von Mädchen Getreiden
Mein Mädchen ist gelb von Hof Getreiden
Ich grüne im Getreide des Jungdorfes

Die Sonne geht den Weg zur Marktstadt
Mein Mädchen geht den Weg zur Marktstadt
Mein grünes Getreidemädchen mein grünes Wiesenmädchen
Mein grünes Jungdorfmädchen geht den Weg zur Marktstadt

Die Marktplätze sind mit Kürbissen
Die Kürbisse sind weisser Staub der Marktplätze
Der weisse Staub der mittäglichen Marktplätze
Der weisse Staub der Weg zum Haus zum Mädchen zum Garten

Ich grüne den Nachmittag im Mädchengarten
Ich grüne nun schon im Mädchengarten
Ein kühles Zimmer ein blaukariertes Tuch
Ein Mittagskrug ein blaues Glas ein Wasser

Eine jüngere Schwester die eifrig das Grün der Kinder spielt
Eine jüngere Schwester die fortgeht und uns alleinlässt
Das Kinderspiel das Wasser plätschert blau
Mein Mädchen im abgesetzten kühlen Zimmer

GREEN MELODY

> . . . green melody blue girl
> holidays are white.

I green in the meadow of the young village
My farm is yellow with girl with grain
My girl is yellow with farm with grain
I green in the grain of the young village

The sun is on the way to market
My girl is on the way to market
My green grain girl my green meadow girl
My green young village girl is on the way to market

The marketplaces are with pumpkins
The pumpkins are white dust of the marketplaces
The white dust of the noonday marketplaces
The white dust the way to the house to the girl to the garden

I green the afternoon in the girl garden
I am greening in the girl garden now
A cool room a blue check cloth
A noonday jug a blue glass a water

A younger sister intently playing the children's green
A younger sister who goes away and leaves us alone
The children's game the water splashes blue
My girl in the cool room apart

Ich bin das kühle Zimmer ich bin im kühlen Zimmer
Ich bin wo das Mädchen ist schliesslich ich bin bei dem Mädchen
Das Mädchen und das Wasser ich trinke das Wasser
Der Krug ist das Zimmer er fasst uns beide

Eine Ameise kriecht über die lateinische Grammatik
Ein Blatt ist zum Fenster hereingekommen
Ein Tropfen Wasser ist über meinen Mund gelaufen
Eine langsame kleine Uhr macht den Nachmittag aus Aluminium

Ich glänze silbern in der Sonne wie Aluminium
Ich habe meine Uhr im Blumentopf in Erde eingegraben
Mein Mädchen ist nicht der Käfer der über das Holz läuft
Mein Mädchen liegt im Sommerkleid auf dem Fensterbrett

Auf dem Fensterbrett auf dem leichten Sessel dem lichten Kasten
Dem Schatten dem Erinnern an die Sonne dem Nachmittag dem
    Garten
Ich begreife den Kleinen gut der Karten spielen geht
Ich begreife die Kleine die in grüne Blätter ihre Finger hält

Ich weiss das Pythagoras wichtig ist und Aristides und Caesar
Ich rebelle auf gegen die eingebundene Schule
Das schwarze Brett die Verordnung den Schularzt dass die Kreide
    trocken ist
Dass das Tafeltuch feucht ist dass das Butterbrotpapier braun ist

Ich vergnüge die Ferien der Kinder der Kleinen der Käfer
Das Wasser den blauen Spiegel den Sonnenbrand die Eisenbahn
Den Hofhund den gelben, die kleine Brut die Fellbälle
Die rote Masche der Katze, die Maus mit dem Speck in der Falle

Ich bin die Ferien ich bin das Grün
Ich grüne auf der Wiese im Getreide
Ich blaue im Zimmer des Mädchens
Im Nachmittag, ich blaue im Mädchen.

I am the cool room I am in the cool room
I am where at last the girl is I am with the girl
The girl and the water I drink the water
The jug is the room it takes us both

An ant crawls across the Latin grammar
A leaf has come in through the window
A drop of water has run across my mouth
A slow small clock makes the afternoon of aluminum

I shine silver in the sun like aluminum
I have buried my clock in earth in the flowerpot
My girl is not the beetle that runs across the wood
My girl lies in her summer dress on the window sill

On the window sill on the slight chair on the light cupboard
On the shadow the memory of sun on the afternoon the garden
I well understand the little boy that goes to play cards
I understand the little girl that keeps her fingers in green leaves

I know that Pythagoras is important and Aristides and Caesar
I am in revolt against the hidebound school
The blackboard the rule the school physician the chalk being dry
The duster being damp the sandwich paper being brown

I please the holidays of the children the little ones the beetles
The water the blue mirror the sunburn the railway
The farmdog the yellow one, the little pups the furballs
The red bow of the cat, the mouse in the trap with the bacon

I am the holidays I am the green
I green on the meadow in the grain
I blue in the room of the girl
In the afternoon, I blue in the girl.

1959

CHRISTOPH MECKEL

POSTSCHIFF

Mit dem Postschiff an Land
kamen Ratten und alte Delphine,
Schnaps und Öl und Goldtabak,
Zeitungen und manche Liebesbriefe.

Mir kam ein Koffer, zerbeult,
voller Hüte und Schuhe, wiewohl
ich nicht arm bin und das Verborgene
nicht für mich zu sorgen braucht.

Wortlos unterschrieb ich
den Rundbrief der Meere, tauschte
die Schuhe heiter, schwang
dem Unbekannten geschenkte Hüte!

DAS ERBE DES SANCHO PANSA

Als er alt war, erbte, wie versprochen,
Sancho Pansa, Bauer und Held,
ein Königreich auf fernverborgenen Inseln,
herrschte über Schatten, Schnee und Rauch,
über Tonnen Tau und Fuder Wind,
über das Licht
und den goldgrubentiefen Mond.

POSTSHIP

To land with the postship
came rats and old dolphins,
schnapps and oil and golden tobacco,
newspapers and a few love letters.

For me came a trunk, battered,
full of hats and shoes, although
I am not poor and what is hidden
has no need to worry about me.

Speechless I signed
the round robin of the seas, swapped
the shoes cheerfully, waved
gift hats to the Unknown!

1959

SANCHO PANZA'S HERITAGE

Sancho Panza, peasant and hero,
inherited when old as promised
a kingdom on some far-off hidden islands,
ruled over shadows, snow and smoke,
barrels of dew, cartloads of wind,
the light
and the goldminehollow moon.

Doch sein Reich verteidigte ihn schlecht;
wenn er ausser Schlaf sein Maultier ritt,
hielt ihn die Öde Spaniens im Exil,
nichts ahnte sein Weib
von Königinnen und Kriegen,
und nur der Stein lag ihm zu Füssen.

Wenn er sein Land betrat im Rausch,
sah er Gärten, Sunde, Residenzen
liegen in Mitternachtssonne, Don Quichote
eilte zu Besuch, durch grosse
Tollkirschparke sah man sie lustwandeln
und durch finstrer Ulmen Rauschgoldwälder.

Doch erwachend fand er leere Krüge,
schrie nach Wein und hörte, staunend,
in dem Schuppen Rosinante stampfen,
den er seinem Kind in Pflege gegeben.

But his estate was a poor defense;
when he rode his mule except in sleep
the Spanish desert kept him exiled,
his wife never knew a thing
of queens and wars,
and only the stone lay at his feet.

When in raptures he walked his land
he saw gardens, straits, palaces
prone in the midnight sun, Don Quixote
paid a flying visit, through big
belladonna parks one saw them ambling,
through rapturous golden woods of somber elms.

But waking he found empty jugs,
shouted for wine and heard, amazed,
stamping in the stable, Rosinante,
whom he had put in the care of his child.

1959

NOTES ON AUTHORS

ARP, HANS. Born 1887 in Strasbourg. Best known as the inventor of modern ageometric sculpture, but he has published poems regularly since 1920. Was with Ball, Huelsenbeck and Tzara, the arch-Dadaist language-dislocators, in Zürich during the First World War (he figures in Otto Flake's novel about the Zürich Dadaists, *Nein und Ja*). Arp has published poems and stories in French as well. Numerous artists of the Expressionist period, e.g., Barlach, Kandinsky, Klee, Kokoschka, Grosz, Schwitters, also wrote verse and prose, but few with Arp's consistency. His verbal agility, love of puns and of the verbally grotesque, make his work as near-untranslatable as that of Ringelnatz (the latter being, however, not nearly as radical as Arp in his abstractness).

wortträume und schwarze sterne [selected poems, 1911–52], Wiesbaden 1953; *auf einem bein*, Wiesbaden 1955.

ARTMANN, HANS CARL. Born 1921 in St. Achaz am Walde, Austria. Translator of Lorca's *Romancero Gitano* and of numerous works in other languages also. His dialect poems are popular in Austria. He also writes non-dialect poems and stories.

med anna schwoazzn dintn, Salzburg 1958.

BACHMANN, INGEBORG. Born 1926 in Klagenfurt, Austria. Radio plays, stories; also the libretto of Henze's opera *Prinz Friedrich von Homburg* (1960). Her verse is ductile and evocative in the extreme, and much is lost in translation.

Die gestundete Zeit (1953), Munich 1957 (2nd edition); *Anrufung des grossen Bären*, Munich 1956.

BALL, HUGO. Born 1886 in Bavaria. Studied philosophy at Munich and Heidelberg. Associated with Max Reinhardt's theatre-productions (1910) and thereafter producer at the Munich Kammerspiele playhouse. He was a friend of the painters Kandinsky and Marc and was extremely well informed about developments in abstract art during the period 1910–14. Ball went to Zürich in 1915—he was one of the pacifist intellectuals of the time. In 1916 he founded, with Tzara and Huelsenbeck, the Dadaist movement; the Cabaret Voltaire in Zürich became the center of the movement (Ball had obtained work there as a pianist), and it was here that he and other poets and artists, as Marcel Janco and Hans Arp, ran a radical anti-bourgeois cabaret at which Dadaist poems were recited and Dadaist antics performed (the multi-national character of the movement being matched by multi-lingual poems). Ball turned away from the movement in 1917 in the conviction that Dada had been not a critical confrontation of the demons at large in the modern European intelligence, but a flirtation with them (he was a ferocious critic of the German intelligentsia). His last years were devoted to theological studies and the writing of a book on three primitive Christian saints (*Byzantinisches Christentum*, 1923). Some of his writings have not yet been published. Ball died in the Ticino (Switzerland) in 1927.

The poem 'Die Sonne' first appeared in *Die Aktion*, 1914; the text used is reprinted from *Lyrik des expressionistischen Jahrzehnts* (ed. M. Niedermayer), Wiesbaden, Limes Verlag, 1955.

BAUER, WALTER. Born 1904 in Merseburg. Working-class background. Was for a time a schoolmaster. His writings were banned in 1933. He fought in the Second World War as a private soldier. Freelance after the war in Stuttgart till 1952, then he emigrated to Canada. He now teaches German at Toronto University. Has published novels, stories and essays, as well as biographies of Nansen, Livingstone, Michelangelo, Pestalozzi, and Van Gogh.

Mein blaues Oktavheft, Hamburg 1954.

BECHER, JOHANNES R. [Robert]. Born 1891 in Munich, the son of a magistrate. His earliest verse, *Der Ringende* (1911) and his novel, *Erde* (1912), prefigure the collision in his Expressionist verse of religious and (in the broadest sense) political emotions. He joined the Communist Party in 1918, at the time when the Russian Revolution was an inspiration to many German leftist intellectuals. Becher's work shows a clear development: from religiously motivated anti-bourgeois aggression (with its emotional disorder), to Communist *Kulturpolitik* and doctrinaire popular verse. His verse of the former phase was later recanted by him in favor of his later work. Becher also wrote novels and many literary and critical essays. He lived in Moscow 1935–45, and became President of the East German Culture Union ("Kulturbund") after the Second World War. He died in 1958.

Um Gott, Leipzig 1921; *Verklärung : Hymne*, Berlin 1922.

BENN, GOTTFRIED. Born 1886 at Mansfeld, Prussia, the son of a Lutheran pastor. Studied medicine and served in the medical corps of the German army during the First World War. His first poems, the pamphlet *Morgue* (1912), were a sensational reflection of his clinical experience and he became known as an Expressionist *enfant terrible*. While in Brussels during the war (he was medical officer to an army jail and also in charge of prostitutes), Benn wrote some of his semi-autobiographical prose sketches which broke new ground in Expressionist prose, and presented in the character Rönne what Benn regarded as the typical split man of the time, torn between the fascination of meaningless facts and the pull of chthonic fantasy. The same division is explored in his verse, with its scientific jargon and deliberately regressive fantasies. For a time he was attracted by the political theories of Nazism, but did not wish to conform to its cultural policies: his work was finally banned, he gave up his medical practice in Berlin and in 1935 rejoined the medical corps of the army, serving with it throughout the Second World War. After the war his work was banned by the Allies; but in 1948 a new collection of poems appeared in Switzerland and by 1949 he had re-emerged as one of the few surviving modernist poets, of the generation of Eliot and Valéry, to whom younger poets could look for guidance (Benn's nihilism was an attraction). His collected works, imaginative and critical prose, dramas and conversation-pieces, are now

being published. For more English translations see Gottfried Benn
Primal Vision (ed. E. B. Ashton), New York 1960. Benn died in West
Berlin in 1956.

Gesammelte Gedichte, Wiesbaden 1956.

BRAMBACH, RAINER. Born 1917 in Basle. He is half Swiss. Has had
various occupations: peat-cutter, farm-laborer, gardener. Lives in
Switzerland. His poems first appeared in the C. Hanser Verlag
annual anthology *Junge Lyrik*, Munich 1956.

Tagwerk, Zürich 1959.

BRECHT, BERTOLT. Born 1898 in Augsburg. His wide fame as a
playwright and theatrical innovator, who spent most of his working
life in and out of exile for political reasons, has somewhat overshadowed his work as a lyric poet—though as a ballad-writer he is
of course well known. There is a bleakness and simplicity in some
of Brecht's poems which is reminiscent of Chinese verse (and he
admired Waley's English translations from the Chinese). The directness of his verse has strongly influenced the post-1945 generation,
and its sense of commitment also. But the "gestic" quality of his
language, even in short aphoristic poems, is a secret not usually
mastered by others. Brecht died in East Berlin in 1956. The poem
'Böser Morgen' ('A Bad Morning') was written soon after the
workers' revolt in East Berlin in 1953. H. R. Hays' translations of
his poems were re-issued by Grove Press in 1959.

Gedichte und Lieder, Frankfurt am Main 1956; *Sinn und Form*, 2nd
Special Brecht Issue, Berlin 1957; *Gedichte* (6 vols), Frankfurt am
Main 1960–61.

BUSTA, CHRISTINE. Born 1915 in Vienna. Librarian in Vienna.
Much of her work, like that of Christine Lavant, has religious
themes. She has also written verse for children.

Die Scheune der Vögel, Salzburg 1958.

CELAN, PAUL. Born 1920 in Czernovitz, Bukovina (Rumania), Jewish background. Has been living for some years in Paris. Celan's verse has a rarity and purity of diction which distinguish it from any other German verse today ("poems are presences", he writes); but his 'Todesfuge' has all the impact of that terror and despair in history which informs many of his poems. He is developing in a radical way the "uprooted" metaphor technique which dates back to the earliest Expressionist verse. His latest book, *Sprachgitter*, appeared in 1959.

Mohn und Gedächtnis, Stuttgart 1952; *Von Schwelle zu Schwelle*, Stuttgart 1955.

COHN, HANS WERNER. Born 1916 in Breslau, where he studied medicine. Expatriate in London since the late 1930's. *Gedichte*, London 1950; poems in the anthologies *Transit* (1956) and *Expeditionen* (1959); also in the magazine *Merkur* (1954). Now secretary of a psychoanalytical association in London. The two poems included have not appeared before.

DÄUBLER, THEODOR. Born 1876 in Trieste, of German parents. Went to sea at 16 but proved as much of a misfit there as in the Austrian army in which he served for a short time. In Vienna he first heard Beethoven's music and read German literature, which were revelations to him; then he returned to North Italy. In 1898 he began to write his vast cosmological epic, *Das Nordlicht* (1910). He travelled in Europe, Asia Minor and Egypt, and lived in Vienna, Berlin, Dresden and Paris. Spent four years wandering all over Greece. He was one of the champions of Expressionist art, also formulating a theory of color-symbolism which parallels the practices of certain Expressionist painters. The poem 'Katzen' is in many ways untypical of Däubler's highly rhetorical and word-inebriated verse, such as his famous poem 'Millionen Nachtigallen schlagen' ('A million nightingales are singing'). Däubler died in 1934.

Dichtungen und Schriften, Munich 1956.

EHRENSTEIN, ALBERT. Born 1886 in Vienna. Studied philosophy and travelled in British and French African colonies. Settled in Berlin. He was a prolific poet, essayist and fiction-writer; of his imaginative prose writings, *Tubutsch* (1912) and *Briefe an Gott* (1922) are outstanding. He was one of the Phase II Expressionists, and a good deal of his pathetic protest seems thin today. He also wrote much erotic verse and some humorous verse. Like Walter Hasenclever, Ernst Toller, Paul Zech, and Johannes R. Becher, Ehrenstein subscribed to the politically revolutionary ideas inherent in later Expressionism. He left Germany in 1932 and went to Switzerland. Later he settled in the U.S. He died in New York in 1950.

Mein Lied, Berlin, E. Rowohlt Verlag, 1931.

EICH, GÜNTER. Born 1907 in Lebus, Brandenburg. Has lived since the Second World War in Bavaria. His first poems appeared in 1930, but he did not reach maturity till after the war: *Abgelegene Gehöfte*, 1948. Many radio plays—a medium in which he has created a style that is all his own. His spare, anti-rhetorical, and direct lyrical style has influenced many of the younger poets of the present.

Botschaften des Regens, Frankfurt am Main 1955; *Träume : Vier Spiele*, Frankfurt am Main 1953 (from which the poem 'Denke daran' is an extract).

ENZENSBERGER, HANS MAGNUS. Born 1929 in Bavaria, and grew up in Nazi Nuremberg. Has been on the staff of the South-West Regional Radio, living in Norway, then, till 1961, in Germany as a publisher's reader. Poet of critical protest and with a caustic style that is packed with shock metaphors.

verteidigung der wölfe, Frankfurt am Main 1956; *landessprache*, Frankfurt am Main 1960.

FRIED, ERICH. Born 1921 in Vienna. Has lived in London since 1938. Translator of Dylan Thomas and of T. S. Eliot. A radio play (based on a Japanese Orpheus legend) was broadcast in 1959. *Deutschland*, 1944; *Oesterreich*, 1945. A large new book of poems is due for publication in 1962. *Ein Soldat und ein Mädchen*, a novel (1961), is being translated.

Gedichte, Hamburg 1958. The poems 'Altes Zimmer' and 'Die Blinden' are from MS.

GOLL, YVAN. Born 1891 at St. Dié in the Vosges. Studies at Strasbourg and Berlin. In Switzerland, during the First World War, he founded the Rhein Verlag which was later to publish the first German edition of Joyce's *Ulysses*. Poems in both German and French; also dramas—highly experimental—and prose. Goll lived for some years in France and was a friend of Picasso and Chagall. Expatriate to the U.S. in 1939; in New York he edited the magazine *Hémisphères*, to which St. John Perse was a contributor. His long cycle of poems, *Jean Sans Terre* (*Landless John*) has appeared in translation in the U.S. Goll returned to Paris in 1947. He died of leukemia in 1950. The poems in his last book, *Traumkraut* (1951), from which 'The Salt Lake' and 'The Rain Palace' are taken, are based on the visions which his last illness induced and which he worked into his own poetic and philosophic system.

Dichtungen (ed. Claire Goll), Berlin-Darmstadt 1960.

GRASS, GÜNTER. Born 1927 in Danzig. Graphic artist and sculptor, also playwright (radically experimental) and novelist: his novel *Die Blechtrommel*, 1959, is being translated. His poems mark a new departure in urbanity and wit from the surrealistic idiom. He lives in Berlin.

Die Vorzüge der Windhühner, Berlin-Darmstadt 1956; the poem 'Wandlung' appeared in the magazine *Akzente*, 1959, 6. *Gleisdreieck* (poems), Berlin-Darmstadt 1960.

HAGELSTANGE, RUDOLF. Born 1912 in Nordhausen (Harz).

Early work shows Rilke's influence. He first became known with his sonnet-cycle *Venezianisches Credo*, 1952. This was written while he was with the German army and it was privately circulated before the end of the war—it was a moral indictment of Nazism. He has also published essays, a novel and a travel-book about the U.S. His *Die Ballade vom verschütteten Leben*, 1945, is the one outstanding attempt by a contemporary German poet to write a narrative poem on a topical theme.

Zwischen Stern und Staub, Wiesbaden 1953.

HEISSENBÜTTEL, HELMUT. Born 1921 in Wilhelmshaven. Producer on *Südwestfunk*. Arch-poet of what Max Picard called "discontinuous consciousness". His second book, *Topographien*, appeared in 1956.

Kombinationen, Esslingen 1954. *Textbuch I*, Olten 1961.

HERRMANN-NEISSE, MAX. Born 1886 at Neisse, Silesia, the son of a business man. Studied German and Art History at Munich and Breslau. After 1917 he lived in Berlin as a freelance writer. Though influenced by Expressionism, and though idiosyncratic and personal, his verse tends to be more traditionally lyrical. He left Germany in 1933, first going to Switzerland, but then moving to Holland, and thence to Paris, and finally to London, where he died in 1941. In the same year his *Letzte Gedichte*, a collection dating from 1932 to 1941, appeared in London.

Empörung. Andacht. Ewigkeit, Leipzig ND [1918]; 'Legende vom Zauber der zärtlichen Zellen' is reprinted from *Verkündigung* (ed. R. Kayser), Munich 1921, though it must have first appeared in one of Herrmann-Neisse's now unobtainable earlier books.

HEYM, GEORG. Born 1887 in Hirschberg, Silesia. Studied law in Berlin. Active there in the literary ferment of the years 1910–12 (the 'Neuer Club' and the magazine *Die Aktion*). His saturnine poems, with their somber prophetic images of ruin, are some of the first urban poems of the early Expressionist period (some influence from Baudelaire is noticeable). His imagery is more experimental than his verse forms, which are mostly traditional. But one of his best poems, a late one, 'Mit den fahrenden Schiffen' (which we have been unable to translate), prefigures Benn's compact and incantatory style of the 1920's. Heym was drowned in 1912, trying to rescue a friend in a skating accident.

Gesammelte Gedichte, Zürich 1947; *Dichtungen*, Munich 1960 (in progress).

HODDIS, JAKOB VAN (pseudonym of Hans Davidsohn). Born 1887 in Berlin, the son of a physician. Associated with Hugo Ball, Emmy Hennings (later Ball's wife) and Ludwig Meidner (best known for his portraits of Expressionist poets). Hoddis' poem 'Weltende', published in the first issue of the magazine *Die Aktion* in 1911, is often regarded as the first Expressionist poem. Both thematically and formally, with its disjunct and catastrophic images (and its near-mechanical rhythm), it established a style that proved congenial to many contemporaries. In 1914 Hoddis went mad. He was in a mental hospital in Thuringia. Deportation and death in 1942.

Weltende, Berlin 1918; *Weltende*, Zürich 1958.

HÖLLERER, WALTER. Born 1922 in Bavaria. Co-editor of the magazine *Akzente* which has published and discovered many younger poets. Essayist and anthologist—he edited the anthology *Transit*, 1956. Now Professor at Berlin and Frankfurt am Main.

Der andere Gast, Munich ND [1952].

HOLTHUSEN, HANS EGON. Born 1913 in Rendsburg. Was widely read as a poet after 1948 (*Hier in der Zeit*, 1949); his verse then showed influences from Rilke and Eliot, but its themes were topical. His more recent work has been as an essayist and definer of current intellectual and literary movements: *Der unbehauste Mensch*, 1951; *Ja und Nein*, 1954; *Das Schöne und das Wahre*, 1958. His last book of poems appeared in 1952.

Labyrinthische Jahre, Munich 1952.

HUCHEL, PETER. Born 1903 in Lichterfelde. After his university studies he spent several years, as a laborer and a freelance, in France. Prisoner of war in Russia at the end of the Second World War. Since 1948 he has been editor of the East German magazine *Sinn und Form*. He is a realistic "Heimatdichter", but his pastoral poems have more a contemplative than a social or Marxist orientation. He has also written verse in support of agricultural reform programs. He has written radio plays and was a program director on Berlin radio in 1948.

Gedichte, Berlin 1948; *Sinn und Form* (Berlin), 1959, 2.

KÄSTNER, ERICH. Born 1899 in Dresden. Originally a poet of the so-called New Realism ("Neue Sachlichkeit") which evolved out of Expressionism in the late 1920's, Kästner is one of the leading satirists of the century. His *Lyrische Hausapotheke* (Zürich 1935), a non-political selection published in Switzerland after his work had been banned by the Nazis, has been one of the most popular books of verse during the period. His numerous writings include children's books, novels, and plays, some of which are familiar in English-speaking countries.

Lyrische Hausapotheke, Zürich 1935; *Gedichte*, Zürich 1959.

KLABUND (pseudonym of Alfred Henschke). Born 1890 in Grossen an der Oder. Was a friend of Gottfried Benn and a versatile poet, novelist, essayist and translator, widely read in the 1920's. Consumptive, he died at Davos in 1928.

Gesammelte Gedichte, Cologne 1930.

KOLMAR, GERTRUD (pseudonym of Gertrud Chodziesner). Born 1894 in Berlin. She had just begun to publish her best work when the Nazis came to power. Last known to be alive in a forced labor camp in 1943. Her last poems have a freedom and sweep that distinguish them from her more conventional earlier work, though there is a purity and seriousness in everything she wrote.

Das lyrische Werk, Heidelberg 1955.

KROLOW, KARL. Born 1915 in Hanover. He has done much to introduce French surrealism into Germany as a new poetic style, and was one of the first new poets to make a mark after the war. He has published seven books of verse.

Die Zeichen der Welt, Stuttgart 1952 ; *Wind und Zeit*, Stuttgart 1954.

LASKER-SCHÜLER, ELSE. Born 1869 at Elberfeld, the daughter of an architect. Was married for a time to Herwarth Walden, and had liaisons with several prominent poets of the time, including Gottfried Benn. She scandalized many of her contemporaries by her bohemian habits and eccentric clothes while living in Berlin between the wars. She wrote plays and prose fantasies—some of which she illustrated with her own drawings—besides the poems whose vivid imagery and oriental color were much admired by experimental poets younger than herself. Her influential *Hebräische Balladen* appeared in 1913. Expatriate, first to Switzerland and then to Palestine in 1937. She died in Jerusalem in 1945.

Gedichte (ed. F. Kemp), Munich 1959.

LAVANT, CHRISTINE. Born 1915 at St. Stefan in Carinthia, Austria, where she lives. She is considered by some to be the best Austrian lyric poet now living. She has also written a remarkable radio play about a young schizophrenic woman (which has been broadcast in England in the translation by Nora Wydenbruck).

Die Bettlerschale, Salzburg 1957.

LEHMANN, WILHELM. Born 1882 at Puerto Cabello, Venezuela, of German parents. Grew up in Hamburg. Was a prisoner-of-war in England during the First World War. Closely associated with Oskar Loerke in initiating a new school of phenomenological and pan-mythical nature poetry. Also the author of several novels and of some distinguished criticism. His work became most widely influential during and immediately after the Second World War. He lives at Plön in Schleswig-Holstein.

Meine Gedichtbücher, Frankfurt am Main 1957.

LICHTENSTEIN, ALFRED. Born 1889 in Berlin. Studied law there till 1913. In the same year he joined a Bavarian regiment for a year's military service, which took him to Belgium at the outbreak of war. He was killed in action at Vermandovillers in September, 1914. He published a small collection of poems, *Die Dämmerung*, in 1913; his collected poems and stories appeared in 1919, in two volumes never reprinted. Lichtenstein belonged among the urban poets of early Expressionism. He was an ironic humanist, at once skeptical and tender, satirical and grave. In an early sequence he ironized himself under the *persona* Kuno Kohn, and even his war-poems are self-deprecating, bitter, and funny. Together with Hoddis, he created a new genre of half-realist, half-surrealist *montage*, distantly related to the new departures of Ezra Pound and T. S. Eliot.

Gedichte und Geschichten (ed. K. Lubasch), Vol. I, Munich 1919.

LOERKE, OSKAR. Born 1884 in West Prussia, the son of a farmer. Lived for most of his life in a suburb of Berlin, where he worked as a reader for S. Fischer Verlag. Seven books of verse appeared in his lifetime, as well as two novels, stories, literary criticism and studies of his favorite composers—Bach and Bruckner. Far removed though his so-called "magical" pastoral poetry is from the mainly urban poetry of Expressionism, his strictness of form is an intrinsic part of Expressionist verse technique (as in Hoddis' 'Weltende' and Lichtenstein's 'Die Dämmerung', 'Prophezeiung', and 'Morgen').

His dramatic development of "uprooted" and self-contained metaphors is also Expressionistic. Loerke was secretary to the poetry section of the Prussian Academy of Arts, but he resigned in 1933 when the Nazis came to power. He spent the last years of his life in lonely retirement, and died in Berlin in 1941.

Gedichte und Prosa, Bd. I, Frankfurt am Main ND [1958].

MECKEL, CHRISTOPH. Born 1935 in Berlin. Was an art student at Freiburg im Breisgau and at Munich. Four books of etchings appeared, 1959-60. Has lived in France and on Corsica, travelled in Scandinavia, Italy and Greece. His first book, *Hotel für Schlafwandler*, appeared in 1958. Prose: *Im Land der Umbramauten*, 1961.

Nebelhörner, Stuttgart 1959.

MORGENSTERN, CHRISTIAN. Born 1871 in Munich, the son of a painter. His serious poems, not represented here, show the influence of Nietzsche, and later that of Rudolf Steiner's anthroposophy. In Norway he met Ibsen and became his translator. It is to his burlesque poems, which are some of the earliest experimental verse of the century, that he owes his fame. "Our language," he wrote, "is the most bourgeois thing about us; to strip it of the bourgeois conventions in which we have taken refuge is the most urgent task of the future." A consumptive since his youth, Morgenstern died at Merano in 1914.

Alle Galgenlieder, Wiesbaden 1956.

OKOPENKO, ANDREAS. Born 1930 in Kaschau (Košice), Czechoslovakia. His family was forced to move in 1939 and settled in Vienna. He is a chemist. Has edited and contributed to various Austrian avant-garde publications.

Grüner November, Munich 1957; the poem 'Grüne Melodie' appeared in the anthology *Expeditionen* (ed. Wolfgang Weyrauch), Munich 1959.

PIONTEK, HEINZ. Born 1925 in Upper Silesia, but has been living in West Germany since the war. Lives in Munich. 'Die Verstreuten' is about refugees; the title means literally 'The Scattered Ones', but has a biblical connotation in German (the diaspora). Stories and criticism. *Die Furt*, his first poems, appeared in 1952, and was subsequently incorporated into a second edition of his second book, *Die Rauchfahne*, in 1956.

Wassermarken, Esslingen 1957.

RILKE, RAINER MARIA. Born 1875 in Prague, of German-speaking parents. Attended military schools 1886–91. At one time he sold his early poems on the streets of Prague. Visited Russia in 1899 and 1900 with Lou Andreas-Salomé to whom Nietzsche had once proposed marriage and who later became an associate of Freud's. In Russia he met Tolstoy. Soon after his marriage in 1901 to Clara Westhoff, the sculptress, he went to Paris to write a book on Rodin, whose secretary he was during the winter months 1905–6. His later life was spent in travels all over Western Europe, often as the guest of his many admirers. His style underwent an important change immediately before the First World War, when he suffered a personal crisis which coincided with the crisis in poetic expression known as Expressionism. He spent his last years at Muzot in Switzerland and died of leukemia in 1926. He is probably best known for his *Duineser Elegien* (1912–22) and his *Sonette an Orpheus* (1922). Many of his writings, and all his verse, are published in English translation.

Werke II, Wiesbaden 1957.

RINGELNATZ, JOACHIM (pseudonym of Hans Bötticher). Born 1883 in Saxony. Ran away from school before his matriculation and became a sailor for many years. Later professions included those of newsboy, window-dresser, cigarette-vendor, bar-poet, librarian and tourist guide. After the First World War, in which he was a naval officer, he earned his living as a cabaret comedian all over German-speaking Europe, reciting his own grotesque and satirical verse.

One of his prose works, . . . *liner Roma* (1924), shows an affinity between him and the Dadaists. Till 1933 he lived in Munich, then he moved to Berlin where he died in 1934.

Und auf einmal steht es neben dir, Berlin 1951.

SCHMIED, WIELAND. Born 1929 in Frankfurt am Main. Lives near Vienna and in Frankfurt. Art-critic and essayist.

Landkarte des Windes, Salzburg 1957.

SCHNACK, ANTON. Born 1892 in Reineck, Franconia. Editor, traveled all over the world. His poems about the First World War are some of the most vivid of the period (he uses the long ryhmed line developed by Stadler). Novels and stories, many in the miniature vein.

Tier rang gewaltig mit Tier, Berlin 1920.

SCHNURRE, WOLFDIETRICH. Born 1920 in Frankfurt am Main. Lives in Berlin. Also writes humorous and grotesque fiction. His work has a spareness and sense of commitment which typify much German verse today.

Kassiber, Frankfurt am Main 1956.

SCHOLL, ALBERT ARNOLD. Born 1926 in the Ruhr. Lives in Bremen. Radio plays and criticism. Poems: *Die gläserne Stadt*, Düsseldorf 1952. Other work in various anthologies and magazines.

Lyrik unserer Zeit (ed. Rudolf Hartung), a special issue of the magazine *Neue Deutsche Hefte*, 1957 (Gütersloh).

STADLER, ERNST. Born 1883 at Colmar in Alsace, the son of a

lawyer. Studied English at Strasbourg and Munich, then went as a Rhodes Scholar to Oxford in 1908. In 1910 he was again in England, writing a thesis on Shakespeare (now lost). Lectured at Brussels University, 1910–14: he was about to take up an appointment at Toronto University when war broke out. Stadler had been associated with the poet René Schickele in cementing Franco-German cultural relations. His early verse was influenced by George; but in the long irregular lines of his later poems he established a style original in German, however much (apart from Stadler's use of rhyme) it may recall Whitman. This line was a liberating example to contemporary and later poets. Stadler was killed in action on the Western front in October, 1914.

Dichtungen (ed. K. L. Schneider), Hamburg ND (1955.)

STEINER, FRANZ BAERMANN. Born 1909 in Prague, the son of orthodox Jewish parents. Studied sociology, oriental languages and anthropology at Prague. After a year in Palestine devoted to Arabic studies, he obtained his doctorate in 1935, but continued studying at Vienna, London, and Oxford, where he remained after the outbreak of war. Both his parents died in a concentration camp in 1942. One of his longest and finest poems, *Gebet im Garten*, is dedicated to their memory, and his comment on the war, included here, must be read in the light of this experience. Steiner himself suffered a breakdown soon after the war, but continued to work intensively at his poetry and his lecturing and research in anthropology. A definitive work on taboos was published posthumously. Steiner died of coronary thrombosis at Oxford in 1952. Only a few of his many poems appeared in periodicals during his life, and only a small selection has been published since his death. His great learning is evident in his poetry, as well as in his scholarly work and his prose aphorisms: his poems included variations on Red Indian, Esquimaux, Siberian and African lore. He belonged to no school or movement; but everything he wrote was distinguished by his delicate sensibility, his intelligence, and his fastidious craftsmanship.

Unruhe ohne Uhr, Heidelberg 1954.

STRAMM, AUGUST. Born 1864 at Münster, Westfalia, the son of a railway official. He himself became a post-office administrator at Bremen, then in Berlin, where he was promoted to the central ministry. In his spare time he studied at Halle and obtained a Ph.D. He was co-editor, with Herwarth Walden, of the magazine *Der Sturm*, the organ of the early Expressionists. His experiments in diction and syntax were some of the most radical of the period. He was killed on the Russian front on September 1, 1915.

Dein Lächeln weint: Gesammelte Gedichte (ed. I. Stramm), Wiesbaden 1956.

THOOR, JESSE (pseudonym of Peter Karl Höfler). Born 1905 in Berlin, the son of a carpenter. Mainly self-educated, he worked in a variety of trades and odd jobs, when he was not out of work or tramping. After the death of his mother, which he attributed to his father's drunkenness and brutality, he lived with his aunt in Vienna. As a member of the Communist Party he was forced to emigrate in 1938, at first to Czechoslovakia, then to England, where he was supported for a time by Prince Hubertus von Löwenstein, broke with the party—he had always been a deviationist—and was imprisoned for a time after being denounced as a Nazi by his former associates. His later religious verse retains the vernacular directness of his earlier Villonesque sonnets on personal and political themes. During his last years in London he worked as a goldsmith and silversmith, under great mental and material stress. He died of coronary thrombosis in 1952, while staying with friends near Lienz in Austria. His collected poems were published after his death.

Sonette und Lieder, Heidelberg 1956.

TRAKL, GEORG. Born 1886 at Salzburg, the son of Protestant parents. Was backward at school, and decided to train as a dispensing chemist, which he did—at Salzburg from 1905 to 1908, then in Vienna. Two of his early plays were performed at Salzburg. After a year in the medical corps of the Austrian army, he considered emigrating to Borneo. But in 1912 he found a patron and publisher in Ludwig von Ficker, editor of *Der Brenner* at Innsbruck, and was able to devote more time to the visionary poems and prose poems to which he owes his posthumous fame. Two collections appeared in his lifetime. From 1913 to the outbreak of war he lived mainly at Innsbruck. Trakl's extreme melancholia and guilt obsessions drove him to drugs and drink. In August 1914 he was posted to Galicia as a lieutenant in the medical corps; after the Battle of Grodek, to which his last poem refers, Trakl was put in charge of ninety serious casualties whom he could do little to help, and suffered a nervous breakdown. Placed in a cell at Cracow for observation as a possible case of schizophrenia, he died there in November 1914 of an overdose of cocaine. Despite its debt to Hölderlin, Rimbaud and others, Trakl's poetry is among the purest and most original of the period.

Gesammelte Werke, Salzburg 1948–53.

WERFEL, FRANZ. Born 1890 in Prague. Publisher's reader, 1912–14, with Kurt Wolff Verlag, which published many important young writers of the period 1912–20, including Kafka. Werfel lived after the First World War in Berlin, then in Vienna; he married the widow of the composer Gustav Mahler. He left Germany for France in 1938, went in 1940 to the U.S., and died at Beverly Hills in 1945. A prolific poet, novelist and playwright, Werfel was regarded in the 1920's as the most outstanding Expressionist lyric poet: in the 1910–24 anthology *Verse der Lebenden* (ed. H. E. Jacob), he is represented with three times as many poems as any other poet excepting Loerke. The rhetorical plush and the pathos of his verse have not worn well. His *Song of Bernadette* (1941) brought him wide fame. His novel *Verdi* (1924) had also sold well over a quarter of a million copies by 1949. Like Becher, though in altogether different ways, Werfel developed out of an Expressionist bourgeois rebel into a popular writer. His poems 1908–45 (*Gedichte aus den Jahren 1908–45*) were first published in Los Angeles (Pacific Press) in 1946. A book of translations by E. A. Snow, *Poems*, appeared in 1945 (Princeton).

Gedichte, Berlin-Vienna-Leipzig 1926 (first collected edition); *Gesammelte Werke: Die Gedichte*, Frankfurt am Main (in progress).

WEYRAUCH, WOLFGANG. Born 1906 in Königsberg. Was an actor for some time. Stories, experimental prose, radio plays and some film scripts. He is a publisher's reader in Hamburg. A good deal of his work has dealt with problems of life in Germany after the Second World War.

Gesang um nicht zu sterben, Hamburg 1956.

WOLFSKEHL, KARL. Born 1869 at Darmstadt. In 1893 he met Stefan George and became a member of his circle, though he was a man of highly independent character. His early poems appeared in 1903, followed by another collection, *Der Umkreis*, in 1927. A considerable scholar and bibliophile, Wolfskehl did not until 1933 emerge as a poet of authentically original vision, identifying himself with the Jewish tradition, without alienating himself from the ideals of the George circle. In 1938 he left Italy where he had been living for some years, and settled at Auckland, New Zealand. He died there in 1948. A collection of his letters from New Zealand was published in 1959.

Sang aus dem Exil, Zürich ND [1950]; *Gesammelte Werke: Gedichte*, Hamburg 1960.

ZEMP, WERNER. Born 1906 in Zürich. Regarded in Switzerland as the most distinguished German-Swiss pastoral poet of his generation; the profound and somber melancholy of much of his verse is central to the mood of German-Swiss verse as a whole. Zemp was also an expert on the 19th century German (Swabian) poet Eduard Mörike. He died in 1959. The scene of 'Landscape before Easter' is quite possibly the same as that described in Zollinger's 'Kloster Fahr'.

Das Hochtal, Olten 1956; *Gedichte* (2nd enlarged ed.), Zürich 1954.

ZOLLINGER, ALBIN. Born 1895 in Canton Zürich, Switzerland. He was a schoolmaster in Oerlikon, near Zürich, and edited the liberal magazine *Die Zeit* (Berne) during the 1930's. He was the outstanding German-Swiss lyric poet of his time, though this has only been recognized in the past few years, and there are various links between many of his poems and German Expressionist verse. He also wrote novels, stories, and criticism. The convent to which the poem reprinted refers is near Zürich; and the graveyard to which it refers is inside the precincts. The Judgement Day painting on the wall of the graveyard, which is an exterior wall of the nun's chapel, is now almost entirely effaced. Zollinger died in 1941.

Gedichte, Zürich 1956.

INDEX OF FIRST LINES

416 INDEX

INDEX OF AUTHORS

DATE DUE

MAY 1 3			
MAR 1.5			
OCT 3 1			
JAN 2 7			
MAR 0 3 2000 FEB 2 2 2010			
GAYLORD			PRINTED IN U.S.A.